GMAT
Math Tests

JEFF KOLBY

DERRICK VAUGHN

GMAT is a registered trademark of the Graduate Management Admission Council, which does not endorse this book.

Additional educational titles from Nova Press (available at novapress.net):

- **GMAT Prep Course** (624 pages)
  Full Potential GMAT Sentence Correction Intensive (372 pages)
- **GRE Prep Course** (624 pages, includes software)
  GRE Math Prep Course (528 pages)
- **Master The LSAT** (608 pages, includes software and 4 official LSAT exams)
- **The MCAT Physics Book** (444 pages)
  The MCAT Biology Book (416 pages)
  The MCAT Chemistry Book (428 pages)
- **SAT Prep Course** (640 pages, includes software)
  SAT Math Prep Course (404 pages)
  SAT Critical Reading and Writing Prep Course (350 pages)
- **ACT Math Prep Course** (402 pages)
  ACT Verbal Prep Course (248 pages)
- **Scoring Strategies for the TOEFL® iBT:** (800 pages, includes audio CD)
  Speaking and Writing Strategies for the TOEFL® iBT: (394 pages, includes audio CD)
  500 Words, Phrases, and Idioms for the TOEFL® iBT: (238 pages, includes audio CD)
  Practice Tests for the TOEFL® iBT: (292 pages, includes audio CD)
  Business Idioms in America: (220 pages)
  Americanize Your Language and Emotionalize Your Speech! (210 pages)
- **Postal Exam Book** (276 pages)
- **Law School Basics:** A Preview of Law School and Legal Reasoning (224 pages)
- **Vocabulary 4000:** The 4000 Words Essential for an Educated Vocabulary (160 pages)

Copyright © 2015 by Nova Press
All rights reserved.

Duplication, distribution, or data base storage of any part of this work is prohibited without prior written approval from the publisher.

ISBN-10: 1–944595-00-7
ISBN-13: 978-1-944595-00-5

GMAT is a registered trademark of the Graduate Management Admission Council.

P. O. Box 692023
West Hollywood, CA 90069

Phone: 1-800-949-6175
E-mail: info@novapress.net
Website: www.novapress.net

ABOUT THIS BOOK

If you don't have a pencil in your hand, get one now! Don't just read this book—write on it, study it, scrutinize it! In short, for the next few weeks, this book should be a part of your life. When you have finished the book, it should be marked-up, dog-eared, tattered and torn.

Although the GMAT is a difficult test, it is a *very* learnable test. This is not to say that the GMAT is "beatable." There is no bag of tricks that will show you how to master it overnight. You probably have already realized this. Some books, nevertheless, offer "inside stuff" or "tricks" which they claim will enable you to beat the test. These include declaring that answer-choices B, C, or D are more likely to be correct than choices A or E. This tactic, like most of its type, does not work. It is offered to give the student the feeling that he or she is getting the scoop on the test.

The GMAT cannot be "beaten." But it can be mastered—through hard work, analytical thought, and by training yourself to think like a test writer.

The GMAT math section is not easy—nor is this book. To improve your GMAT math score, you must be willing to work; if you study hard and master the techniques in this book, your score will improve—significantly.

This book contains 13 full-length GMAT Math Tests with detailed solutions to all the problems! These problems and solutions will introduce you to numerous analytic techniques that will help you immensely, not only on the GMAT but in business school as well. For this reason, studying for the GMAT can be a rewarding and satisfying experience.

CONTENTS

	ORIENTATION	7
Part One	**THE TESTS**	11
	Test 1	13
	Test 2	41
	Test 3	69
	Test 4	95
	Test 5	121
	Test 6	149
	Test 7	175
	Test 8	201
	Test 9	229
	Test 10	255
	Test 11	283
	Test 12	313
	Test 13	341
Part Two:	**SUMMARY OF MATH PROPERTIES**	371

ORIENTATION

Format of the Math Sections

The Math section consists of 37 multiple-choice questions. The questions come in two formats: the standard multiple-choice question and the Data Sufficiency question. The math section is designed to test your ability to solve problems, not to test your mathematical knowledge.

The math section is 75 minutes long and contains 37 questions. The questions can appear in any order.

FORMAT
Standard Multiple-Choice
Data Sufficiency

GMAT VS. SAT

GMAT math is very similar to SAT math, though a little harder. The mathematical skills tested are very basic: only first year high school algebra and geometry (no proofs). However, this does not mean that the math section is easy. The medium of basic mathematics is chosen so that everyone taking the test will be on a fairly even playing field. Although the questions require only basic mathematics and **all** have **simple** solutions, it can require considerable ingenuity to find the simple solution. If you have taken a course in calculus or another advanced math topic, don't assume that you will find the math section easy. Other than increasing your mathematical maturity, little you learned in calculus will help on the GMAT.

As mentioned above, every GMAT math problem has a simple solution, but finding that simple solution may not be easy. The intent of the math section is to test how skilled you are at finding the simple solutions. The premise is that if you spend a lot of time working out long solutions you will not finish as much of the test as students who spot the short, simple solutions. So if you find yourself performing long calculations or applying advanced mathematics—stop. You're heading in the wrong direction.

Experimental Questions

The GMAT is a standardized test. Each time it is offered, the test has, as close as possible, the same level of difficulty as every previous test. Maintaining this consistency is very difficult—hence the experimental questions (questions that are not scored). The effectiveness of each question must be assessed before it can be used on the GMAT. A problem that one person finds easy another person may find hard, and vice versa. The experimental questions measure the relative difficulty of potential questions; if responses to a question do not perform to strict specifications, the question is rejected.

About one quarter of the questions are experimental. The experimental questions can be standard math, data sufficiency, reading comprehension, arguments, sentence correction, or integrated reasoning. You won't know which questions are experimental.

Because the "bugs" have not been worked out of the experimental questions—or, to put it more directly, because you are being used as a guinea pig to work out the "bugs"—these unscored questions are often more difficult and confusing than the scored questions.

This brings up an ethical issue: How many students have run into experimental questions early in the test and have been confused and discouraged by them? Crestfallen by having done poorly on a few experimental questions, they lose confidence and perform below their ability on the other parts of the test. Some testing companies are becoming more enlightened in this regard and are administering experimental questions as separate practice tests. Unfortunately, the GMAT has yet to see the light.

Knowing that the experimental questions can be disproportionately difficult, if you do poorly on a particular question you can take some solace in the hope that it may have been experimental. In other words, do not allow a few difficult questions to discourage your performance on the rest of the test.

The CAT & the Old Paper-&-Pencil Test

The computerized GMAT uses the same type of questions as did the old Paper & Pencil Test. The only thing that has changed is medium, that is the way the questions are presented.

There are advantages and disadvantages to the CAT. Probably the biggest advantages are that you can take the CAT just about any time and you can take it in a small room with just a few other people—instead of in a large auditorium with hundreds of other stressed people. One the other hand, you cannot return to previous questions, it is easier to misread a computer screen than it is to misread printed material, and it can be distracting looking back and forth from the computer screen to your scratch paper.

Pacing

Although time is limited on the GMAT, working too quickly can damage your score. Many problems hinge on subtle points, and most require careful reading of the setup. Because undergraduate school puts such heavy reading loads on students, many will follow their academic conditioning and read the questions quickly, looking only for the gist of what the question is asking. Once they have found it, they mark their answer and move on, confident they have answered it correctly. Later, many are startled to discover that they missed questions because they either misread the problems or overlooked subtle points.

To do well in your undergraduate classes, you had to attempt to solve every, or nearly every, problem on a test. Not so with the GMAT. For the vast majority of people, the key to performing well on the GMAT is not the number of questions they solve, within reason, but the percentage they solve correctly.

Scoring the GMAT

The two major parts of the test are scored independently. You will receive a verbal score (0 to 60) and a math score (0 to 60). You will also receive a total score (200 to 800), and a writing score (0 to 6). The average Verbal score is about 27, the average Math score is about 31, and the average total score is about 500.

In addition, you will be assigned a percentile ranking, which gives the percentage of students with scores below yours.

Skipping and Guessing

On the test, you cannot skip questions; each question must be answered before moving on to the next question. However, if you can eliminate even one of the answer-choices, guessing can be advantageous. We'll talk more about this later. Unfortunately, you cannot return to previously answered questions.

On the test, your first question will be of medium difficulty. If you answer it correctly, the next question will be a little harder. If you again answer it correctly, the next question will be harder still, and so on. If your GMAT skills are strong and you are not making any mistakes, you should reach the medium-hard or hard problems by about the fifth problem. Although this is not very precise, it can be quite helpful. Once you have passed the fifth question, you should be alert to subtleties in any seemingly simple problems.

Often students become obsessed with a particular problem and waste time trying to solve it. To get a top score, learn to cut your losses and move on. The exception to this rule is the first five questions of each section. Because of the importance of the first five questions to your score, you should read and solve these questions slowly and carefully.

Because the total number of questions answered contributes to the calculation of your score, you should answer ALL the questions—even if this means guessing randomly before time runs

Part One
THE TESTS

Test 1

The Directions

Standard Multiple-choice

Directions
Solve each problem and decide which one of the choices given is best.

Notes
1. All numbers used are real numbers.
2. Figures are drawn as accurately as possible EXCEPT when it is stated that the figure is not drawn to scale. All figures lie in a plane unless otherwise indicated. Position of points, angles, regions, etc. can be assumed to be in the order shown; and angle measures can be assumed to be positive.

Note 1 indicates that complex numbers, $i = \sqrt{-1}$, do not appear on the test.

Note 2 indicates that figures are drawn accurately. Hence, you can check your work and in some cases even solve a problem by "eyeballing" the figure. If a drawing is labeled "Figure not drawn to scale," then the drawing is not accurate. In this case, an angle that appears to be $90°$ may not be or an object that appears congruent to another object may not be. The statement "All figures lie in a plane unless otherwise indicated" indicates that two-dimensional figures do not represent three-dimensional objects. That is, the drawing of a circle is not representing a sphere, and the drawing of a square is not representing a cube.

Reference Information

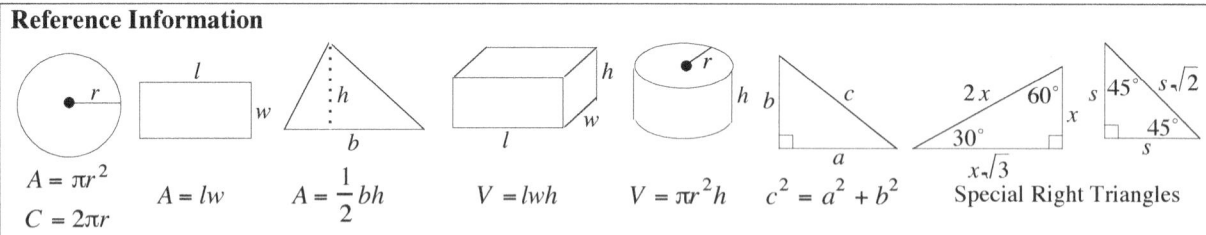

$A = \pi r^2$
$C = 2\pi r$
$A = lw$
$A = \frac{1}{2}bh$
$V = lwh$
$V = \pi r^2 h$
$c^2 = a^2 + b^2$
Special Right Triangles

The number of degrees of arc in a circle is 360.
The sum of the measures in degrees of the angles of a triangle is 180.

Although this reference material can be handy, be sure you know it well so that you do not waste time looking it up during the test.

Data Sufficiency

The directions for Data Sufficiency questions are rather complicated. Before reading any further, take some time to learn the directions cold. Some of the wording in the directions below has been changed from the GMAT to make it clearer. You should never have to look at the instructions during the test.

Directions: Each of the following Data Sufficiency problems contains a question followed by two statements, numbered (1) and (2). You need not solve the problem; rather you must decide whether the information given is sufficient to solve the problem.

The correct answer to a question is
- A if statement (1) ALONE is sufficient to answer the question but statement (2) alone is not sufficient;
- B if statement (2) ALONE is sufficient to answer the question but statement (1) alone is not sufficient;
- C if the two statements TAKEN TOGETHER are sufficient to answer the question, but NEITHER statement ALONE is sufficient;
- D if EACH statement ALONE is sufficient to answer the question;
- E if the two statements TAKEN TOGETHER are still NOT sufficient to answer the question.

Numbers: Only real numbers are used. That is, there are no complex numbers.

Drawings: A figure accompanying a data sufficiency question will conform to the information given in the question, but may conflict with the information given in statements (1) and (2).

You can assume that a line that appears straight is straight and that angle measures cannot be zero.

You can assume that the relative positions of points, angles, and objects are as shown.

All drawings lie in a plane unless stated otherwise.

Example:

In $\triangle ABC$, what is the value of y?

(1) $AB = AC$
(2) $x = 30$

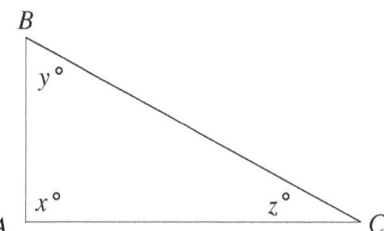

Explanation: By statement (1), $\triangle ABC$ is isosceles. Hence, its base angles are equal: $y = z$. Since the angle sum of a triangle is $180°$, we get $x + y + z = 180$. Replacing z with y in this equation and then simplifying yields $x + 2y = 180$. Since statement (1) does not give a value for x, we cannot determine the value of y from statement (1) alone. By statement (2), $x = 30$. Hence, $x + y + z = 180$ becomes $30 + y + z = 180$, or $y + z = 150$. Since statement (2) does not give a value for z, we cannot determine the value of y from statement (2) alone. However, using both statements in combination, we can find both x and z and therefore y. Hence, the answer is C.

Notice in the above example that the triangle appears to be a right triangle. However, that cannot be assumed: angle A may be $89°$ or $91°$, we can't tell from the drawing. **You must be very careful not to assume any more than what is explicitly given in a Data Sufficiency problem.**

Questions: 37
Time: 75 minutes

---

1. By how much is the greatest of five consecutive even integers greater than the smallest among them?

(A) 1
(B) 2
(C) 4
(D) 8
(E) 10

USE THIS SPACE FOR SCRATCHWORK.

---

2. A function * is defined for all even positive integers *n* as the number of even factors of *n* other than *n* itself. What is the value of *(48) ?

(A) 3
(B) 5
(C) 6
(D) 7
(E) 8

USE THIS SPACE FOR SCRATCHWORK.

---

3. If A, B, C, D, and E are points in a plane such that line CD bisects $\angle ACB$ and line CB bisects right angle $\angle ACE$, then $\angle DCE$ =

(A) 22.5°
(B) 45°
(C) 57.5°
(D) 67.5°
(E) 72.5°

USE THIS SPACE FOR SCRATCHWORK.

[Data Sufficiency Question (see Directions, page 15)]
4. What is the value of $l + 2t$?

   (1) $l + t = 4$
   (2) $l + 3t = 9$

5. Three workers A, B, and C are hired for 4 days. The daily wages of the three workers are as follows:

   A's first day wage is $4.
   Each day, his wage increases by 2 dollars.

   B's first day wage is $3.
   Each day, his wage increases by 2 dollars.

   C's first day wage is $1.
   Each day, his wage increases by the prime numbers 2, 3, and 5 in that order.

   Which one of the following is true about the wages earned by A, B, and C in the first 4 days?

   (A) $A > B > C$
   (B) $C > B > A$
   (C) $A > C > B$
   (D) $B > A > C$
   (E) $C > A > B$

6. Which one of the following does the expression $\dfrac{2^x + 2^{x-1}}{2^{x+1} - 2^x}$ equal?

   (A) 1
   (B) 3/2
   (C) 2
   (D) 5/2
   (E) 3

[Data Sufficiency Question]
7. Is xy a multiple of 48?

   (1) x is a multiple of 4.
   (2) y is a multiple of 6.

8. If $p + q = 7$ and $pq = 12$, then what is the value of $\dfrac{1}{p^2} + \dfrac{1}{q^2}$?

   (A) 1/6
   (B) 25/144
   (C) 49/144
   (D) 7/12
   (E) 73/144

9. The arithmetic mean (average) of the numbers a and b is 5, and the geometric mean of the numbers a and b is 8. Then $a^2 - 10a =$

(A) –64
(B) 76
(C) 82
(D) 96
(E) 102

USE THIS SPACE FOR SCRATCHWORK.

[Data Sufficiency Question]
10. Is $x^2 > y^2$?

(1) $x > y > 0$
(2) $x > 1 > y$

USE THIS SPACE FOR SCRATCHWORK.

[Data Sufficiency Question]
11. What fraction of the students in a class have blue eyes?

(1) 10% of the girls have blue eyes.
(2) 20% of the boys have blue eyes.

USE THIS SPACE FOR SCRATCHWORK.

12. In the figure, what is the value of y if $x : y = 2 : 3$?

   (A) 16
   (B) 32
   (C) 48
   (D) 54
   (E) 72

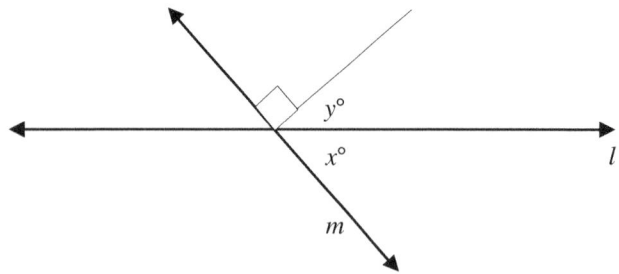

13. $\dfrac{\dfrac{\left(\left(\sqrt{7}\right)^x\right)^2}{\left(\sqrt{7}\right)^{11}}}{\dfrac{7^x}{7^{11}}} =$

   (A) $\sqrt{7}$
   (B) 7
   (C) 7^2
   (D) $7^{11/2}$
   (E) 7^{11}

[Data Sufficiency Question]
14. If Ms. Ana and Mr. Mathew are children of Mrs. Smith, how many brothers and sisters are there in Mrs. Smith's family?

   (1) Ms. Ana has the same number of brothers and sisters.
   (2) Mr. Mathew has twice as many sisters as brothers.

15. If $x - 3 = 10/x$ and $x > 0$, then what is the value of x ?

   (A) -2
   (B) -1
   (C) 3
   (D) 5
   (E) 10

[Data Sufficiency Question]
16. $A, B, C,$ and D are points on a line in that order. If $AD = 13$, what is the length of BC ?

   (1) $AC = 5$
   (2) $BD = 10$

17. If $|3x| \neq 2$, what is the value of $\frac{9x^2 - 4}{3x + 2} - \frac{9x^2 - 4}{3x - 2}$?

(A) –9
(B) –4
(C) 0
(D) 4
(E) 9

USE THIS SPACE FOR SCRATCHWORK.

18. Williams has x eggs. He sells 12 of them at a profit of 10 percent and the rest of the eggs at a loss of 10 percent. He made neither a profit nor a loss overall. Which one of the following equals x?

(A) 10
(B) 12
(C) 13
(D) 14
(E) 24

USE THIS SPACE FOR SCRATCHWORK.

[Data Sufficiency Question]
19. Which one of the expressions x^2y and x^2/y is greater?

(1) $y > x$
(2) $y < -1$

USE THIS SPACE FOR SCRATCHWORK.

The next two questions refer to the following discussion:
Mike and Fritz ran a 30-mile Marathon. Mike ran 10 miles at 10 miles per hour and then ran at 5 miles per hour for the remaining 20 miles. Fritz ran for the first one-third of the time of the run at 10 miles per hour, and for the remaining two-thirds of his time at 5 miles per hour.

20. How much time in hours did Mike take to complete the Marathon?

    (A)   3
    (B)   3.5
    (C)   4
    (D)   4.5
    (E)   5

21. How much time in hours did Fritz take to complete the Marathon?

    (A)   3
    (B)   3.5
    (C)   4
    (D)   4.5
    (E)   5

[Data Sufficiency Question]
22. In a sequence, the nth term a_n is defined by the rule $(a_{n-1} - 3)^2$. What is the value of a_4?

    (1) $a_1 = 1$
    (2) $a_2 = 4$

Questions 23–25 refer to the following graph.

The graph below shows historical exchange rates between the Indian Rupee (INR) and the US Dollar (USD) between January 9 and February 8 of a particular year.

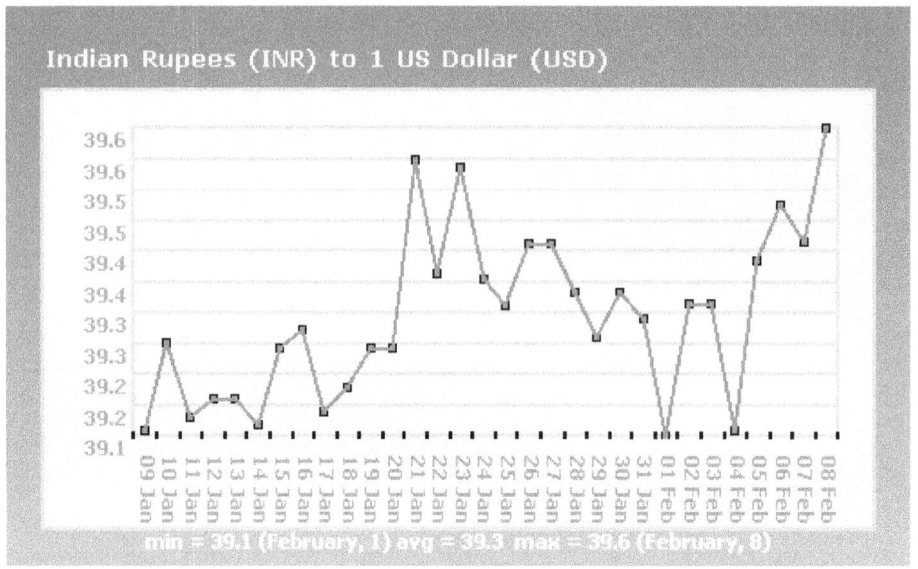

23. On which day shown on the graph did the value of the US dollar increase against the Rupee by the greatest amount?

    (A) Jan. 10
    (B) Jan. 14
    (C) Jan. 21
    (D) Jan. 23
    (E) Feb. 4

24. John had 100 dollars. The exchange rate converts the amount in US dollars to a number in Indian Rupees by directly multiplying by the value of the exchange rate. By what amount did John's $100 increase in terms of Indian Rupees from Jan. 9 to Feb. 8?

    (A) 5
    (B) 10
    (C) 15
    (D) 25
    (E) 50

25. On February 8, the dollar value was approximately what percent of the dollar value on January 9?

    (A) 1.28
    (B) 12.8
    (C) 101.28
    (D) 112.8
    (E) 128

26. A sequence of numbers $a_1, a_2, a_3, \ldots, a_n$ is generated by the rule $a_{n+1} = 2a_n$. If $a_7 - a_6 = 96$, then what is the value of a_7 ?

(A) 48
(B) 96
(C) 98
(D) 192
(E) 198

USE THIS SPACE FOR SCRATCHWORK.

27. There are 750 male and female participants in a meeting. Half the female participants and one-quarter of the male participants are Democrats. One-third of all the participants are Democrats. How many of the Democrats are female?

(A) 75
(B) 100
(C) 125
(D) 175
(E) 225

USE THIS SPACE FOR SCRATCHWORK.

[Data Sufficiency Question]
28. Can x equal 0 ?

(1) $x^2 + 1 > 2x + 4$
(2) $(x + 1)^2 - 2x > 2(x + 1) + 2$

USE THIS SPACE FOR SCRATCHWORK.

GMAT Math Tests

[Data Sufficiency Question]
29. Is x greater than y ?

    (1) $x = 2y$
    (2) $y = 2k$

[Data Sufficiency Question]
30. If $y = -x$, then is $y > -1$?

    (1) $x^4 > x^2$
    (2) $x^3 < x^2$

31. The functions f and g are defined as $f(x, y) = 2x + y$ and $g(x, y) = x + 2y$. What is the value of $f(3, 4)$?

    (A) $f(4, 3)$
    (B) $f(3, 7)$
    (C) $f(7, 4)$
    (D) $g(3, 4)$
    (E) $g(4, 3)$

[Data Sufficiency Question]
32. $2x - y =$

    (1) $3x + y = x + 2y$
    (2) $(x + y) + 3(x - y) = 0$

33. John was born on February 28, 1999. It was a Sunday. February of that year had only 28 days, and the year had exactly 365 days. His brother Jack was born on the same day of the year 2000. February of the year 2000 had 29 days. On which day was Jack born?

   (A) Monday
   (B) Tuesday
   (C) Friday
   (D) Saturday
   (E) Sunday

[Data Sufficiency Question]

34. What is the value of $\dfrac{xy}{x+y}$?

   (1) $1/x + 1/y = 1/3$
   (2) $x + y = xy/3$

35. In the triangle, what is the value of x ?

   (A) 25
   (B) 55
   (C) 60
   (D) 77
   (E) 85

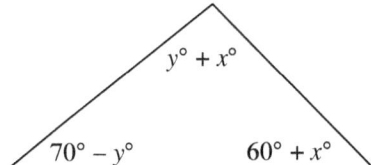

GMAT Math Tests

[Data Sufficiency Question]
36. What is the value of $(x-2)^2$?

    (1) $x^2 - 4x + 3 = 0$
    (2) $x^2 - 7x + 12 = 0$

37. If $\dfrac{a^2 - 9}{12a} = \dfrac{a-3}{a+3}$, $a + 3 \neq 0$, and $a \neq 0$, then $a =$

    (A)   1
    (B)   2
    (C)   3
    (D)   6
    (E)   9

Test 1—Answers and Solutions

Answers and Solutions Test 1:

1. D	11. E	21. D	31. E
2. D	12. D	22. D	32. D
3. D	13. D	23. C	33. A
4. C	14. C	24. E	34. D
5. A	15. D	25. C	35. A
6. B	16. C	26. D	36. A
7. A	17. B	27. C	37. C
8. B	18. E	28. D	
9. A	19. B	29. E	
10. A	20. E	30. B	

---

1. Choose any 5 consecutive even integers—say—2, 4, 6, 8, 10. The largest in this group is 10, and the smallest is 2. Their difference is $10 - 2 = 8$. The answer is (D).

---

2. $48 = 2 \cdot 2 \cdot 2 \cdot 2 \cdot 3$. The even factors of 48 are

$$2$$
$$2 \cdot 2 \; (= 4)$$
$$2 \cdot 2 \cdot 2 \; (= 8)$$
$$2 \cdot 2 \cdot 2 \cdot 2 \; (= 16)$$
$$3 \cdot 2 \; (= 6)$$
$$3 \cdot 2 \cdot 2 \; (= 12)$$
$$3 \cdot 2 \cdot 2 \cdot 2 \; (= 24)$$
$$3 \cdot 2 \cdot 2 \cdot 2 \cdot 2 \; (= 48)$$

Not counting the last factor (48 itself), the total number of factors is 7. The answer is (D).

---

3. Drawing the figure given in the question yields

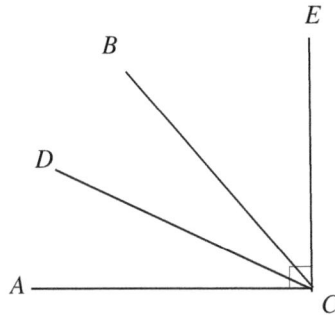

Figure not drawn to scale.

CD bisects ∠ACB
CB bisects ∠ACE

We are given that *CB* bisects the right-angle ∠*ACE*. Hence, ∠*ACB* = ∠*BCE* = ∠*ACE*/2 = 90°/2 = 45°. Also, since *CD* bisects ∠*ACB*, ∠*ACD* = ∠*DCB* = ∠*ACB*/2 = 45°/2 = 22.5°. Now, ∠*DCE* = ∠*DCB* + ∠*BCE* = 22.5° + 45° = 67.5°. The answer is (D).

GMAT Math Tests

4. Statement (1) contains two variables and only one equation. Hence, it cannot determine the value of $l + 2t$. So, Statement (1) alone is *not* sufficient.

Similarly, Statement (2) contains two variables and only one equation. Hence, it cannot determine the value of $l + 2t$. So, Statement (2) alone is *not* sufficient.

With Statement (1) and Statement (2) together, we have two equations in two unknowns:

$$l + t = 4$$
$$l + 3t = 9$$

This system may have a solution. To find out, add the equations:

$$(l + t) + (l + 3t) = 4 + 9$$

$$2l + 4t = 13$$

$$l + 2t = 13/2$$

Hence, the statements together answer the question. The answer is (C).

5. The payments to Worker *A* for the 4 days are the four integers 4, 6, 8, and 10. The sum of the payments is $4 + 6 + 8 + 10 = 28$.

The payments to Worker *B* for the 4 days are the four integers 3, 5, 7, and 9. The sum of the payments is $3 + 5 + 7 + 9 = 24$.

The payments to Worker *C* for the 4 days are 1, $1 + 2 = 3$, $3 + 3 = 6$, and $6 + 5 = 11$. The sum of the payments is $1 + 3 + 6 + 11 = 21$.

From the calculations, $A > B > C$. The answer is (A).

6. The term 2^{x-1} equals $\dfrac{2^x}{2}$, and the term 2^{x+1} equals $2^x \cdot 2$. Hence, the given expression $\dfrac{2^x + 2^{x-1}}{2^{x+1} - 2^x}$ becomes

$$\dfrac{2^x + \dfrac{2^x}{2}}{2^x \cdot 2 - 2^x} =$$

$$\dfrac{2^x\left(1 + \dfrac{1}{2}\right)}{2^x(2 - 1)} = \quad \text{by factoring out } 2^x \text{ from both numerator and denominator}$$

$$\dfrac{\left(1 + \dfrac{1}{2}\right)}{2 - 1} = \quad \text{by canceling } 2^x \text{ from both numerator and denominator}$$

$$\dfrac{3/2}{1} =$$

$$\dfrac{3}{2}$$

The answer is (B).

7. Not every multiple of 4 is a multiple of 48 (For example, 8 [= 4 · 2] is a multiple of 4, but 8 is not a multiple of 48). Hence, Statement (1) alone is not sufficient to answer the question.

Not every multiple of 6 is a multiple of 48 (For example, 12 [= 6 · 2] is a multiple of 6, but 12 is not a multiple of 48). Hence, Statement (2) alone is not sufficient to answer the question.

A multiple of both 4 and 6 must be a multiple of the least common multiple of 4 and 6, which is 24. But again, not every multiple of 24 is a multiple of 48 (For example, 72 [= 24 · 3] is a multiple of 24, but 72 is not a multiple of 48). Hence, statements (1) and (2) together cannot answer the question. The answer is (E).

---

8. Solving the equation $p + q = 7$ for q yields $q = 7 - p$. Plugging this into the equation $pq = 12$ yields

$$p(7 - p) = 12$$
$$7p - p^2 = 12$$
$$p^2 - 7p + 12 = 0$$
$$(p - 3)(p - 4) = 0$$
$$p - 3 = 0 \text{ or } p - 4 = 0$$
$$p = 3 \text{ or } p = 4$$

If $p = 3$, then $q = 7 - p = 7 - 3 = 4$. Plugging these values into the expression $\frac{1}{p^2} + \frac{1}{q^2}$ yields

$$\frac{1}{3^2} + \frac{1}{4^2} =$$
$$\frac{1}{9} + \frac{1}{16} =$$
$$\frac{25}{144}$$

The result is the same for the other solution $p = 4$ (and then $q = 7 - p = 7 - 4 = 3$). The answer is (B).

Method II:
$\frac{1}{p^2} + \frac{1}{q^2} = \frac{(q^2 + p^2)}{p^2 q^2} = \frac{(p+q)^2 - 2pq}{(pq)^2} = \frac{(7)^2 - 2(12)}{12^2} = \frac{49 - 24}{144} = \frac{25}{144}$. The answer is (B).

---

9. The arithmetic mean of the numbers a and b is 5. Hence, we have $(a + b)/2 = 5$, or $a + b = 10$.

The geometric mean of the numbers a and b is 8. Hence, we have $\sqrt{ab} = 8$, or $ab = 8^2 = 64$. Hence, $b = 64/a$.

Substituting this into the equation $a + b = 10$ yields

$$a + 64/a = 10$$
$$a^2 + 64 = 10a$$
$$a^2 - 10a = -64$$

The answer is (A).

10. From the inequality $x > y > 0$ in Statement (1), we have that both x and y are positive. Multiplying the inequality $x > y$ by x yields $x^2 > xy$, and multiplying by y yields $xy > y^2$. Combining the two results yields $x^2 > xy > y^2$. So, we have $x^2 > y^2$. Hence, Statement (1) alone is sufficient to answer the question.

From Statement (2) alone, we have $x > 1 > y$. Now, if $x = 2$ and $y = -3$, then x^2 is not greater than y^2. But, if $x = 2$ and $y = -1$, then x^2 is greater than y^2. Hence, we have a double case and Statement (2) alone is *not* sufficient.

The answer is (A).

11. Let the number of girls be g, and the number of boys be b. Hence, the number of students is $b + g$. From the statements together, we have that

10% of girls are blue eyed. 10% of g is $\dfrac{10}{100}g = \dfrac{g}{10}$.

20% of boys are blue eyed. 20% of b is $\dfrac{20}{100}b = \dfrac{b}{5}$.

Hence, the total number of blue-eyed students is $\dfrac{g}{10} + \dfrac{b}{5}$.

Hence, the required fraction is $\dfrac{\dfrac{g}{10} + \dfrac{b}{5}}{b + g}$.

Dividing both the numerator and the denominator of the fraction by b yields $\dfrac{\dfrac{g}{10b} + \dfrac{1}{5}}{1 + \dfrac{g}{b}}$. Hence, to find the value of the required fraction, we need at least the ratio of b/g. Since we do not have means to evaluate the ratio, the statements together are not sufficient to answer the question. The answer is (E).

12. We know that the angle made by a line is 180°. Applying this to line m yields $x + y + 90 = 180$. Subtracting 90 from both sides of this equation yields $x + y = 90$. We are also given that $x : y = 2 : 3$. Hence, $x/y = 2/3$. Multiplying this equation by y yields $x = 2y/3$. Plugging this into the equation $x + y = 90$ yields

$$2y/3 + y = 90$$
$$5y/3 = 90$$
$$5y = 270$$
$$y = 54$$

The answer is (D).

13. The numerator $\dfrac{\left(\left(\sqrt{7}\right)^x\right)^2}{\left(\sqrt{7}\right)^{11}}$ equals

$$\dfrac{\left(\left(7^{1/2}\right)^x\right)^2}{\left(7^{1/2}\right)^{11}} \qquad \text{since } \sqrt{7} = 7^{1/2}$$

$$= \dfrac{7^{\frac{2x}{2}}}{7^{\frac{11}{2}}}$$

$$= \dfrac{7^x}{7^{\frac{11}{2}}}$$

Substituting this in the given expression $\dfrac{\dfrac{\left(\left(\sqrt{7}\right)^x\right)^2}{\left(\sqrt{7}\right)^{11}}}{\dfrac{7^x}{7^{11}}}$ yields

$$\dfrac{\dfrac{7^x}{7^{\frac{11}{2}}}}{\dfrac{7^x}{7^{11}}} =$$

$$\dfrac{\dfrac{1}{7^{\frac{11}{2}}}}{\dfrac{1}{7^{11}}} = \qquad \text{canceling } 7^x \text{ from both numerator and denominator}$$

$$\dfrac{7^{11}}{7^{\frac{11}{2}}} =$$

$$7^{\frac{11}{2}}$$

The answer is (D).

14. From Statement (1) alone, we have that Ms. Anna has the same number of brothers as sisters. If m is the number of male children Mrs. Smith has (so Anna has this many brothers), then she must have m sisters also. Hence, including Ms. Anna, Mrs. Smith must have $m + 1$ female children. Now, the number of children Mrs. Smith has equals $m + (m + 1) = 2m + 1$. But, we still do not know the value of m. Hence, Statement (1) alone is not sufficient.

From Statement (2) alone, we have that Mr. Mathew has twice as many sisters as brothers. Hence, if Mathew has, say, $m - 1$ brothers, then he must have $2(m - 1)$ sisters. Hence, the total number of children of Mrs. Smith equals

$m - 1$ brothers of Mathew $+ 1$ (Mathew himself) $+ 2(m - 1)$ sisters $= m + 2(m - 1) = 3m - 2$

Since we do not know the value m, Statement (2) alone is not sufficient.

Equating the number of children from both statements yields $2m + 1 = 3m - 2$. Solving this equation for m yields $m = 3$. Hence, the number of children of Mrs. Smith is $2m + 1 = 2 \cdot 3 + 1 = 7$. Hence, the statements together answer the question.

The answer is (C).

15. We have the equation $x - 3 = 10/x$. Multiplying the equation by x yields $x^2 - 3x = 10$. Subtracting 10 from both sides yields $x^2 - 3x - 10 = 0$. Factoring the equation yields $(x - 5)(x + 2) = 0$. The possible solutions are 5 and –2. The only solution that also satisfies the given inequality $x > 0$ is $x = 5$. The answer is (D).

16. Drawing a number line with the points A, B, C, and D yields

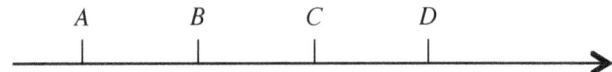

From the number line, we have the equations

$AC = AB + BC$
$BD = BC + CD$
$AD = AB + BC + CD$

Adding the first two equations yields

$AC + BD = (AB + BC) + (BC + CD) = AB + 2BC + CD$

Subtracting the third equation from this equation yields

$AC + BD - AD = AB + 2BC + CD - (AB + BC + CD)$
$= BC$

Hence, $BC = AC + BD - AD = AC + BD - 13$. Now, the side lengths of BD and AC are independent of each other. Hence, the value of BC depends on both AC and BC. Hence, both statements are required to answer the question. Hence, the answer is (C), and $BC = AC + BD - 13 = 5 + 10 - 13 = 2$.

17. $\dfrac{9x^2-4}{3x+2} - \dfrac{9x^2-4}{3x-2}$

$\quad = (9x^2-4)\left(\dfrac{1}{3x+2} - \dfrac{1}{3x-2}\right)$ by factoring out the common term $9x^2-4$

$\quad = (9x^2-4)\dfrac{(3x-2)-(3x+2)}{(3x+2)(3x-2)}$

$\quad = (9x^2-4)\dfrac{3x-2-3x-2}{(3x)^2-2^2}$

$\quad = (9x^2-4)\dfrac{-4}{9x^2-4}$ Since $|3x| \neq 2$, $(3x)^2 \neq 4$, and therefore $9x^2-4 \neq 0$.

                 Hence, we can safely cancel $9x^2-4$ from numerator and denominator.

$\quad = -4$

The answer is (B).

---

18. Let a dollars be the cost of each egg to Williams. Hence, the net cost of the x eggs is ax dollars.

Now, the selling price of the eggs when selling at a 10% profit is $a(1 + 10/100) = 11a/10$. Selling 12 eggs now returns $12(11a/10)$ dollars.

The selling price of the eggs when selling at a 10% loss is $a(1 - 10/100) = 9a/10$. Selling the remaining $x - 12$ eggs now returns $(x - 12)(9a/10)$ dollars.

The net return equals $12(11a/10) + (x - 12)(9a/10) = a(0.9x + 2.4)$.

Since overall he made neither a profit nor a loss, the net returns equals the net cost. So, we have $a(0.9x + 2.4) = ax$. Dividing both sides by a yields $0.9x + 2.4 = x$. Multiplying each side by 10 yields $9x + 24 = 10x$. Subtracting $9x$ from both sides yields $x = 24$. Hence, the answer is (E).

---

19. We can reword the question as either "Is $x^2y > x^2/y$?" or "Is $x^2y < x^2/y$?" A valid assumption is $x^2y \neq x^2/y$ since the original question asks for the greater one of the two. Let's work on "Is $x^2y > x^2/y$?" Dividing this inequality by the positive value x^2 changes the question to "Is $y > 1/y$?" Since the inequality in the question no longer has x^2, any further information about x is irrelevant. So, Statement (1) is *not* required.

From Statement (2) alone, we have that $y < -1$. Hence, y is negative. Dividing both sides of this inequality by $-y$, a positive number, yields $-1 < 1/y$. Combining the inequalities $y < -1$ and $-1 < 1/y$ yields $y < -1 < 1/y$ from which we have $y < 1/y$. Hence, Statement (2) alone answers the question. Hence, the answer is (B). The answer to the question is "No. y is not greater than $1/y$." So, the answer to the original question is "No. x^2y is *not* greater than x^2/y," or "x^2/y is the greater one."

GMAT Math Tests

---

20. Mike ran 10 miles at 10 miles per hour:

$$Time = Distance/Rate = 10 \text{ miles}/10 \text{ miles per hour} = 1 \text{ hour}$$

He ran at 5 miles per hour for the remaining 20 miles:

$$Time = Distance/Rate = 20 \text{ miles}/5 \text{ miles per hour} = 4 \text{ hrs.}$$

The total length of the Marathon track is 30 miles, and the total time taken to cover the track is 5 hours. Hence, the answer is (E).

---

21. Suppose Fritz took t hours to complete the 30-mile Marathon. Then as given, Fritz ran at 10 miles per hour for $t/3$ hours and 5 miles per hour for the remaining $2t/3$ hours. Now, by formula, *Distance = Rate · Time*, the total distance covered would be

$$(10 \text{ miles per hour}) \cdot t/3 + (5 \text{ miles per hour}) \cdot 2t/3 = (10/3 + 10/3)t = 30 \text{ miles}$$

Solving the equation for t yields $t = 90/20$ hours $= 4.5$ hours. The answer is (D).

---

22. The question is asking for the value of a_4. Substituting $n = 4$ in the formula of the sequence $a_n = (a_{n-1} - 3)^2$ yields $a_4 = (a_{4-1} - 3)^2 = (a_3 - 3)^2$. From this equation, it is clear that we need the value of a_3 to evaluate a_4. Similarly, to evaluate a_3, we need the value of a_2 (a_2 alone is sufficient). Hence, a_4 can be evaluated if we have a_2 alone. Hence, Statement (2) alone is sufficient to answer the question. Similarly, a_2 can also be evaluated from a_1 and therefore the value of a_1 alone is sufficient to evaluate a_4. Since each statement alone is sufficient, the answer is (D).

---

23. Here, the scale of the x-axis is uniform. Hence, growth is greatest when the curve is steepest. The growth curve of the US dollar against the Indian Rupee is the steepest (increased by a bit more than six horizontal lines on the graph) on January 21. Hence, the answer is (C). On February 5th, the growth is the next greatest, growing by a bit less than 6 horizontal lines.

---

24. One dollar converted to 39.1 Rupees on Jan. 9. Hence, 100 dollars converts to $39.15 \times 100 = 3915$ Indian Rupees. On February 8, it converted to 39.65 Rupees. Hence, on that day, 100 dollars converted to $39.65 \times 100 = 3965$ Rupees. The increase in terms of Indian Rupees is $3965 - 3915 = 50$. The answer is (E).

---

25. On January 9, the dollar value was 39.15 Rupees, and on February 8 the dollar value was 39.65 Rupees. Hence, the dollar value on February 8th was $39.65/39.15 \times 100 = (39.15 + 0.5)/39.15 \times 100 = 100 + 0.5/39.15 \times 100 = (100 + 1.28) = 101.28$ percent of the value on January 9th. Hence, the answer is (C).

---

26. Putting $n = 6$ in the given rule $a_{n+1} = 2a_n$ yields $a_{6+1} = 2a_6$, or $a_7 = 2a_6$. Since we are given that $a_7 - a_6 = 96$, we have $2a_6 - a_6 = 96$, or $a_6 = 96$. Hence, $a_7 = 2a_6 = 2 \cdot 96 = 192$. The answer is (D).

27. Let m be the number of male participants and f be the number of female participants in the meeting. The total number of participants is given as 750. Hence, we have

$$m + f = 750$$

Now, we have that half the female participants and one-quarter of the male participants are Democrats. Let d equal the number of the Democrats. Then we have the equation

$$f/2 + m/4 = d$$

Now, we have that one-third of the total participants are Democrats. Hence, we have the equation

$$d = 750/3 = 250$$

Solving the three equations yields the solution $f = 250$, $m = 500$, and $d = 250$. The number of female democratic participants equals half the female participants equals $250/2 = 125$. The answer is (C).

28. From Statement (1), we have the inequality:

$x^2 + 1 > 2x + 4$
$x^2 - 2x + 1 > 4$ subtracting $2x$ from both sides
$x^2 - 2(x)(1) + 1^2 > 4$ expressing the left side in the form $a^2 - 2ab + b^2$
$(x - 1)^2 > 4$ using the formula $a^2 - 2ab + b^2 = (a - b)^2$

Square rooting both sides of the inequality yields two new inequalities: $x - 1 > 2$ or $x - 1 < -2$. Adding 1 to both sides of these inequalities yields $x > 3$ and $x < -1$. So, x is either less than -1 or x is greater than 3. In either case, x does not equal 0. Hence, Statement (1) alone answers the question.

Now, the given inequality in Statement (2) is

$(x + 1)^2 - 2x > 2(x + 1) + 2$
$x^2 + 2x + 1 - 2x > 2x + 2 + 2$
$x^2 + 1 > 2x + 4$

This inequality is same as the inequality in Statement (1). Hence, each statement alone is sufficient to answer the question, and the answer is (D).

29. From statements (1) and (2) together, we have $x = 2y$ and $y = 2k$.

Let k equal -1. Then from the second equation, $y = 2k = 2(-1) = -2$; and from the first equation, $x = 2y = 2(-2) = -4$. In this case, x ($= -4$) is not greater than y ($= -2$).

Now, let k equal 1. Then from the second equation, we have $y = 2k = 2(1) = 2$ and $x = 2y = 2(2) = 4$. In this case, x ($= 4$) is greater than y ($= 2$). We have a double case here with statements (1) and (2) taken together.

Hence, statements (1) and (2) together are not sufficient to answer the question. The answer is (E).

30. The question asks is $y > -1$? We are also given the equation $y = -x$. Substituting this into the inequality $y > -1$ yields $-x > -1$. Multiplying this inequality by -1 and flipping the direction of the inequality yields $x < 1$. Hence, effectively, we are asked "Is $x < 1$."

Now, dividing the inequality in Statement (1) by the positive value x^2 yields $x^2 > 1$. The solutions for this inequality are $x < -1$ and $x > 1$. The first solution says x is less than 1 and the second solution says x is greater than 1. Hence, we have a double case with Statement (1) alone. So, the statement is not sufficient.

Now, dividing the inequality in Statement (2), $x^3 < x^2$, by x^2 yields $x < 1$. Hence, Statement (2) says x is less than 1. Hence, Statement (2) alone is sufficient to answer the question.

The answer is (B).

---

31. We are given the function rules $f(x, y) = 2x + y$ and $g(x, y) = x + 2y$. Swapping arguments in g yields

$$g(y, x) = y + 2x = f(x, y)$$

Hence, $f(3, 4) = g(4, 3)$. The answer is (E).

---

32. From Statement (1) alone, we have

$$3x + y = x + 2y$$
$$3x + y - x - 2y = 0 \qquad \text{by subtracting } x \text{ and } 2y \text{ from both sides}$$
$$2x - y = 0$$

Hence, Statement (1) alone answers the question: $2x - y = 0$.

Now, from Statement (2), we have

$$(x + y) + 3(x - y) = 0$$
$$x + y + 3x - 3y = 0$$
$$4x - 2y = 0$$
$$2x - y = 0$$

Hence, Statement (2) alone also answers the question: $2x - y = 0$.

Hence, each statement alone is sufficient to answer the question. The answer is (D).

---

33. The period February 28, 1999 through February 28, 2000 (not including the former date) does not include the complete month of February 2000 (which actually had 29 days). Hence, the length of the period is exactly 365 days (equal to the length of a normal year). Now, dividing 365 by 7 (the number of days in a week) yields a quotient of 52 and a remainder of 1. Hence, the exact length of the period is 52 weeks and one day. Hence, the day February 28 of the year 2000 would advance by one day over the date February 28 of the year 1999. Hence, since February 28, 1999 is a Sunday, the date February 28, 2000 is a Monday. The answer is (A).

Test 1—Answers and Solutions

34. Multiplying the equation $1/x + 1/y = 1/3$ given in Statement (1) by xy yields $y + x = xy/3$, or $x + y = xy/3$. This equation is the same as the equation given in Statement (2). Hence, Statement (2) is the same as Statement (1).

Now, multiplying both sides of the equation $x + y = \dfrac{xy}{3}$ by $\dfrac{3}{x+y}$ yields $\dfrac{xy}{x+y} = 3$. Hence, Statement (1) alone, and therefore Statement (2) alone, is sufficient to answer the question.

The answer is (D).

---

35. The angle sum of a triangle is 180°. Hence, $(y + x) + (60 + x) + (70 - y) = 180$. Simplifying the equation yields $2x + 130 = 180$. Solving for x yields $x = 25$. The answer is (A).

---

36. $(x - 2)^2 = x^2 - 4x + 2^2 = x^2 - 4x + 4$. Hence, the question is "What is the value of $x^2 - 4x + 4$?"

From Statement (1) alone, we have that $x^2 - 4x + 3 = 0$. Adding 1 to both sides yields $x^2 - 4x + 4 = 1$. The answer is 1. Hence, Statement (1) alone is sufficient.

From Statement (2) alone, we have that $x^2 - 7x + 12 = 0$. Adding $3x - 8$ to both sides yields

$$x^2 - 7x + 12 + (3x - 8) = 0 + 3x - 8, \text{ or } x^2 - 4x + 4 = 3x - 8$$

Here, the value of $x^2 - 4x + 4$ depends on x, an unknown, so Statement (2) alone is not sufficient.

Hence, the answer is (A).

---

37. The given equation is

$$\dfrac{a^2 - 9}{12a} = \dfrac{a - 3}{a + 3}$$

$$\dfrac{a^2 - 9}{12a} - \dfrac{a - 3}{a + 3} = 0$$

$$\dfrac{(a-3)(a+3)}{12a} - \dfrac{a-3}{a+3} = 0 \qquad \text{by the formula } a^2 - b^2 = (a - b)(a + b)$$

$$(a - 3)\left(\dfrac{a+3}{12a} - \dfrac{1}{a+3}\right) = 0 \qquad \text{by factoring out the common factor } a - 3$$

$$(a - 3)\left(\dfrac{(a+3)^2 - 12a}{12a(a+3)}\right) = 0$$

$$(a - 3)\left((a+3)^2 - 12a\right) = 0 \qquad \text{by multiplying both sides by } 12a(a+3)$$

$$(a - 3)(a^2 + 6a + 9 - 12a) = 0$$
$$(a - 3)(a^2 - 6a + 9) = 0$$
$$(a - 3)(a^2 - 2a3 + 9) = 0$$
$$(a - 3)(a - 3)^2 = 0 \qquad \text{by the Perfect Square Trinomial formula}$$
$$(a - 3)^3 = 0$$
$$a - 3 = 0 \qquad \text{by cube rooting both sides}$$
$$a = 3$$

Hence, the answer is (C).

Test 2

GMAT Math Tests

Questions: 37
Time: 75 minutes

1. Which one of the following could be an integer?

   (A) Average of two consecutive integers.
   (B) Average of three consecutive integers.
   (C) Average of four consecutive integers.
   (D) Average of six consecutive integers.
   (E) Average of 6 and 9.

2. For any positive integer n, $\pi(n)$ represents the number of factors of n, inclusive of 1 and itself. If a and b are unequal prime numbers, then $\pi(a) + \pi(b) - \pi(a \times b) =$

   (A) −4
   (B) −2
   (C) 0
   (D) −2
   (E) 4

3. Which one of the following is the minimum value of the sum of two integers whose product is 36?

   (A) 37
   (B) 20
   (C) 15
   (D) 13
   (E) 12

[Data Sufficiency Question (see Directions, page 15)]
4. What is the last digit of the positive integer n ?

   (1) The last digit of n equals the last digit of n^2.
   (2) n is an even number.

5. What is the value of y in the figure?

   (A) 20
   (B) 30
   (C) 35
   (D) 45
   (E) 50

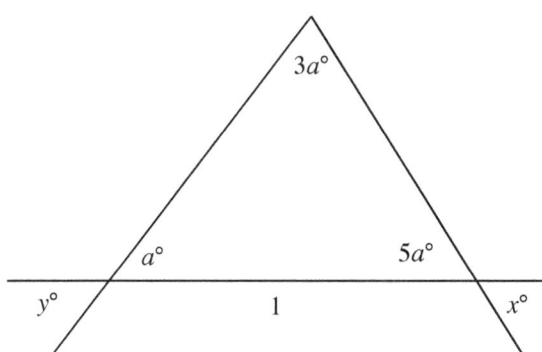

6. ΔABC is a right-angled isosceles triangle, and $\angle B$ is the right angle in the triangle. If AC measures $7\sqrt{2}$, then which one of the following would equal the lengths of AB and BC, respectively?

(A) 7, 7
(B) 9, 9
(C) 10, 10
(D) 11, 12
(E) 7, 12

USE THIS SPACE FOR SCRATCHWORK.

[Data Sufficiency Question]

7. $\frac{1}{p^4} + \frac{1}{q^4} =$

(1) $p + q = 12$
(2) $pq = 35$

USE THIS SPACE FOR SCRATCHWORK.

[Data Sufficiency Question]

8. If $H = \frac{T\sqrt{1 - R^2}}{k\sqrt{1 - g^k}}$, then $H =$

(1) $T = 3, R = 1/2$
(2) $k = 4, g = 1/3$

USE THIS SPACE FOR SCRATCHWORK.

9. If $a = x + 2y$, and $b = y + 2x$, and $3x + 7y > 7x + 3y$, then which one of the following is true?

   (I) $a > b$
   (II) $a = b$
   (III) $a < b$

   (A)   I only
   (B)   II only
   (C)   III only
   (D)   I and II only
   (E)   II and III only

[Data Sufficiency Question]
10. If n is a positive integer, then is $(n + 1)(n + 3)$ a multiple of 4?

   (1) $(n + 2)(n + 4)$ is odd.
   (2) $(n + 3)(n + 6)$ is even.

[Data Sufficiency Question]
11. X is a 4-digit integer, and Y is a 3-digit integer. Is the sum of the digits of X greater than the sum of the digits of Y?

   (1)   All the digits of X are greater than 5.
   (2)   All the digits of Y are less than 5.

12. If x is not equal to 1 and $y = \dfrac{1}{x-1}$, then which one of the following cannot be the value of y?

    (A) 0
    (B) 1
    (C) 2
    (D) 3
    (E) 4

13. If $(x+5) \div \left(\dfrac{1}{x} + \dfrac{1}{5}\right) = 5$, then $x =$

    (A) -5
    (B) $1/2$
    (C) 1
    (D) 5
    (E) 10

[Data Sufficiency Question]
14. If x is not equal to 1, then is y equal to zero?

   (1) $y = \dfrac{1}{x-1}$
   (2) $y = \dfrac{x}{6}$

[Data Sufficiency Question]
15. What is the average temperature from Monday through Saturday of a week?

   (1) The average temperature from Monday through Wednesday of the week is 36°C.
   (2) The minimum and maximum temperatures between Thursday and Saturday of the week are 25°C and 38°C, respectively.

16. A cyclist travels at 12 miles per hour. How many minutes will it take him to travel 24 miles?

   (A) 1
   (B) 2
   (C) 30
   (D) 60
   (E) 120

17. The nth term of the sequence $a_1, a_2, a_3, \ldots, a_n$ is defined as $a_n = -(a_{n-1})$. The first term a_1 equals -1. What is the value of a_5 ?

   (A) -2
   (B) -1
   (C) 0
   (D) 1
   (E) 2

18. In a zoo, each pigeon has 2 legs, and each rabbit has 4 legs. The head count of the two species together is 12, and the leg count is 32. How many pigeons and how many rabbits are there in the zoo?

   (A) 4, 8
   (B) 6, 6
   (C) 6, 8
   (D) 8, 4
   (E) 8, 6

[Data Sufficiency Question]
19. The length and width of a rectangular box are 6 feet and 5 feet, respectively. A hose supplies water at a rate of 6 cubic feet per minute. How long would it take to fill a conical box whose volume is three times the volume of the rectangle box?

   (1) The depth of the rectangular box is 7 feet.
   (2) The radius of the base of the conical box is 6 feet.

20. (The average of five consecutive integers starting from m) − (the average of six consecutive integers starting from m) =

   (A) −1/4
   (B) −1/2
   (C) 0
   (D) 1/2
   (E) 1/4

21. The function $\Delta(m)$ is defined for all positive integers m as the product of $m + 4$, $m + 5$, and $m + 6$. If n is a positive integer, then $\Delta(n)$ must be divisible by which one of the following numbers?

   (A) 4
   (B) 5
   (C) 6
   (D) 7
   (E) 11

22. A palindrome number is a number that reads the same forward or backward. For example, 787 is a palindrome number. By how much is the first palindrome larger than 233 greater than 233?

   (A) 9
   (B) 11
   (C) 13
   (D) 14
   (E) 16

Questions 23–25 refer to the following graph.

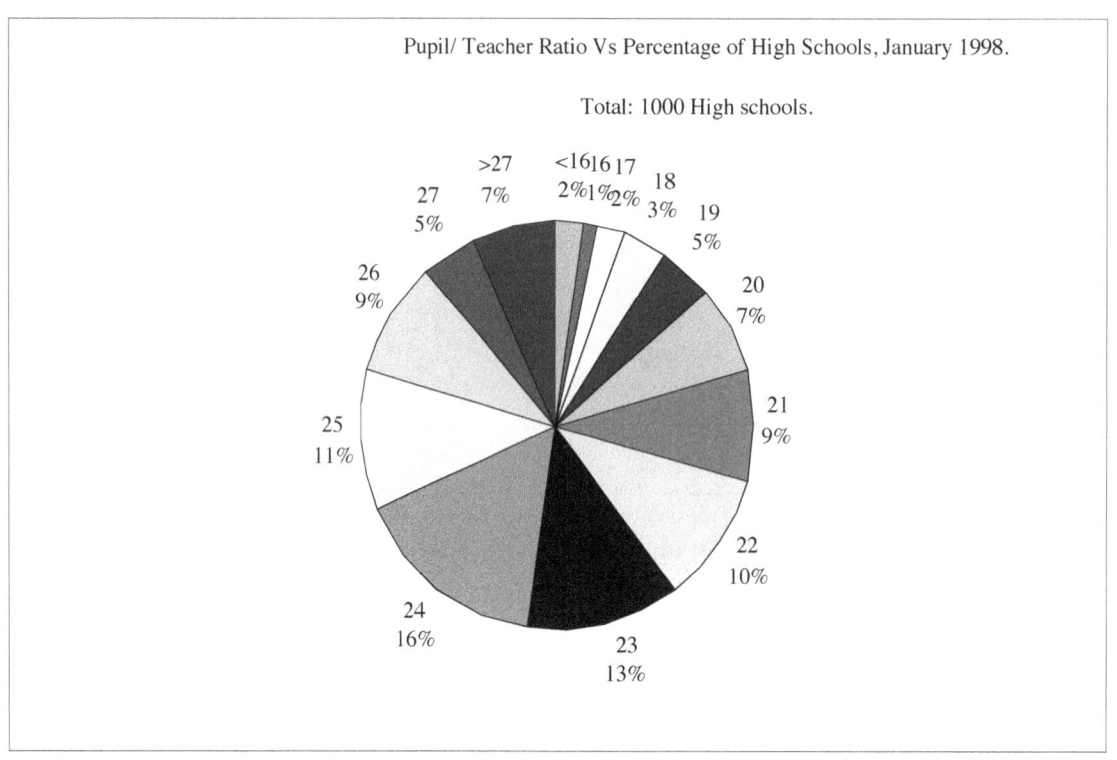

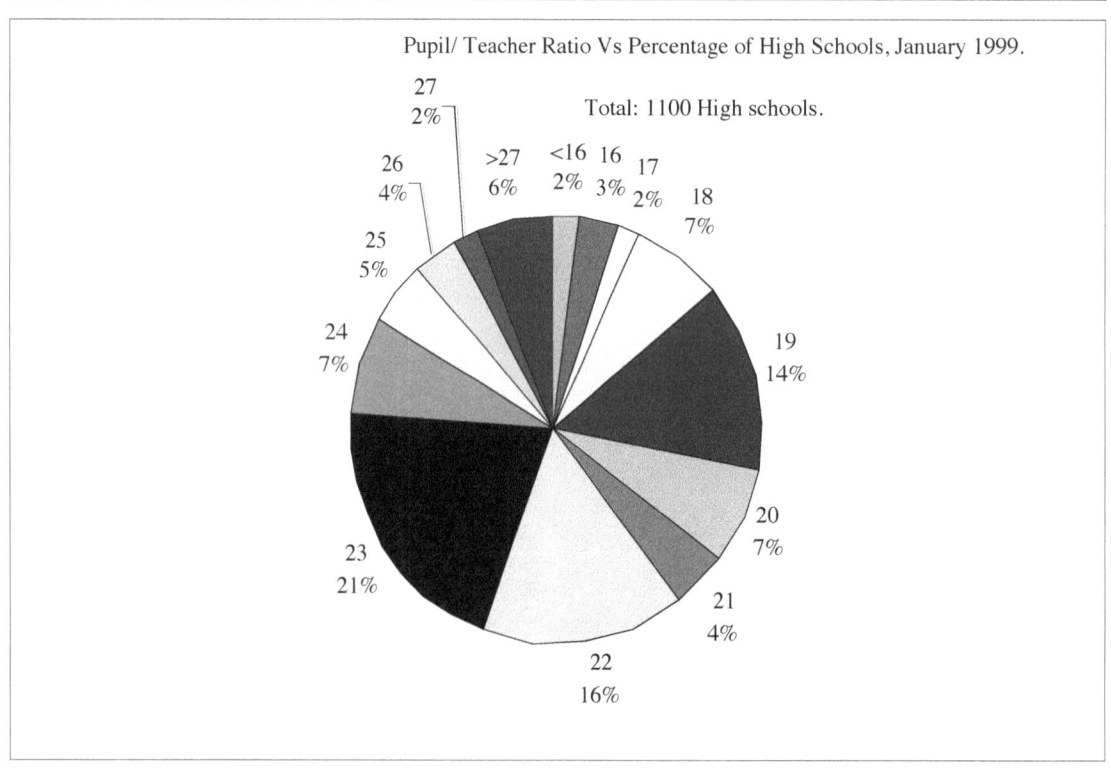

23. By what percent did the number of schools with Pupil/Teacher ratio less than 16 increase in January 1999 over January 1998?

   (A) −2%
   (B) 0%
   (C) 2%
   (D) 10%
   (E) 12%

24. In January 1998, what percent of high schools had a Pupil/Teacher ratio less than 23?

   (A) 25%
   (B) 39%
   (C) 50%
   (D) 60%
   (E) 75%

25. If the areas of the sectors in the circle graphs are drawn in proportion to the percent shown, what is the measure, in degrees, of the sector representing the number of high schools with Pupil/Teacher ratio greater than 27 in 1999?

   (A) 21.6
   (B) 30
   (C) 45.7
   (D) 56.3
   (E) 72

26. In the figure, what is the area of △ABC ?

(A) 2
(B) √2
(C) 1
(D) $\frac{1}{\sqrt{2}}$
(E) 1/2

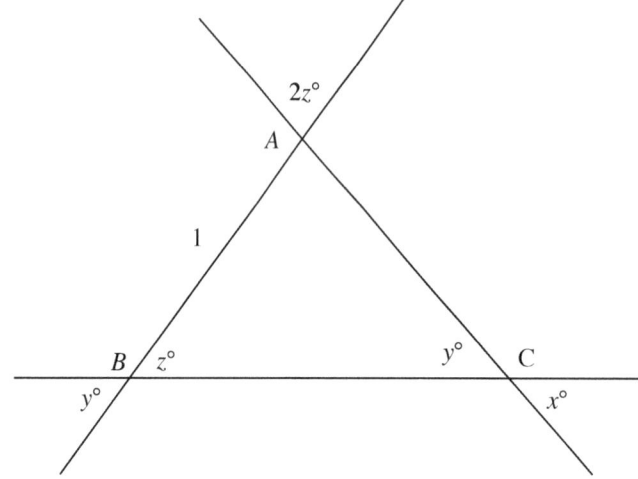

27. In the figure, O is the center of the circle. Which one of the following must be true about the perimeter of the triangle shown?

   (A) Always less than 10
   (B) Always greater than 40
   (C) Always greater than 30
   (D) Always less than 30
   (E) Less than 40 and greater than 20

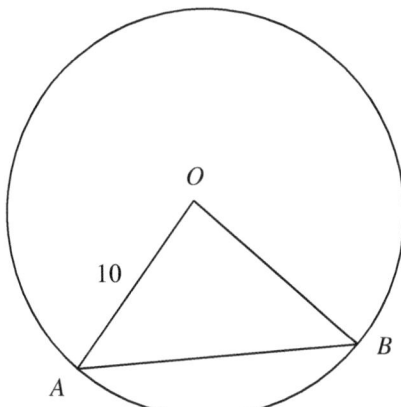

[Data Sufficiency Question]
28. If x equals $y/7$, then is x less than 30?

   (1) $y > 210$
   (2) $y < 217$

[Data Sufficiency Question]

29. Is $\dfrac{(a-b)+(c-b)}{d} > 0$?

   (1) $a + c < 2b$
   (2) $d < 0$

[Data Sufficiency Question]

30. Does the integer m have at least 4 positive prime factors?

   (1) $m/14$ is a positive integer.
   (2) $m/15$ is a positive integer.

31. What is the slope of the line passing through $(-3, -4)$ and the origin?

   (A) 3/7
   (B) 4/7
   (C) 3/4
   (D) 1
   (E) 4/3

[Data Sufficiency Question]

32. Is $x > y$?

   (1) $x = y + 1$
   (2) $x + y = 1$

33. If $|x| + x = 4$, then which one of the following is odd?

    (A) $x^2 + 3x$
    (B) $x^2 + 3x + 2$
    (C) $x^2 + 4x$
    (D) $x^2 + 4x + 2$
    (E) $x^2 + 4x + 3$

[Data Sufficiency Question]
34. What is the value of x ?

    (1) $x - 3 = 10/x$
    (2) $x > 0$

35. If a is $\dfrac{30}{31}$ of $\dfrac{31}{32}$ and $b = \dfrac{30}{31}$, then $\dfrac{a}{b} =$

    (A) 900/992
    (B) 30/32
    (C) 30/31
    (D) 31/32
    (E) 992/900

[Data Sufficiency Question]

36. What number is 25 percent of x ?

    (1) 50 percent of x is 50.
    (2) 9/100 of x is 9.

37. Which one of the following numbers can be removed from the set $S = \{0, 2, 4, 5, 9\}$ without changing the average of set S?

    (A) 0
    (B) 2
    (C) 4
    (D) 5
    (E) 9

Test 2—Answers and Solutions

Answers and Solutions Test 2:

1. B	11. C	21. C	31. E
2. D	12. A	22. A	32. A
3. E	13. C	23. D	33. E
4. E	14. A	24. B	34. C
5. A	15. E	25. A	35. D
6. A	16. B	26. E	36. D
7. C	17. B	27. E	37. C
8. C	18. D	28. A	
9. A	19. A	29. C	
10. A	20. B	30. C	

---

1. Choose any three consecutive integers, say, 1, 2, and 3. Forming their average yields $\frac{1+2+3}{3} = \frac{6}{3} = 2$. Since 2 is an integer, the answer is (B).

Method II (without substitution):

Choice (A): Let a and $a + 1$ be the consecutive integers. The average of the two is $\frac{a+(a+1)}{2} = \frac{2a+1}{2} = a + \frac{1}{2}$, certainly not an integer since a is an integer. Reject.

Choice (B): Let $a, a + 1$, and $a + 2$ be the three consecutive integers. The average of the three numbers is $\frac{a+(a+1)+(a+2)}{3} = \frac{3a+3}{3} = a+1$, certainly an integer since a is an integer. Correct.

Choice (C): Let $a, a + 1, a + 2$, and $a + 3$ be the four consecutive integers. The average of the four numbers is $\frac{a+(a+1)+(a+2)+(a+3)}{4} = \frac{4a+6}{4} = a + \frac{3}{2}$, certainly not an integer since a is an integer. Reject.

Choice (D): Let $a, a + 1, a + 2, a + 3, a + 4$, and $a + 5$ be the six consecutive integers. The average of the six numbers is $\frac{a+(a+1)+(a+2)+(a+3)+(a+4)+(a+5)}{6} = \frac{6a+15}{6} = a + \frac{5}{2}$, certainly not an integer since a is an integer. Reject.

Choice (E): The average of 6 and 9 is $\frac{6+9}{2} = \frac{15}{2} = 7.5$, not an integer. Reject.

The answer is (B).

---

2. The only factors of a prime number are 1 and itself. Hence, π(any prime number) = 2. So, π(a) = 2 and π(b) = 2, and therefore π(a) + π(b) = 2 + 2 = 4.

Now, the factors of ab are 1, a, b, and ab itself. Since a and b are different, the total number of factors of $a \times b$ is 4. In other words, π($a \times b$) = 4.

Hence, π(a) + π(b) − π($a \times b$) = 4 − 4 = 0. The answer is (C).

3. List all possible factors *x* and *y* whose product is 36, and calculate the corresponding sum *x* + *y*:

x	y	xy	x + y
1	36	36	37
2	18	36	20
3	12	36	15
4	9	36	13
6	6	36	12

From the table, the minimum sum is 12. The answer is (E).

4. The last digit of a positive integer is the same as the last digit of n^2 only when the last digit is 0, 1, 5, or 6. For example, the last digit of 10 is 0 and the last digit of 10^2 (= 100) is also 0. The last digit of 11 is 1 and the last digit of 11^2 (= 121) is also 1. The last digit of 15 is 5, and the last digit of 15^2 (= 225) is also 5. The last digit of 16 is 6, and the last digit of 16^2 (= 256) is also 6. Since we have multiple cases with Statement (1) alone, it is *not* sufficient.

Now, the last digit of an even number is 0, 2, 4, 6, or 8. Hence, Statement (2) alone is *not* sufficient.

The common solutions from the two statements are 0 and 6 (which means *n* ends with either 0 or 6). Since we do not have a single solution, the statements together are not sufficient. The answer is (E).

5. Summing the angles of the triangle in the figure to 180° yields $a + 3a + 5a = 180$. Solving this equation for *a* yields $a = 180/9 = 20$. Angles *y* and *a* in the figure are vertical and therefore are equal. So, $y = a = 20$. The answer is (A).

6.

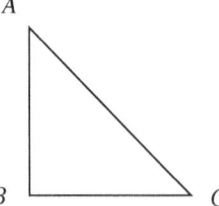

In a right-angled isosceles triangle, the sides of the right angle are equal. Now, in the given right-angled isosceles triangle $\triangle ABC$, $\angle B$ is given to be the right angle. Hence, the sides of the angle, *AB* and *BC*, are equal. Applying The Pythagorean Theorem to the triangle yields

$AB^2 + BC^2 = AC^2$
$BC^2 + BC^2 = \left(7\sqrt{2}\right)^2$ since $AB = BC$
$2(BC)^2 = 7^2 \times 2$
$BC^2 = 7^2$
$BC = 7$ by square rooting both sides

Hence, $AB = BC = 7$. The answer is (A).

Test 2—Answers and Solutions

7. Statement (1) contains two variables, but only one equation. Hence, we cannot determine the values of p and q using the statement alone.

Similarly, we cannot determine the value of the given expression from Statement (2) alone.

Together, statements (1) and (2) form a system of two equations in two unknowns that may have a solution. Solving the equation $pq = 35$ for q yields $q = 35/p$. Plugging this into the equation $p + q = 12$ yields

$p + 35/p = 12$

$p^2 + 35 = 12p$ by multiplying both sides by p

$p^2 - 12p + 35 = 0$ by subtracting $12p$ from both sides

$(p - 5)(p - 7) = 0$

$p - 5 = 0$ or $p - 7 = 0$

$p = 5$ or $p = 7$

When $p = 5$, the equation $p + q = 12$ yields $q = 7$. Similarly, when $p = 7$, $q = 5$. Hence, the solutions of the system are the ordered pairs (5, 7) and (7, 5). From the symmetry in the expression $\frac{1}{p^4} + \frac{1}{q^4}$, both ordered pairs will return the same value when plugged into the expression. Thus, the value of the expression $\frac{1}{p^4} + \frac{1}{q^4}$ can be determined only by using both statements. The answer is (C).

---

8. The expression on the right-hand side of the equation cannot be further reduced. Hence, the variable H (the only variable on the left-hand side) is dependent only on the variables: T, R, k, and g (the only variables on the right-hand side). We can collect the values for all four variables on the right-hand side only by using both statements and thereby determine the value of H. Hence, both statements are required, and the answer is (C).

---

9. We are given the inequality $3x + 7y > 7x + 3y$. Subtracting $3x + 3y$ from both sides of the inequality yields $4y > 4x$, and dividing both sides of this inequality by 4 yields $y > x$.

Suppose Statement (I) $a > b$ is true. Now, $a > b$ if $x + 2y > y + 2x$ since we are given that $a = x + 2y$ and $b = y + 2x$. Subtracting $x + y$ from both sides yields $y > x$, which we know is true. So, Statement (I) $a > b$ is true, and therefore Statement (II) $a = b$ and Statement (III) $a < b$ are false. The answer is (A).

Note the strategy we used here: We assumed something to be true ($a > b$) and then reduced it to something that we know is true ($y > x$). If all the steps are reversible (and they are here), then we have proven that our assumption is in fact true. This is a common strategy in mathematics.

Method II:
Solve the given equations $a = x + 2y$ and $b = y + 2x$ for x and y and substitute the results in the given inequality $3x + 7y > 7x + 3y$ to derive $a > b$. Thus, I is true, and II and III are false.

10. If *n* is odd, then both *n* + 1 and *n* + 3 are even and their product (*n* + 1)(*n* + 3) is a multiple of 4 (For example, 6 × 10 = 60, a multiple of 4).

If *n* is even, then both *n* + 1 and *n* + 3 are odd and their product (*n* + 1)(*n* + 3) is odd, which is not a multiple of 4.

These are the only two significant cases.

Hence, (*n* + 1)(*n* + 3) is a multiple of 4 only when *n* is odd. Hence, the question can be reduced to "Is *n* odd?"

Now, from Statement (1) alone, we have that (*n* + 2)(*n* + 4) is odd. Hence, we have

$(n + 2)(n + 4)$ = Odd

$n^2 + 6n + 8$ = Odd

$n^2 + 2(3n + 4)$ = Odd

n^2 + Even Number = Odd

n^2 = An Odd Number – An Even Number = An Odd Number

n^2 = Square Root of an Odd Number = Odd Number

Hence, Statement (1) alone is sufficient to answer the question: "Is *n* odd?". The answer is "Yes."

From Statement (2) alone, we have that (*n* + 3)(*n* + 6) is even.

Now, suppose *n* is even. Then *n* + 3 must be odd and *n* + 6 must be even and the product (*n* + 3)(*n* + 6) must be even. Now, suppose *n* is odd. Then *n* + 3 must be even and *n* + 6 must be odd and the product (*n* + 3)(*n* + 6) is even, again.

Hence, (*n* + 3)(*n* + 6) is even, whether *n* is odd or whether *n* is even. Hence, Statement (2) alone is *not* sufficient to answer the question.

The answer is (A).

---

11. From Statement (1) alone, we have that all 4-digits of *X* are greater than 5. Hence, each digit must be at least 6 or greater. Hence, the sum of its digits must be at least 4 × 6 = 24.

Now, suppose *Y* = 111. Then the sum of its digits is 1 + 1 + 1 = 3, which is less than 24 (a possible value of the sum of the digits of *X*).

Now, suppose *Y* = 999. Then the sum of its digits is 9 + 9 + 9 = 27, which is greater than 24 (a possible value of the sum of the digits of *X*).

Hence, we have a double case, and Statement (1) alone is *not* sufficient.

From Statement (2) alone, we have that the 3 digits of *Y* are less than 5. Hence, none of the digits is greater than 4. Hence, the sum of the digits of *Y* is not greater than 3 × 4 = 12.

Now, suppose *X* = 1111. Then the sum of its digits is 1 + 1 + 1 + 1 = 4, which is less than 12 (a possible value of the sum of the digits of *Y*).

Now, suppose *X* = 4444. Then the sum of its digits is 4 + 4 + 4 + 4 = 16, which is greater than 12 (a possible value of the sum of the digits of *Y*).

Test 2—Answers and Solutions

Hence, we have a double case, and Statement (2) alone is *not* sufficient.

From the statements together, we have that the sum of the digits of *X* is greater than or equal to 24, and the sum of the digits of *Y* is less than or equal to 12. Hence, the sum of the digits of *X* is greater than the sum of the digits of *Y*. Hence, the statements together answer the question, and the answer is (C).

---

12. Since the numerator of the fraction $\dfrac{1}{x-1}$ does not contain a variable, it can never equal 0. Hence, the fraction can never equal 0. The answer is (A).

---

13. We are given the equation

$$(x+5) \div \left(\frac{1}{x} + \frac{1}{5}\right) = 5$$

$$(x+5) \div \left(\frac{x+5}{5x}\right) = 5$$

$$(x+5) \cdot \left(\frac{5x}{x+5}\right) = 5$$

$$5x = 5$$

$$x = 1$$

The answer is (C). Note: If you solved the equation without getting a common denominator, you may have gotten –5 as a possible solution. But, –5 is not a solution. Why? *

---

14. From Statement (1) alone, we have that $y = \dfrac{1}{x-1}$. For any value of *x*, $\dfrac{1}{x-1}$ cannot equal 0. For example, suppose $\dfrac{1}{x-1} = 0$. Then multiplying the equation by $x - 1$ yields a false result $1 = 0$. Hence, the assumption that $y = \dfrac{1}{x-1} = 0$ is false. Hence, Statement (1) alone is sufficient to answer the question. The answer is "No. *y* is not equal to 0."

From Statement (2) alone, we have that $y = x/6$. Now, suppose $x = 0$. Then $y = x/6 = 0/6 = 0$. But if *x* is not zero, say $x = 2$, then $y = x/6 = 2/6 \neq 0$. Hence, we have a double case, and therefore Statement (2) alone is not sufficient to answer the question.

The answer is (A).

---

15. From Statement (1), we have information about the average temperature only for the period Monday through Wednesday. Since there is no relevant information for the rest of the week, Statement (1) alone is not sufficient.

Statement (2) has information about the minimum and the maximum temperatures for the period Thursday through Saturday. It does not help us evaluate the average temperature for the period.

With two statements together, we do not have information about average temperatures for the complete week. Hence, the statements together are not sufficient to answer the question.

The answer is (E).

---

* Because –5 is not in the domain of the original equation since it causes the denominator to be 0. When you solve an equation, you are only finding possible solutions. The "solutions" may not work when plugged back into the equation.

16. Since the answer is in minutes, we must convert the cyclist's speed (12 miles per hour) into miles per minute. Since there are 60 minutes in an hour, his speed is 12/60 = 1/5 miles per minute.

Remember that *Distance = Rate × Time*. Hence,

$$24 = \frac{1}{5} \times t$$

Solving for *t* yields *t* = 5 × 24 = 120. The answer is (E). [If you forgot to convert hours to minutes, you may have mistakenly answered (B).]

17. The rule for the sequence a_n is $a_n = -(a_{n-1})$. Putting *n* = 2 and 3 in the rule yields

$a_2 = -(a_{2-1}) = -a_1 = -(-1) = 1$ (given that $a_1 = -1$)
$a_3 = -(a_{3-1}) = -a_2 = -1$

Similarly, we get that *each* even numbered term (when *n* is even) equals 1 and *each* odd numbered term (when *n* is odd) equals –1. Since a_5 is an odd numbered term, it equals –1. The answer is (B).

18. Let the number of pigeons be *p* and the number of rabbits be *r*. Since the head count together is 12,

$$p + r = 12 \quad (1)$$

Since each pigeon has 2 legs and each rabbit has 4 legs, the total leg count is

$$2p + 4r = 32 \quad (2)$$

Dividing equation (2) by 2 yields *p* + 2*r* = 16. Subtracting this equation from equation (1) yields

$(p + r) - (p + 2r) = 12 - 16$
$p + r - p - 2r = -4$
$r = 4$

Substituting this into equation (1) yields *p* + 4 = 12, which reduces to *p* = 8.

Hence, the number of pigeons is *p* = 8, and the number of rabbits is *r* = 4. The answer is (D).

19. The volume of a rectangular tank is *length × width × depth* = 6 feet × 5 feet × *depth*. Hence, the volume of the conical box, which is 3 times the volume of rectangular box, is 3(6 × 5 × *depth*). Since the time taken to fill a tank equals the (volume of the tank) ÷ (the rate of filling), the conical box should be filled in

3(6 × 5 × *depth*)/6 cubic feet per minute

The only unknown in the expression is the *depth* (of the rectangular box). Hence, Statement (1) alone is sufficient to answer the question. Since the radius of the conical box alone does not determine the volume of the conical box, Statement (2) alone is not sufficient. Hence, the answer is (A).

20. Choose any five consecutive integers, say, –2, –1, 0, 1 and 2. (We chose these particular numbers to make the calculation as easy as possible. But any five consecutive integers will do. For example, 1, 2, 3, 4, and 5.) Forming the average yields (–1 + (–2) + 0 + 1 + 2)/5 = 0/5 = 0. Now, add 3 to the set to form 6 consecutive integers: –2, –1, 0, 1, 2, and 3. Forming the average yields

$$\frac{-1+(-2)+0+1+2+3}{6} =$$

$$\frac{[-1+(-2)+0+1+2]+3}{6} =$$

$$\frac{[0]+3}{6} = \qquad \text{since the average of } -1 + (-2) + 0 + 1 + 2 \text{ is zero, their sum must be zero}$$

$$3/6 =$$

$$1/2$$

(The average of five consecutive integers starting from m) – (The average of six consecutive integers starting from m) = (0) – (1/2) = –1/2.

The answer is (B).

---

21. By the given definition, $\Delta(n) = (n + 4)(n + 5)(n + 6)$, a product of three consecutive integers. There is exactly one multiple of 3 in every three consecutive positive integers. Also, at least one of the three numbers must be an even number. Hence, $\Delta(n)$ must be a multiple of both 2 and 3. Hence, $\Delta(n)$ must be a multiple of 6 (= 2 × 3), because 2 and 3 are primes. The answer is (C).

---

22. A palindrome number reads the same forward or backward. The first palindrome larger than 233 will have the last digit 2 (same as the first digit), and the middle digit will be 1 unit greater than the middle digit of 233. Hence, the first palindrome larger than 233 is 242. Now, 242 – 233 = 9. The answer is (A).

---

23. In January 1998, the Pupil/Teacher ratio is less than 16 in 2% of the schools. The number of schools in 1998 is 1000. Hence, 2% of 1000 is 2/100 × 1000 = 20. So, 20 schools have pupil/Teacher ratio less than 16.

In January 1999, the pupil/Teacher ratio is less than 16 in 2% of schools again. The number of schools in 1999 is 1100. Hence, 2% of 1100 is 2/100 × 1100 = 22. In 1999, there are 22 schools with the ratio less than 16.

The percentage increase equals (22 – 20)/20 × 100 = 2/20 × 100 = 10%. The answer is (D).

24. The number of schools having a ratio less than 23 is

> The number of schools having the Pupil/Teacher ratio less than 16
> + The number of schools having the Pupil/Teacher ratio equal to 16
> + The number of schools having the Pupil/Teacher ratio equal to 17
> + The number of schools having the Pupil/Teacher ratio equal to 18
> + The number of schools having the Pupil/Teacher ratio equal to 19
> + The number of schools having the Pupil/Teacher ratio equal to 20
> + The number of schools having the Pupil/Teacher ratio equal to 21
> + The number of schools having the Pupil/Teacher ratio equal to 22
> = 2% + 1% + 2% + 3% + 5% + 7% + 9% + 10%
> = 39%

The answer is (B).

Method II:
The number of schools having the ratio less than 23 equals

> 100%
> − (The number of schools having the Pupil Teacher ratio greater than 27
> + The number of schools having the Pupil/Teacher ratio equal to 27
> + The number of schools having the Pupil/Teacher ratio equal to 26
> + The number of schools having the Pupil/Teacher ratio equal to 25
> + The number of schools having the Pupil/Teacher ratio equal to 24
> + The number of schools having the Pupil/Teacher ratio equal to 23
>)
> = 100 − (7% + 5% + 9% + 11% + 16% + 13%) = 100 − 61% = 39%.

The answer is (B).

---

25. From the chart, in 1999, 6% of schools have a Pupil/Teacher ratio greater than 27. Hence, the fraction of the angle that the sector makes in the complete angle of the circle also equals 6% = 6/100. Since the complete angle is 360°, the part of the angle equals 6/100 × 360 = 21.6°. The answer is (A).

---

26. Equating vertical angles at point B in the figure yields $y = z$ and $\angle A = 2z$. So, the triangle is isosceles ($\angle B = \angle C = y$). Now, the angle sum of a triangle is 180°, so $2z + z + z = 180$. Solving for z yields $z = 180/4 = 45$. Hence, we have $2z = 2 \times 45 = 90$. So, $\triangle ABC$ is a right-angled isosceles triangle with right angle at vertex A and equal angles at $\angle B$ and $\angle C$ (both equaling 45°). Since sides opposite equal angles in a triangle are equal, sides AB and AC are equal and each is 1 unit (given that AB is 1 unit). Now, the area of the right triangle ABC is $1/2 \times AB \times AC = 1/2 \times 1 \times 1 = 1/2$. The answer is (E).

---

27. In $\triangle AOB$, OA and OB are radii of the circle. Hence, both equal 10 (since $OA = 10$ in the figure).

Now, the perimeter of a triangle equals the sum of the lengths of the sides of the triangle. Hence, Perimeter of $\triangle AOB = OA + OB + AB = 10 + 10 + AB = 20 + AB$.

In a triangle, the length of any side is less than the sum of the lengths of the other two sides and is greater than their difference. So, AB is less than $AO + OB$ (= 10 + 10 = 20) and is greater than $10 − 10 = 0$. So, we have $0 < AB < 20$. Adding 20 to each part of this inequality yields $20 < 20 + AB < 20 + 20$, or $20 <$ Perimeter < 40. Hence, the answer is (E).

Test 2—Answers and Solutions

28. We are given that $x = y/7$.

From Statement (1) alone, we have $y > 210$. Dividing this inequality by 7 yields $y/7 > 210/7 = 30$. Replacing $y/7$ with x yields $x > 30$. Hence, x is not less than 30. Hence, Statement (1) alone is sufficient to answer the question.

From Statement (2) alone, we have $y < 217$. Dividing this inequality by 7 yields $y/7 < 217/7 = 31$. Replacing $y/7$ with x yields $x < 31$. Now, suppose x equals 29 ($x < 31$), then x is less than 30. Now, suppose $x = 30$ ($x < 31$), then x is not less than 30. Hence, we have a double case, and Statement (2) alone is not sufficient to answer the question.

Hence, the answer is (A).

29. The question is about the fraction $\dfrac{(a-b)+(c-b)}{d}$. The numerator of the fraction is $(a-b)+(c-b)$ and the denominator is d.

From Statement (1), we do not have any information about d. So, if $(a-b)+(c-b)$ is negative and d is positive, the fraction is negative; and if $(a-b)+(c-b)$ is negative and d is negative, the fraction is positive. Hence, Statement (1) alone is *not* sufficient.

From Statement (2), we do not have information about the numerator $(a-b)+(c-b)$. So, if the numerator is negative and the denominator d is negative, the fraction is positive; and if the numerator is positive and the denominator d is negative, the fraction is negative. Hence, we have a double case and Statement (2) alone is *not* sufficient.

Now, the numerator is $(a-b)+(c-b) = a+c-2b$ and according to Statement (1) alone, we have the expression is negative (< 0). Now, from statement (2) alone, we have the denominator d is negative. So, the fraction Numerator/Denominator = a Negative Number ÷ a Negative Number = a Positive Number. So, the answer is "Yes. $\dfrac{(a-b)+(c-b)}{d} > 0$". Hence, the answer is (C), the statements together are sufficient.

30. From Statement (1) alone, we have that $m/14$ is an integer. Now, suppose $m = 42$. Then $m/14 = 3$, a positive integer.

Now, $m = 42 = 2 \cdot 3 \cdot 7$. The prime factors of m are 2, 3, and 7. Hence, the number of prime factors of m is 3. Here, the answer is "No. m does not have even 4 prime factors."

Now, suppose $m = 210 = 2 \cdot 3 \cdot 5 \cdot 7$. Here, $m/14 = 3 \cdot 5$, a positive integer, and m has 4 prime factors: 2, 3, 5, and 7.

Here, the answer is "Yes. m has exactly 4 prime factors." Hence, we have a double case, and Statement (1) alone is not sufficient.

From Statement (2) alone, we have that $m/15$ is an integer.

Now, suppose $m = 30$. Then $m/15 = 2$, a positive integer. Now, $m = 30 = 2 \cdot 3 \cdot 5$, so the prime factors of m are 2, 3, and 5. Hence, the number of prime factors of m is 3. Here, the answer is "No. m does not have even 4 prime factors."

Now, suppose $m = 2 \cdot 3 \cdot 5 \cdot 7 = 210$. Here, $m/15 = 2 \cdot 7$, a positive integer, and m has 4 prime factors: 2, 3, 5, and 7. Here, the answer is "Yes. m has exactly 4 prime factors." Hence, we have a double case, and Statement (2) alone is not sufficient.

GMAT Math Tests

Now, with statements (1) and (2) together, we have that m is divisible by both 14 and 15. Hence, m is a multiple of both 14 and 15. Hence, m must equal the least common multiple of 14 and 15 or its multiple. Let's assume that m is only equal to the LCM. The LCM of 14 ($= 2 \cdot 7$) and 15 ($= 3 \cdot 5$) is $2 \cdot 7 \cdot 3 \cdot 5$ ($= 210$). The LCM itself has 4 prime factors 2, 7, 3, and 5. Hence, its multiples might have more prime factors. Hence, both statements are required to answer that m has at least 4 prime factors. Hence, the statements together answer the question. The answer is (C).

---

31. The formula for the slope of a line passing through two points (x_1, y_1) and (x_2, y_2) is $\dfrac{y_2 - y_1}{x_2 - x_1}$. Hence, the slope of the line through $(-3, -4)$ and the origin $(0, 0)$ is $\dfrac{0 - (-4)}{0 - (-3)} = \dfrac{4}{3}$. The answer is (E).

---

32. From Statement (1) alone, we have that x is 1 unit greater than y. Hence, Statement (1) alone answers the question. The answer is "Yes. x is greater than y."

From Statement (2) alone, we have the equation $x + y = 1$. This equation is symmetric in x and y. Hence, the relation between x and y cannot be established. For example,

If $x = 1$ and $y = 0$, then $x + y = 1 + 0 = 1$ and $x > y$.

If $x = 0$ and $y = 1$, then $x + y = 0 + 1 = 1$ and $x < y$.

Hence, we have a double case, and Statement (2) alone is not sufficient to answer the question.

Hence, the answer is (A).

---

33. We are given that $|x| + x = 4$. If x is negative or zero, then $|x|$ equals $-x$ and $|x| + x$ equals $-x + x = 0$. This conflicts with the given equation, so x is not negative nor equal to 0. Hence, x is positive and therefore $|x|$ equals x. Putting this in the given equation yields

$$|x| + x = 4$$
$$x + x = 4$$
$$2x = 4$$
$$x = 2$$

Now, select the answer-choice that results in an odd number when $x = 2$.

Choice (A): $x^2 + 3x = 2^2 + 3(2) = 4 + 6 = 10$, an even number. Reject.
Choice (B): $x^2 + 3x + 2 = 2^2 + 3(2) + 2 = 4 + 6 + 2 = 12$, an even number. Reject.
Choice (C): $x^2 + 4x = 2^2 + 4(2) = 4 + 8 = 12$, an even number. Reject.
Choice (D): $x^2 + 4x + 2 = 2^2 + 4(2) + 2 = 4 + 8 + 2 = 14$, an even number. Reject.
Choice (E): $x^2 + 4x + 3 = 2^2 + 4(2) + 3 = 4 + 8 + 3 = 15$, an odd number. Accept.

The answer is (E).

Test 2—Answers and Solutions

34. From Statement (1) alone, we have the equation $x - 3 = 10/x$. Multiplying the equation by x yields $x^2 - 3x = 10$. Subtracting 10 from both sides yields $x^2 - 3x - 10 = 0$. Factoring the equation yields $(x - 5)(x + 2) = 0$. Now, the left-hand side of the equation is 0 when x equals 5 or –2. Since we have two solutions for x, Statement (1) alone is not sufficient.

From Statement (2) alone, we have a range of values for x ($x > 0$, x is positive), not a single value. Hence, Statement (2) alone is not sufficient to answer the question.

Combining the results from the two statements, we eliminate the chance of x being equal to –2 since now we know that x is positive. So, we are left with only one solution $x = 5$. Hence, the answer is (C).

35. a is $\frac{30}{31}$ of $\frac{31}{32} = \frac{30}{31} \cdot \frac{31}{32} = \frac{30}{32}$.

$b = \frac{30}{31}$.

Hence, $\frac{a}{b} = \frac{30}{32} / \frac{30}{31} = \frac{30}{32} \cdot \frac{31}{30} = \frac{31}{32}$. The answer is (D).

36. 25 percent of x is $25/100 \cdot x$. We can evaluate this if we have the value of x. Hence, the question effectively is "What is the value of x?"

From Statement (1) alone, we have that 50 percent of x is 50. Hence, we have the equation $\frac{50}{100} x = 50$, or $\frac{x}{2} = 50$, or $x = 100$. Hence, Statement (1) alone is sufficient to answer the question.

From Statement (2) alone, we have that 9/100 of x is 9. Hence, we have the equation $\frac{9}{100} x = 9$, or $x = \frac{100}{9} \times 9 = 100$. Hence, Statement (2) alone is sufficient to answer the question.

Hence, the answer is (D).

37. The average of the elements in the original set S is $(0 + 2 + 4 + 5 + 9)/5 = 20/5 = 4$. If we remove an element that equals the average, then the average of the new set will remain unchanged. The new set after removing 4 is {0, 2, 5, 9}. The average of the elements is $(0 + 2 + 5 + 9)/4 = 16/4 = 4$. The answer is (C).

Test 3

GMAT Math Tests

Questions: 37
Time: 75 minutes

1. Which one of the following is divisible by both 2 and 3?

    (A) 1005
    (B) 1296
    (C) 1351
    (D) 1406
    (E) 1414

2. Define x^* by the equation $x^* = \pi/x$. Then $((-\pi)^*)^* =$

    (A) $-1/\pi$
    (B) $-1/2$
    (C) $-\pi$
    (D) $1/\pi$
    (E) π

3. The remainder when the positive integer m is divided by n is r. What is the remainder when $2m$ is divided by $2n$?

    (A) r
    (B) $2r$
    (C) $2n$
    (D) $m - nr$
    (E) $2(m - nr)$

4. *A* and *B* are centers of two circles that touch each other externally, as shown in the figure. What is the area of the circle whose diameter is *AB* ?

   (A) 4π
   (B) $25\pi/4$
   (C) 9π
   (D) 16π
   (E) 25π

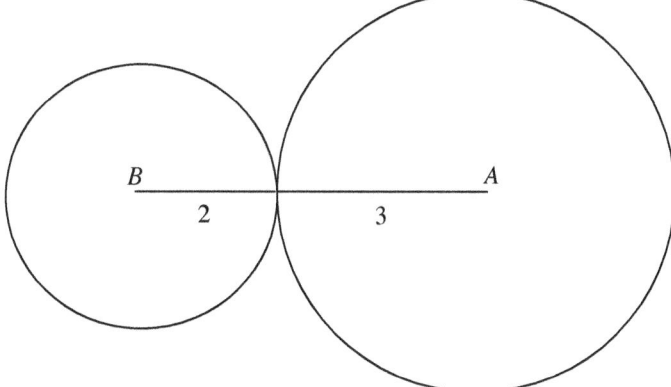

[Data Sufficiency Question (see Directions, page 15)]

5. Is $\dfrac{a^2 - b^2}{a - b} > \dfrac{a^2 - b^2}{a + b}$?

   (1) $a = 49$
   (2) $b = 59$

6. The side length of a square inscribed in a circle is 2. What is the area of the circle?

   (A) π
   (B) $\sqrt{2}\pi$
   (C) 2π
   (D) $2\sqrt{2}\pi$
   (E) π^2

[Data Sufficiency Question]
7. Is the number x a multiple of 12?

   (1) Both 3 and 4 divide into x evenly.
   (2) Both 2 and 6 divide into x evenly.

8. The slope of the line $2x + y = 3$ is NOT the same as the slope of which one of the following lines?

   (A) $2x + y = 5$
   (B) $x + y/2 = 3$
   (C) $x = -y/2 - 3$
   (D) $y = 7 - 2x$
   (E) $x + 2y = 9$

[Data Sufficiency Question]
9. Is △ABC a right triangle?

   (1) The angles of △ABC are in the ratio 1 : 2 : 3.
   (2) One of the angles of △ABC equals the sum of the other two angles.

10. If $5 < x < 10$ and $y = x + 5$, what is the greatest possible integer value of $x + y$?

    (A) 18
    (B) 20
    (C) 23
    (D) 24
    (E) 25

[Data Sufficiency Question]
11. Are the two triangles similar?

    (1) The ratio of the measures of the angles in one triangle is 2 : 3 : 4.
    (2) The ratio of the measures of the angles in the other triangle is 4 : 3 : 2.

12. Kate ate 1/3 of a cake, Fritz ate 1/2 of the remaining cake, and what was left was eaten by Emily. The fraction of the cake eaten by Emily equals

    (A) 1/5
    (B) 1/3
    (C) 2/3
    (D) 1/2
    (E) 3/5

[Data Sufficiency Question]
13. Are the two triangles similar?

    (1) The ratio of the measures of the angles in one triangle is 2 : 3 : 4.
    (2) The ratio of the measures of the angles in the other triangle is 1 : 1 : 1.

[Data Sufficiency Question]
14. What is the minimum area of cardboard required to make a rectangular box with no top?

    (1) The area of the bottom of the box is 23 square feet.
    (2) The volume of the box is 23 cubic feet.

[Data Sufficiency Question]
15. What is the value of $ab + bc$?

    (1) $b = a + c$
    (2) $b = 3$

16. The sum of two numbers is 13, and their product is 30. What is the sum of the squares of the two numbers?

    (A) −229
    (B) −109
    (C) 139
    (D) 109
    (E) 229

17. The difference between two angles of a triangle is 24°. The average of the same two angles is 54°. Which one of the following is the value of the greatest angle of the triangle?

    (A) 45°
    (B) 60°
    (C) 66°
    (D) 72°
    (E) 78°

18. At Stephen Stores, 3 pounds of cashews cost $8. What is the cost in cents of a bag weighing 9 ounces?

    (A) 30
    (B) 60
    (C) 90
    (D) 120
    (E) 150

[Data Sufficiency Question]

19. Steve deposited $100 to open a savings account. If there are no other transactions in the account, what amount of money would the account accrue in 6 months after opening the account?

    (1) The interest rate is 4%.
    (2) Interest is compounded quarterly.

20. Point M is located 8 miles East of point P. If point P is located 6 miles North of another point A, then how far is point A from point M?

    (A) 4
    (B) 5
    (C) 6
    (D) 7
    (E) 10

21. The sum of the first n terms of an arithmetic series whose nth term is n can be calculated by the formula $n(n + 1)/2$. Which one of the following equals the sum of the first eight terms in a series whose nth term is $2n$?

(A) 24
(B) 48
(C) 56
(D) 72
(E) 96

USE THIS SPACE FOR SCRATCHWORK.

22. For how many integers n between 5 and 20, inclusive, is the sum of $3n$, $9n$, and $11n$ greater than 200?

(A) 4
(B) 8
(C) 12
(D) 16
(E) 20

USE THIS SPACE FOR SCRATCHWORK.

Questions 23–25 refer to the following graph.

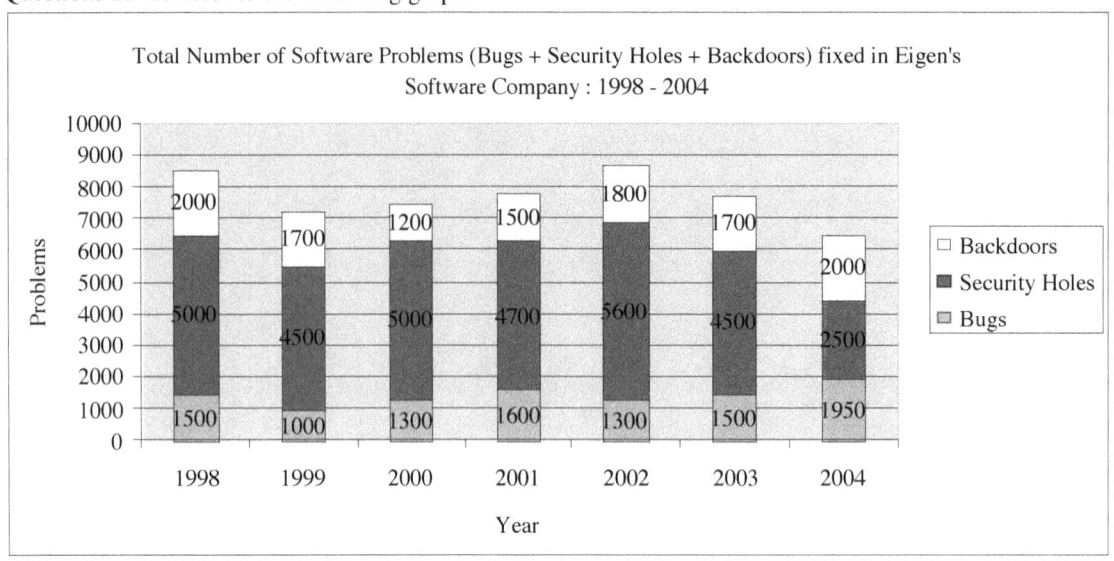

23. What was the number of security holes fixed in 2003?

    (A) 1500
    (B) 1700
    (C) 4500
    (D) 6000
    (E) 6300

24. For which year was the ratio of the Security holes to Bugs fixed by the software company the greatest?

    (A) 1998
    (B) 1999
    (C) 2000
    (D) 2001
    (E) 2002

25. If the total number of software problems solved is a direct measure of the company's capability, then by approximately what percent did capability increase from 1999 to 2002?

   (A) 10%
   (B) 20%
   (C) 30%
   (D) 40%
   (E) 50%

26. A bag of wheat weighs 5 pounds and 12 ounces. How much does the bag of wheat weigh in pounds?

   (A) 5 1/4
   (B) 5 1/2
   (C) 5 3/4
   (D) 6 1/4
   (E) 6 3/4

27. The function f is defined for all positive integers n as $f(n) = n/(n + 1)$. Then $f(1) \cdot f(2) - f(2) \cdot f(3) =$

   (A) $-1/6$
   (B) $1/5$
   (C) $1/4$
   (D) $1/3$
   (E) $1/2$

[Data Sufficiency Question]
28. $m =$

    (1) $7m + 5n = 29$
    (2) m and n are positive integers.

[Data Sufficiency Question]
29. In the figure, l, m, and k are straight lines. Are the lines l and m parallel to each other?

    (1) $x = q$
    (2) $y = q$

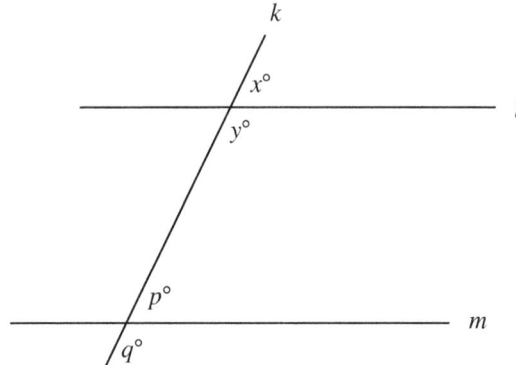

[Data Sufficiency Question]
30. Is x divisible by 14?

    (1) $x/4$ is a positive integer.
    (2) $x/6$ is a positive integer.

31. If $1 < p < 3$, then which of the following could be true?

    (I) $p^2 < 2p$
    (II) $p^2 = 2p$
    (III) $p^2 > 2p$

    (A) I only
    (B) II only
    (C) III only
    (D) I and II only
    (E) I, II, and III

[Data Sufficiency Question]
32. Waugh jogged to a restaurant at x miles per hour, and jogged back home along the same route at y miles per hour. He took 30 minutes for the whole trip. What is the average speed at which he jogged for the whole trip?

    (1) The restaurant is 2 miles from home.
    (2) $x = 12$ and $y = 6$.

33. $a, b,$ and c are consecutive integers in increasing order of size. If $p = a/5 - b/6$ and $q = b/5 - c/6$, then $q - p =$

    (A) 1/60
    (B) 1/30
    (C) 1/12
    (D) 1/6
    (E) 1/5

[Data Sufficiency Question]
34. In the figure, ABCD is a rectangle and E is a point on the side AB. What is the area of the shaded region in the figure?

   (1) $AB = 10$ and $AD = 5$
   (2) $AE = 4$ and $EB = 6$

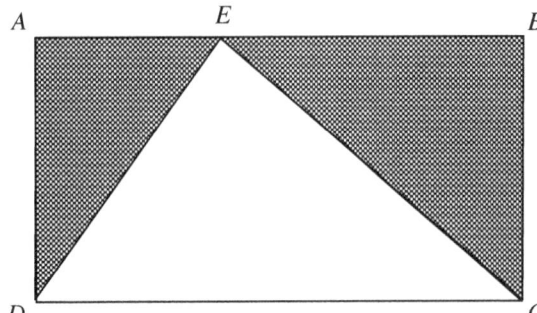

35. If $x > 2$ and $x < 3$, then which of the following is positive?

   (I) $(x-2)(x-3)$
   (II) $(2-x)(x-3)$
   (III) $(2-x)(3-x)$

   (A)   I only
   (B)   II only
   (C)   III only
   (D)   I and II only
   (E)   I and III only

[Data Sufficiency Question]
36. If $x^2 - y^2 = 15$, is $x + y > x - y$?

   (1) $x - y = 5$
   (2) $x + y = 3$

37. 3/8 of a number is what fraction of 2 times the number?

   (A)   3/16
   (B)   3/8
   (C)   1/2
   (D)   4/6
   (E)   3/4

Answers and Solutions Test 3:

1.	B	11.	C	21.	D	31.	E
2.	C	12.	B	22.	C	32.	D
3.	B	13.	C	23.	C	33.	E
4.	B	14.	E	24.	B	34.	A
5.	A	15.	C	25.	B	35.	B
6.	C	16.	D	26.	C	36.	D
7.	A	17.	D	27.	A	37.	D
8.	E	18.	E	28.	C		
9.	D	19.	C	29.	B		
10.	D	20.	E	30.	E		

---

1. A number divisible by 2 ends with one of the digits 0, 2, 4, 6, or 8.

If a number is divisible by 3, then the sum of its digits is also divisible by 3.

Hence, a number divisible by both 2 and 3 will follow both of the above rules.

Choices (A) and (C) do not end with an even digit. Hence, eliminate them.

The sum of digits of Choice (B) is $1 + 2 + 9 + 6 = 18$, which is divisible by 3. Also, the last digit is 6. Hence, choice (B) is correct.

Next, the sum of the digits of choices (D) and (E) are $1 + 4 + 0 + 6$ (= 11) and $1 + 4 + 1 + 4$ (= 10), respectively, and neither is divisible by 3. Hence, reject the two choices.

Hence, the answer is (B).

---

2. Working from the inner parentheses out, we get

$$((-\pi)^*)^* =$$
$$(\pi/(-\pi))^* =$$
$$(-1)^* =$$
$$\pi/(-1) =$$
$$-\pi$$

The answer is (C).

Method II:

We can rewrite this problem using ordinary function notation. Replacing the odd symbol x^* with $f(x)$ gives $f(x) = \pi/x$. Now, the expression $((-\pi)^*)^*$ becomes the ordinary composite function

$$f(f(-\pi)) =$$
$$f(\pi/(-\pi)) =$$
$$f(-1) =$$
$$\pi/(-1) =$$
$$-\pi$$

3. As a particular case, suppose $m = 7$ and $n = 4$. Then $m/n = 7/4 = 1 + 3/4$. Here, the remainder r equals 3.

Now, $2m = 2 \cdot 7 = 14$ and $2n = 2 \cdot 4 = 8$. Hence, $2m/2n = 14/8 = 1 + 6/8^*$. Here, the remainder is 6. Now, let's choose the answer-choice that equals 6.

    Choice (A): $r = 3 \neq 6$. Reject.
    Choice (B): $2r = 2 \cdot 3 = 6$. Possible answer.
    Choice (C): $2n = 2 \cdot 4 = 8 \neq 6$. Reject.
    Choice (D): $m - nr = 7 - 4 \cdot 3 = -5 \neq 6$. Reject.
    Choice (E): $2(m - nr) = 2(7 - 4 \cdot 3) = 2(-5) = -10 \neq 6$. Reject.

Hence, the answer is (B).

Method II (without substitution):
Since the remainder when m is divided by n is r, we can represent m as $m = kn + r$, where k is some integer. Now, $2m$ equals $2kn + 2r$. Hence, dividing $2m$ by $2n$ yields $2m/2n = (2kn + 2r)/2n = k + 2r/2n$. Since we are dividing by $2n$ (not by n), the remainder when divided by $2n$ is $2r$. The answer is (B).

4. Since the two circles touch each other, the distance between their centers, AB, equals the sum of the radii of the two circles, which is $2 + 3 = 5$. Hence, the area of a circle with diameter AB (or radius = $AB/2$) is

$$\pi \times radius^2 =$$
$$\pi(AB/2)^2 =$$
$$\pi(5/2)^2 =$$
$$25\pi/4$$

The answer is (B).

5. Applying the Difference of Squares formula to the numerator of $\dfrac{a^2-b^2}{a-b}$ yields $\dfrac{(a+b)(a-b)}{a-b} = a+b$, and doing the same to $\dfrac{a^2-b^2}{a+b}$ yields $\dfrac{(a+b)(a-b)}{a+b} = a-b$. So, the question reduces to "Is $a + b > a - b$?" Adding $-a + b$ to both sides of the inequality further reduces the question to "Is $2b > 0$?", or finally "Is $b > 0$?" Statement (2): $b = 59$ alone can answer the question. Statement (1): $a = 49$ alone is not relevant since it does not tell us the value of b. The answer is (B).

Z10. From Statement (1), we have x is divisible by 3 and 4. So, x must be a common multiple of 3 and 4. The least common multiple of 3 and 4 is 12. So, x is a multiple of 12. Hence, Statement (1) answers the question, "Is x multiple of 12?"

From Statement (2), we have 2 and 6 divide x evenly. The LCM of 2 and 6 is 6, so x is a multiple of 6. But, not all multiples of 6 are multiples of 12 (for example, 18). Hence, Statement (2) alone is not sufficient to answer the question, "Is x is multiple of 12?"

The answer is (A).

---

* Note that we do not reduce 6/8 to 3/4 because the devisor is 8. If we were to reduce 6/8 to 3/4, then we would be finding the remainder when dividing by 4.

6.

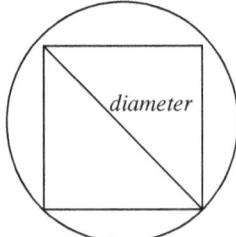

The diagonal of a square inscribed in a circle is a diameter of the circle. The formula for the diagonal of a square is $\sqrt{2} \times side$. Hence, the diameter of the circle inscribing the square of side length 2 is $\sqrt{2} \times 2 = 2\sqrt{2}$. Since $radius = diameter/2$, the radius of the circle is $\frac{2\sqrt{2}}{2} = \sqrt{2}$. Hence, the area of the circle is $\pi \cdot radius^2 = \pi(\sqrt{2})^2 = 2\pi$. The answer is (C).

7. From Statement (1), we have x is divisible by 3 and 4. So, x must be a common multiple of 3 and 4. The least common multiple of 3 and 4 is 12. So, x is a multiple of 12. Hence, Statement (1) answers the question, "Is x multiple of 12?"

From Statement (2), we have 2 and 6 divide x evenly. The LCM of 2 and 6 is 6, so x is a multiple of 6. But, not all multiples of 6 are multiples of 12 (for example, 18). Hence, Statement (2) alone is not sufficient to answer the question, "Is x is multiple of 12?"

The answer is (A).

8. The slope of a line expressed as $y = mx + b$ is m. Expressing the given line $2x + y = 3$ in that format yields $y = -2x + 3$. Hence, the slope is -2, the coefficient of x. Let's express each line in the form $y = mx + b$ and pick the line whose slope is not -2.

Choice (A): $2x + y = 5$; $y = -2x + 5$, slope is -2. Reject.
Choice (B): $x + y/2 = 3$; $y = -2x + 6$, slope is -2. Reject.
Choice (C): $x = -y/2 - 3$; $y = -2x - 6$, slope is -2. Reject.
Choice (D): $y = 7 - 2x$; $y = -2x + 7$, slope is -2. Reject.
Choice (E): $x + 2y = 9$; $y = -\frac{1}{2}x + \frac{9}{2}$, slope is $-\frac{1}{2} \neq -2$. Accept the choice.

The answer is (E).

9. From Statement (1) alone, we have that the ratio of the three angles of the triangle is $1 : 2 : 3$. Let $k°$, $2k°$, and $3k°$ be the three angles. Summing the three angles to 180° yields $k + 2k + 3k = 180$; $6k = 180$; $k = 180/6 = 30$. Now that we have the value of k, we can calculate the three angles and determine whether the triangle is a right triangle or not. Hence, Statement (1) alone is sufficient. The third angle equals $3k = 3 \times 30° = 90°$ and therefore the triangle is right angled. Hence, the answer to the question is "Yes. The triangle is right angled."

From Statement (2) alone, we have that one angle of the triangle equals the sum of the other two angles. Let $\angle A = \angle B + \angle C$. Summing the angles of the triangle to 180° yields $\angle A + \angle B + \angle C = 180$; $\angle A + \angle A = 180$ (since $\angle B + \angle C = \angle A$); $2\angle A = 180$; $\angle A = 180/2 = 90$. Hence, the triangle is a right triangle, and therefore Statement (2) alone is also sufficient.

Hence, the answer is (D).

Test 3—Answers and Solutions

10. Adding x to both sides of the equation $y = x + 5$ yields $x + y = x + (x + 5)$, or $x + y = 2x + 5$. Hence, the greatest possible value of $x + y$ is the maximum possible value of $2x + 5$. Now, let's create this expression out of the given inequality $5 < x < 10$. Multiplying the inequality by 2 yields $10 < 2x < 20$. Adding 5 to each part of the inequality yields $10 + 5 < 2x + 5 < 20 + 5$, or $15 < 2x + 5 < 25$. So, $2x + 5$ is less than 25. The greatest possible integer value of $2x + 5$ is 24. Hence, the answer is (D).

11. Name the first triangle ABC and the second triangle DEF. From statements (1) and (2) together, let $\angle A : \angle B : \angle C = 2 : 3 : 4$, and let $\angle D : \angle E : \angle F = 4 : 3 : 2$. The ordering of the ratio can be reversed and doing this for the second ratio equation yields $\angle F : \angle E : \angle D = 2 : 3 : 4$. Now since the ratios of the corresponding angles in triangle ABC equals the ratio of angles in triangle DEF, we have that triangles ABC and FED are similar. The statements can together answer the question. Hence, the answer is (C).

12. We are given that Kate ate 1/3 of the cake. So, the uneaten part of the cake is $1 - 1/3 = 2/3$. Exactly 1/2 of this part is eaten by Fritz. Hence, $1 - 1/2 = 1/2$ of this part is uneaten. The uneaten part of the complete cake is now $1/2 \times 2/3 = 1/3$. This was eaten by Emily, and the answer is (B).

13. The angle ratio of the triangle given in Statement (1) is $2 : 3 : 4$ which in any order is not equal to the ratio of angles of the triangle in Statement (2), which is $1 : 1 : 1$. Hence, the statements together say that the two triangles are not similar. We need both statements (1) and (2) to solve it. Hence, the answer is (C).

Method II: The ratio of the angles of the triangle in Statement (1) is $2 : 3 : 4$. So, let the three angles of the triangle be $2x$, $3x$, and $4x$. Since the sum of the angles of a triangle is $180°$, $2x + 3x + 4x = 180$. Solving this equation for x yields $x = 180/9 = 20$. Hence, the three angles are $2x = 2 \times 20 = 40$, $3x = 3 \times 20 = 60$, and $4x = 4 \times 20 = 80$.

Now, the ratio of the angles of the triangle in Statement (2) is $1 : 1 : 1$. Let the three angles of the triangle be y, y, and y. Summing the three to $180°$ yields $y + y + y = 180$, so $3y = 180/3 = 60$. Hence, each of the three angles in the triangle is $60°$.

Thus, not all three angles of the two triangles are equal. Hence, the two triangles are not similar. We need both statements (1) and (2) to solve it. Hence, the answer is (C).

14. Let the rectangular box be as shown in the figure:

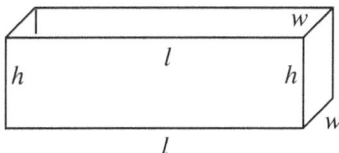

The surface area of the box is $lw + 2lh + 2hw$, and the volume is lwh.

From Statement (1), we have that the area of the base, which equals lw, is 23.

From Statement (2), we have that the volume of the box, which equals lwh, is 23.

Dividing the value in Statement (2) by the value in Statement (1) yields

$$\frac{lwh}{lw} = h = \frac{23}{23} = 1$$

So, we have the height of the box. Since we have the values of only h and lw, there is not enough information to determine the value of the expression $lw + 2lh + 2hw$, which has to be evaluated.

Hence, the statements together are insufficient to answer the question.

The answer is (E).

---

15. Factoring the common factor b from the expression $ab + bc$ yields $b(a + c)$.

From Statement (1) alone, we have $b = a + c$. Replacing $a + c$ with b in the expression $b(a + c)$ yields $b \cdot b$, or b^2. Since we do not have the value of b or $a + c$, which equals b, the expression cannot be evaluated. Hence, Statement (1) alone is not sufficient.

From Statement (2) alone, we have that $b = 3$. Substituting this in the expression $b(a + c)$ yields the expression $3(a + c)$. Since we do not know the value of $a + c$, we cannot evaluate the expression. Hence, Statement (2) alone is not sufficient.

Now, let's combine the statements. From Statement (1), we have that the expression $b(a + c)$ equals b^2; and since from Statement (2) we have that b equals 3, the value of the expression is $b^2 = 3^2 = 9$. Hence, the answer is (C).

---

16. Let the two numbers be x and y. Since their sum is 13, $x + y = 13$. Since their product is 30, $xy = 30$. Solving the equation $xy = 30$ for y yields $y = 30/x$. Plugging this into the equation $x + y = 13$ yields

$x + 30/x = 13$
$x^2 + 30 = 13x$ by multiplying both sides of the equation by x
$x^2 - 13x + 30 = 0$ by subtracting $13x$ from both sides of the equation
$(x - 3)(x - 10) = 0$
$x = 3$ or $x = 10$

Now, if $x = 3$, then $y = 13 - x = 13 - 3 = 10$. Hence, $x^2 + y^2 = 3^2 + 10^2 = 9 + 100 = 109$. The answer is (D).

Method II:
$(x + y)^2 = x^2 + y^2 + 2xy$. Hence, $x^2 + y^2 = (x + y)^2 - 2xy = 13^2 - 2(30) = 169 - 60 = 109$.

---

17. Let a and b be the two angles in the question, with $a > b$. We are given that the difference between the angles is 24°, so $a - b = 24$. Since the average of the two angles is 54°, we have $(a + b)/2 = 54$. Solving for b in the first equation yields $b = a - 24$, and substituting this into the second equation yields

$$\frac{a + (a - 24)}{2} = 54$$
$$\frac{2a - 24}{2} = 54$$
$$2a - 24 = 54 \times 2$$
$$2a - 24 = 108$$
$$2a = 108 + 24$$
$$2a = 132$$
$$a = 66$$

Also, $b = a - 24 = 66 - 24 = 42$.

Now, let c be the third angle of the triangle. Since the sum of the angles in the triangle is 180°, $a + b + c = 180$. Plugging the previous results into the equation yields $66 + 42 + c = 180$. Solving for c yields $c = 72$. Hence, the greatest of the three angles a, b and c is c, which equals 72°. The answer is (D).

18. This problem can be solved by setting up a proportion. Note that 1 pound has 16 ounces, so 3 pounds has 48 (= 3 × 16) ounces. Now, the proportion, in cents to ounces, is

$$\frac{800}{48} = \frac{\text{cents}}{9}$$

or

$$\text{cents} = 9 \cdot \frac{800}{48} = 150$$

The answer is (E).

---

19. Compound interest is the concept of adding accumulated interest to the principal so that interest is earned on the new principal from that moment onward. The act of declaring interest to be principal is called compounding (i.e., interest is compounded).

To calculate the interest earned or the balance at any point, apart from the interest earned, we also need the frequency of compounding of the interest. Hence, both statements are required to answer the question. The answer is (C).

---

20. First, place point A arbitrarily. Then locate point P 6 miles North of point A, and then locate a new point 8 miles East of P. Name the new point M. The figure looks like this:

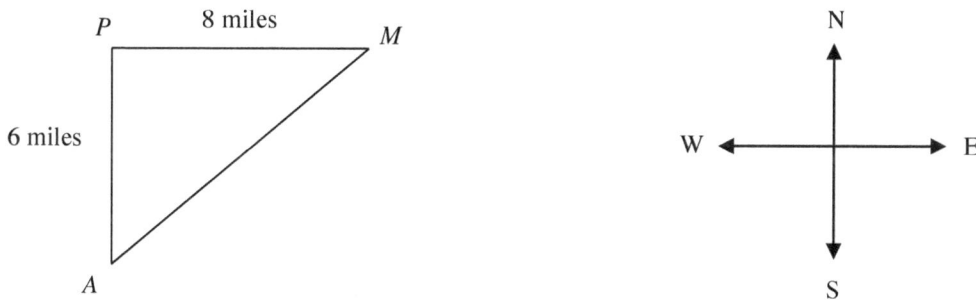

Since the angle between the standard directions East and South is 90°, the three points A, P and M form a right triangle with right angle at P. So, AM is the hypotenuse. By The Pythagorean Theorem, the hypotenuse equals the square root of the sum of squares of the other two sides. Hence,
$AM = \sqrt{AP^2 + PM^2} = \sqrt{6^2 + 8^2} = \sqrt{36 + 64} = \sqrt{100} = 10$. The answer is (E).

---

21. The sum of the first n terms of an arithmetic series whose nth term is n is $n(n + 1)/2$. Hence, we have

$$1 + 2 + 3 + \ldots + n = n(n + 1)/2$$

Multiplying each side by 2 yields

$$2 + 4 + 6 + \ldots + 2n = 2n(n + 1)/2 = n(n + 1)$$

Hence, the sum to 8 terms equals $n(n + 1) = 8(8 + 1) = 8(9) = 72$. The answer is (D).

---

22. The sum of $3n$, $9n$, and $11n$ is $23n$. Since this is to be greater than 200, we get the inequality $23n > 200$. From this, we get $n > 200/23 \approx 8.7$. Since n is an integer, $n > 8$. Now, we are given that $5 \le n \le 20$. Hence, the values for n are 9 through 20, a total of 12 numbers. The answer is (C).

23. From the graph, the number of security holes fixed in 2003 is 4500. The answer is (C).

24. Let's calculate the ratio and find the year in which the ratio is the greatest:

Choice (A): Year 1998. The number of security holes to bugs fixed is 5000/1500 = 10/3 = 3.33.

Choice (B): Year 1999. The number of security holes to bugs fixed is 4500/1000 = 9/2 = 4.5 > Choice (A). Reject choice (A).

Choice (C): Year 2000. The number of security holes to bugs fixed is 5000/1300 = 50/13 = 3.86 < Choice (B). Reject choice (C).

Choice (D): Year 2001. The number of security holes to bugs fixed is 4700/1600 = 47/16 = 2.9375 < Choice (B). Reject choice (D).

Choice (E): Year 2002. The number of security holes to bugs fixed is 5600/1300 = 56/13 = 4.3 < Choice (B). Reject choice (E).

The ratio is greatest in the year 1999. Hence, the answer is (B).

25. In 1999, the total number of software problems solved by Eigen's Software Company is Bugs + Security holes + Backdoors = 1000 + 4500 + 1700 = 7200.

In 2002, the total number of software problems solved by Eigen's Software Company is Bugs + Security holes + Backdoors = 1300 + 5600 + 1800 = 8700.

Hence, the percent increase in the number in the period is $\frac{8700-7200}{7200} \times 100 = 20.88\%$. The nearest answer is (B).

26. There are 16 ounces in a pound. Hence, each ounce equals 1/16 pounds. Now, 12 ounces equals $12 \times 1/16 = 3/4$ pounds. Hence, 5 pounds + 12 ounces equals 5 3/4 pounds. The answer is (C).

27. The function f is defined as $f(n) = n/(n+1)$. Putting,

$n = 1$ yields $f(1) = \frac{1}{1+1} = \frac{1}{2}$.

$n = 2$ yields $f(2) = \frac{2}{2+1} = \frac{2}{3}$.

$n = 3$ yields $f(3) = \frac{3}{3+1} = \frac{3}{4}$.

Hence, $f(1) \cdot f(2) - f(2) \cdot f(3) = 1/2 \cdot 2/3 - 2/3 \cdot 3/4 = 1/3 - 2/4 = 1/3 - 1/2 = -1/6$.

The answer is (A).

Test 3—Answers and Solutions

28. Statement (1) is just one constraint in 2 unknowns, and Statement (2) is also just one constraint in 2 unknowns. To solve for the two unknowns m and n we need at least 2 constraints. So, either statement alone is not sufficient.

Using both statements, we have $7m + 5n = 29$ and m and n are positive integers. Suppose $p = 7m$ and $q = 5n$. Then $p + q = 29$ and $q = 29 - p$ [(a positive multiple of 5) equals 29 − (a positive multiple of 7)]. Since m and n are positive integers, p is a multiple of 7 and q is a multiple of 5. Now,

If $p = 7$, $q = 29 - 7 = 22$, not a multiple of 5. Reject.

If $p = 14$, $q = 29 - 14 = 15$, a multiple of 5. Accept.

If $p = 21$, $q = 29 - 21 = 8$, not a multiple of 5. Reject.

If $p = 28$, $q = 29 - 28 = 1$, not a multiple of 5. Reject.

If $p \geq 35$, $q \leq 29 - 35 = -6$, not positive. Reject.

So, we have a unique solution $m = p/7 = 14/7 = 2$ and $n = q/5 = 15/5 = 3$. Hence, the answer is (C).

---

29. Two lines (here l and m) cut by a third line (a transversal, here k) are parallel when any one of the following can be shown:

   (1) Corresponding angles are equal: $y = q$. Hence, Statement (2) alone is sufficient.
   (2) Alternate interior angles are equal: No information is given about such angles in the problem.
   (3) Alternate exterior angles are equal: No information is given about such angles in the problem.
   (4) Interior angles are supplementary. $y + p = 180°$. No information is given about such the angles in problem.
   (5) Exterior angles are supplementary. $x + q = 180°$. We are told that the exterior angles x and q are equal in Statement (1), but this does not determine whether their sum is 180°.

Hence, Statement (1) alone is *not* sufficient, and Statement (2) alone is sufficient. The answer is (B).

---

30. $x/4$ is a positive integer when x is a multiple of 4. Now, not every multiple of 4 is divisible by 14. For example, 28 is a multiple of 4 and divisible by 14, but 32 is a multiple of 4 and not divisible by 14. Hence, Statement (1) alone is not sufficient.

$x/6$ is a positive integer when x is a multiple of 6. Now, not every multiple of 6 is divisible by 14. For example, 42 is a multiple of 6 and divisible by 14, but 48 is a multiple of 6 and not divisible by 14. Hence, Statement (2) alone is not sufficient.

With statements (1) and (2) together, we have that x is a multiple of both 4 and 6. Hence, x must be a multiple of the least common multiple of 4 and 6, which is 12. Hence, x is a multiple of 12. Now, not every multiple of 12 is divisible by 14. For example, 84 is a multiple of 12 and divisible by 14, but 24 is a multiple of 12 and not divisible by 14. Hence, even statements (1) and (2) together do not answer the question. The answer is (E).

31. If $p = 3/2$, then $p^2 = (3/2)^2 = 9/4 = 2.25$ and $2p = 2 \cdot 3/2 = 3$. Hence, $p^2 < 2p$, I is true, and clearly II ($p^2 = 2p$) and III ($p^2 > 2p$) are both false. This is true for all $1 < p < 2$.

If $p = 2$, then $p^2 = 2^2 = 4$ and $2p = 2 \cdot 2 = 4$. Hence, $p^2 = 2p$, II is true, and clearly I ($p^2 < 2p$) and III ($p^2 > 2p$) are both false.

If $p = 5/2$, then $p^2 = (5/2)^2 = 25/4 = 6.25$ and $2p = 2 \cdot 5/2 = 5$. Hence, $p^2 > 2p$, III is true, and clearly I ($p^2 < 2p$) and II ($p^2 = 2p$) are both false. This is true for any $2 < p < 3$.

Hence, exactly one of the three choices I, II, and III is true simultaneously (for a given value of p). The answer is (E).

---

32. Remember that *Average Speed = Net Distance ÷ Time Taken*. We are given that the time taken for the full trip is 30 minutes. Hence, we need only the distance traveled.

From Statement (1) alone, we have that the restaurant is 2 miles from home. Since Waugh jogs back along the same route, the net distance he traveled is 2 miles + 2 miles = 4 miles. Hence, his average speed is 4 miles ÷ 30 minutes, which can be calculated. Hence, Statement (1) alone is sufficient.

From Statement (2) alone, we have that $x = 12$ and $y = 6$. Let d be the distance to the restaurant. Then the time taken to jog to the restaurant, by the formula *Time = Distance ÷ Speed*, equals $d \div x = d/12$; and to return home from restaurant, the time taken equals $d \div y = d \div 6$. Hence, the total time taken equals $d/12 + d/6$, which is given to be 30 minutes (1/2 hour). Hence, d can be calculated from this formula, and therefore the average speed can be calculated using *Distance ÷ Time* $= \dfrac{2d}{\frac{1}{2} \text{ hours}} = 4d$. Hence, Statement (2) alone is also sufficient.

Hence, the answer is (D).

---

33. The consecutive integers $a, b,$ and c in the increasing order can be expressed as $a, a + 1, a + 2$, respectively.

$$p = \frac{a}{5} - \frac{b}{6} = \frac{a}{5} - \frac{a+1}{6} = \frac{6a - 5a - 5}{30} = \frac{a-5}{30}.$$

$$q = \frac{b}{5} - \frac{c}{6} = \frac{a+1}{5} - \frac{a+2}{6}$$

$$= \frac{6a + 6 - 5a - 10}{30}$$

$$= \frac{a-4}{30}$$

$$= \frac{a-4-1+1}{30} \qquad \text{by adding and subtracting 1 from the numerator}$$

$$= \frac{a-5+1}{30}$$

$$= \frac{a-5}{30} + \frac{1}{30}$$

$$= p + \frac{1}{30}$$

$$q - p = \frac{1}{30} \qquad \text{by subtracting } p \text{ from both sides}$$

The answer is (E).

34. The shaded region contains two triangles $\triangle AED$ and $\triangle EBC$. Hence, the area of the shaded region equals the sum of the areas of these two triangles.

Now, the formula for the area of a triangle is $1/2 \times base \times height$. Hence, the area of $\triangle AED = 1/2 \times AE \times AD$, and the area of $\triangle EBC = 1/2 \times EB \times BC = 1/2 \times EB \times AD$ (since $BC = AD$).

So, the area of the shaded region equals

$$1/2 \times AE \times AD + 1/2 \times EB \times AD =$$
$$1/2 \times AD(AE + EB) =$$
$$1/2 \times AD \times AB \quad (\text{since } AB = AE + EB)$$

Hence, to evaluate the area of the shaded region, we need AD and AB, which are given in Statement (1). Hence, Statement (1) alone is sufficient.

Statement (2) gives the lengths of AE and EB, which are only horizontal lengths. Since we do not have any vertical lengths (AD and BC) in the figure, the vertical lengths are free to take any values and therefore Statement (2) alone is *not* sufficient.

Hence, the answer is (A).

---

35. Combining the given inequalities $x > 2$ and $x < 3$ yields $2 < x < 3$. So, x lies between 2 and 3. Hence,

$x - 2$ is positive and $x - 3$ is negative. Hence, the product $(x - 2)(x - 3)$ is negative. I is false.

$2 - x$ is negative and $x - 3$ is negative. Hence, the product $(x - 2)(x - 3)$ is positive. II is true.

$2 - x$ is negative and $3 - x$ is positive. Hence, the product $(2 - x)(3 - x)$ is negative. III is false.

Hence, the answer is (B), II only is correct.

---

36. We are given the expression $x^2 - y^2 = 15$. Applying the Difference of Squares formula $(a + b)(a - b) = a^2 - b^2$ to the left-hand side yields $(x + y)(x - y) = 15$.

From Statement (1) alone, we have $x - y = 5$. Plugging this in the equation $(x + y)(x - y) = 15$ yields $(x + y)(5) = 15$. Dividing both sides by 5 yields $x + y = 3$. Hence, we have the values of both $x + y$ and $x - y$. Now, we can compare the two and answer the question. So, Statement (1) alone is sufficient. The answer is "No. $x + y > x - y$ is false."

From Statement (2) alone, we have $x + y = 3$. Plugging this in the equation $(x + y)(x - y) = 15$ yields $3(x - y) = 15$. Dividing both sides by 3 yields $x - y = 5$. Hence, we have the values of both $x + y$ and $x - y$. Now, we can compare the two and answer the question. Hence, Statement (2) alone is sufficient. The answer to the question is "No. $x + y$ is not greater than $x - y$."

Hence, the answer is (D).

37. Let the number be x. Now, 3/8 of the number is $3x/8$, and 2 times the number is $2x$. Forming the fraction yields $\dfrac{\frac{3}{8}x}{2x} = \dfrac{\frac{3}{8}}{2} = \dfrac{3}{8} \cdot \dfrac{1}{2} = \dfrac{3}{16}$. The answer is (A).

J4. a is $\dfrac{30}{31}$ of $\dfrac{31}{32} = \dfrac{30}{31} \cdot \dfrac{31}{32} = \dfrac{30}{32}$.

$b = \dfrac{30}{31}$.

Hence, $\dfrac{a}{b} = \dfrac{30}{32} / \dfrac{30}{31} = \dfrac{30}{32} \cdot \dfrac{31}{30} = \dfrac{31}{32}$. The answer is (D).

Test 4

Questions: 37
Time: 75 minutes

1. If $(x - 3)(x + 2) = (x - 2)(x + 3)$, then $x =$

    (A) –3
    (B) –2
    (C) 0
    (D) 2
    (E) 3

2. If $A*B$ is the greatest common factor of A and B, $A\$B$ is defined as the least common multiple of A and B, and $A \cap B$ is defined as equal to $(A*B) \$ (A\$B)$, then what is the value of $12 \cap 15$?

    (A) 42
    (B) 45
    (C) 48
    (D) 52
    (E) 60

3. How many numbers between 100 and 300, inclusive, are multiples of both 5 and 6?

    (A) 7
    (B) 12
    (C) 15
    (D) 20
    (E) 30

[Data Sufficiency Question]
4. Is $a - b > 2.5$?

    (1) $a > b + 2.5$
    (2) $a = 3 + b$

5. Which of the following could be the four angles of a parallelogram?

    (I) $50°, 130°, 50°, 130°$
    (II) $125°, 50°, 125°, 60°$
    (III) $60°, 110°, 60°, 110°$

    (A)   I only
    (B)   II only
    (C)   I and II only
    (D)   I and III only
    (E)   I, II and III

6. If $a^2 + 7a < 0$, then which one of the following could be the value of a?

    (A) -3
    (B) 0
    (C) 1
    (D) 2
    (E) 3

[Data Sufficiency Question]
7. Is the positive integer x an odd number?

   (1) $x^2 + 3x + 4$ is even.
   (2) $x^2 + 4x + 3$ is odd.

[Data Sufficiency Question]
8. What is the value of $x + y$?

   (1) $2x + 3y = 11$
   (2) $3x + 2y = 9$

9. The length of a rectangular banner is 3 feet 2 inches, and the width is 2 feet 4 inches. Which one of the following equals the area of the banner?

   (A) 5 sq. feet
   (B) 5 1/2 sq. feet
   (C) 6 1/3 sq. feet
   (D) 7 sq. feet
   (E) 7 7/18 sq. feet

[Data Sufficiency Question]
10. Is $x > y$?

    (1) $2x = 2y + 1$
    (2) $3x = 4y - 1$

[Data Sufficiency Question]
11. Is x positive?

    (1) $x + 3$ is positive.
    (2) $x - 3$ is positive.

12. $2 \times 10^1 + 3 \times 10^0 + 4 \times 10^{-1} + 5 \times 10^{-2} =$

    (A) 11.15
    (B) 20.131
    (C) 23.45
    (D) 45.321
    (E) 53.231

13. If *p* is the sum of *q* and *r*, then which one of the following must equal $q - r$?

    (A) $p - r$
    (B) $p + r$
    (C) $p - 2r$
    (D) $p + 2r$
    (E) $2q + p$

[Data Sufficiency Question]
14. Is $2p - 3q$ not equal to 0?

    (1) $4p$ is not equal to $6q$.
    (2) p is not equal to q.

[Data Sufficiency Question]
15. If *m* and *n* are positive integers, then is $m + 2n$ an even integer?

    (1) $m = 3n + 1$
    (2) Exactly one of the two numbers *m* and *n* is even.

16. In a set of three numbers, the average of first two numbers is 2, the average of the last two numbers is 3, and the average of the first and the last numbers is 4. What is the average of three numbers?

   (A) 2
   (B) 2.5
   (C) 3
   (D) 3.5
   (E) 4

17. In the figure, ABCD is a rectangle and points E, F, G and H are midpoints of its sides. What is the ratio of the area of the shaded region to the area of the un-shaded region in the rectangle?

   (A) 1 : 1
   (B) 1 : 2
   (C) 2 : 1
   (D) 1 : 3
   (E) 3 : 1

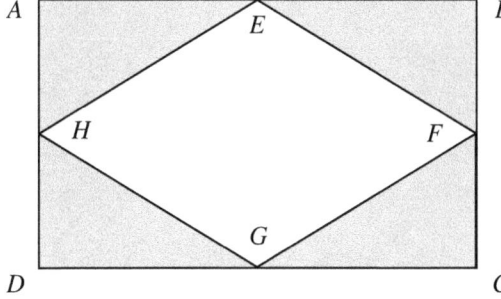

18. If $xy = 1$ and x is not equal to y, then $\left(7^{\frac{1}{x-y}}\right)^{\frac{1}{x}-\frac{1}{y}} =$

(A) $\frac{1}{7^2}$
(B) 1/7
(C) 1
(D) 7
(E) 7^2

USE THIS SPACE FOR SCRATCHWORK.

[Data Sufficiency Question]
19. What is the value of x ?

(1) $2x + 1 = 10$
(2) $(2x + 1)^2 = 100$

USE THIS SPACE FOR SCRATCHWORK.

20. If $a = 49$ and $b = 59$, then $\frac{a^2 - b^2}{a - b} - \frac{a^2 - b^2}{a + b} =$

(A) 39/49
(B) 37/45
(C) 59
(D) 108
(E) 118

USE THIS SPACE FOR SCRATCHWORK.

21. If $x \neq 3$ and $x \neq 6$, then $\dfrac{2x^2 - 72}{x - 6} - \dfrac{2x^2 - 18}{x - 3} =$

    (A) 3
    (B) 6
    (C) 9
    (D) 12
    (E) 15

22. Which one of the following must $p - q$ equal if 60% of m equals p and 3/5 of m equals q ?

    (A) 0
    (B) $m/11$
    (C) $2m/11$
    (D) $3m/55$
    (E) $6m/55$

Questions 23–27 refer to the following discussion.

The graphs below provide data on a common entrance examination conducted in different years.

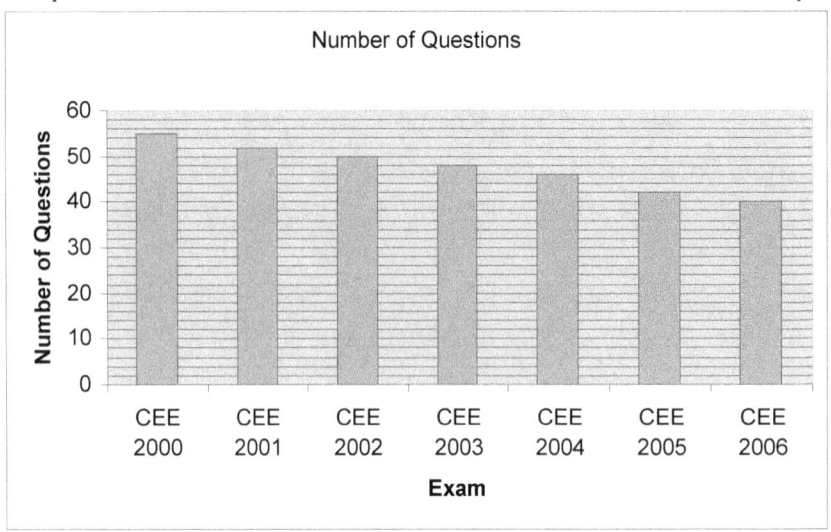

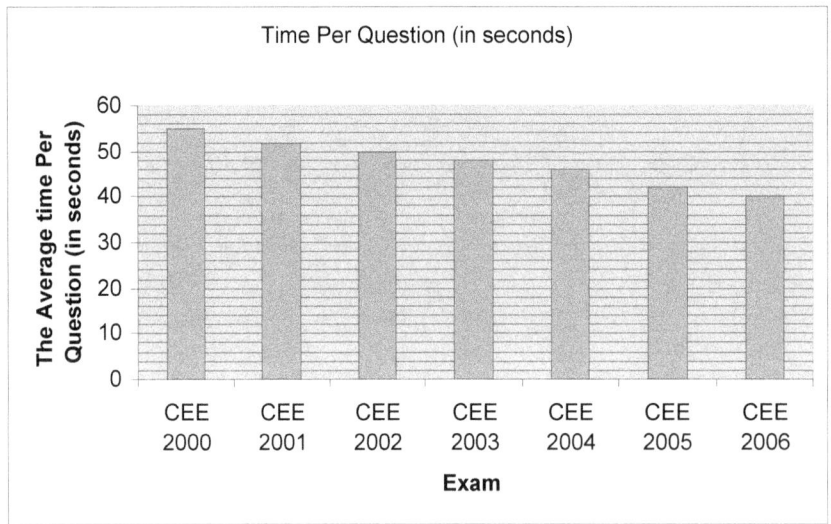

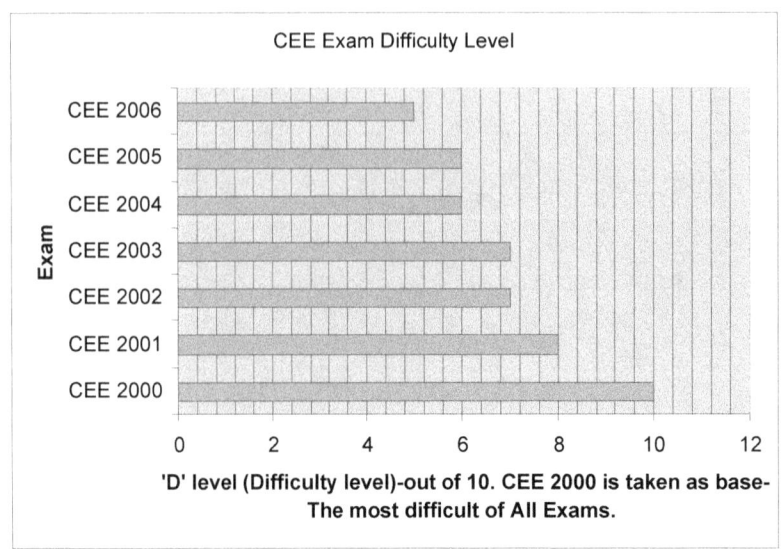

23. Which year had the second most difficult exam?

(A) 2000
(B) 2001
(C) 2002
(D) 2004
(E) 2006

USE THIS SPACE FOR SCRATCHWORK.

24. By approximately what percent did the number of questions decrease from CEE 2000 to CEE 2006?

(A) 11
(B) 22
(C) 27
(D) 33
(E) 37

USE THIS SPACE FOR SCRATCHWORK.

25. In which year were the test takers given the least time to answer all the questions?

(A) 2000
(B) 2001
(C) 2002
(D) 2004
(E) 2006

USE THIS SPACE FOR SCRATCHWORK.

GMAT Math Tests

26. If the Pressure Factor for the examinees in an exam is defined as Difficulty level divided by Average Time (in minutes) given per question, then the Pressure Factor equals which one of the following in CEE 2006?

    (A) 7.5
    (B) 10
    (C) 12.5
    (D) 15
    (E) 17.5

27. If the Stress Factor for the examinees in an exam is defined as the product of the Difficulty level and the Number of questions divided by the average time given per question, then the Stress Factor equals which one of the following in the exam CEE 2005?

    (A) 2 per second
    (B) 3 per second
    (C) 4 per second
    (D) 6 per second
    (E) 9 per second

[Data Sufficiency Question]
28. What is the numerical difference between the 5th and 6th terms in the sequence of numbers $a_0, a_1, a_2, ..., a_n$?

    (1) The mth term is defined by the rule $2m + 1$.
    (2) The 6th term is 81.

[Data Sufficiency Question]
29. What is the value of $x - y$?

   (1) x is 50% more than y.
   (2) x is the sum of y and 20.

[Data Sufficiency Question]
30. Is $x/15 > y/25$?

   (1) $5y + 3x > 8x + 2y$
   (2) $6y + 5x > 10x + 3y$

31. An old man distributed all the gold coins he had to his two sons into two different numbers such that the difference between the squares of the two numbers is 36 times the difference between the two numbers. How many coins did the old man have?

   (A) 24
   (B) 26
   (C) 30
   (D) 36
   (E) 40

[Data Sufficiency Question]
32. Is $a > b$?

    (1)   The arithmetic mean of a and b is 25.
    (2)   The geometric mean of a and b is 25.

33. The sum of the first n terms of a series is 31, and the sum of the first $n - 1$ terms of the series is 20. What is the value of nth term in the series?

    (A)   9
    (B)   11
    (C)   20
    (D)   31
    (E)   51

[Data Sufficiency Question]
34. What is the value of $x^2 - y^2$?

    (1) $x + y = 12$
    (2) $xy = 35$

35. Ana is a girl and has the same number of brothers as sisters. Andrew is a boy and has twice as many sisters as brothers. Ana and Andrew are the children of Emma. How many children does Emma have?

   (A) 2
   (B) 3
   (C) 5
   (D) 7
   (E) 8

[Data Sufficiency Question]

36. What is the value of $\dfrac{a+b}{\sqrt{ab}}$?

   (1) a is 4 times b.
   (2) b is one-fourth of a.

37. If p and q are both positive integers such that $p/9 + q/10$ is also an integer, then which one of the following numbers could p equal?

   (A) 3
   (B) 4
   (C) 9
   (D) 11
   (E) 19

Answers and Solutions Test 4:

1.	C	11.	B	21.	B	31.	D
2.	E	12.	C	22.	A	32.	C
3.	A	13.	C	23.	B	33.	B
4.	D	14.	A	24.	C	34.	E
5.	E	15.	E	25.	E	35.	D
6.	A	16.	C	26.	A	36.	D
7.	B	17.	A	27.	D	37.	C
8.	C	18.	B	28.	A		
9.	E	19.	A	29.	B		
10.	A	20.	E	30.	D		

---

1. If $x = 0$, then the equation $(x - 3)(x + 2) = (x - 2)(x + 3)$ becomes

$$(0 - 3)(0 + 2) = (0 - 2)(0 + 3)$$

$$(-3)(2) = (-2)(3)$$

$$-6 = -6$$

Hence, 0 is a solution of the equation, and the answer is (C).

---

2. According to the definitions given, $12 \cap 15$ equals $(12*15) \$ (12\$15) = $ (GCF of 12 and 15) $\$$ (LCM of 12 and 15) = $3 \$ 60$ = LCM of 3 and 60 = 60. The answer is (E).

---

3. The least common multiple of the numbers 5 and 6 is the product of the two (since 5 and 6 have no common factors), which is $5 \times 6 = 30$. Hence, if a number is a multiple of both 5 and 6, the number must be a multiple of 30. For example, the numbers 30, 60, 90, ... are divisible by both 5 and 6. The multiples of 30 between 100 and 300, inclusive, are 120, 150, 180, 210, 240, 270, and 300. The count of the numbers is 7. The answer is (A).

---

4. From Statement (1) alone, we have the inequality $a > b + 2.5$. Subtracting b from both sides yields $a - b > 2.5$. Hence, Statement (1) alone is sufficient to answer the question.

From Statement (2) alone, we have that $a = 3 + b$. Subtracting b from both sides yields $a - b = 3$. Since 3 is greater than 2.5, $a - b$ is greater than 2.5. Hence, Statement (2) alone is also sufficient to answer the question.

The answer is (D).

Test 4—Answers and Solutions

5. A quadrilateral is a parallelogram if it satisfies two conditions:

   1) The opposite angles are equal.
   2) The angles sum to 360°.

Now, in (I), opposite angles are equal (one pair of opposite angles equals 50°, and the other pair of opposite angles equals 130°). Also, all the angles sum to 360° (= 50° + 130° + 50° + 130° = 360°). Hence, (I) is true.

In (II), not all opposite angles are equal (50° ≠ 60°). Hence, (II) is not a parallelogram.

In (III), the angle sum is not equal to 360° (60° + 110° + 60° + 110° = 340° ≠ 360°). Hence, (III) does not represent a quadrilateral.

Hence, only (I) is true, and the answer is (A).

6. Factoring out the common factor a on the left-hand side of the inequality $a^2 + 7a < 0$ yields $a(a + 7) < 0$. The product of two numbers (here, a and $a + 7$) is negative when one is negative and the other is positive. Hence, we have two cases:

$$1)\ a < 0 \text{ and } a + 7 > 0$$
$$2)\ a > 0 \text{ and } a + 7 < 0$$

Case 2) is impossible since if a is positive then $a + 7$ cannot be negative.

Case 1) is valid for all values of a between 0 and –7. Hence, a must be negative, so a could equal –3. The answer is (A).

7. From Statement (1) alone, we have that $x^2 + 3x + 4$ is an even number. Hence,

$x^2 + 3x$ = (an even number) – 4 = an even number. So, $x^2 + 3x = x(x + 3)$ is an even number

The product of the two positive integers is even when at least one of them is even. So, whether x is even or $x + 3$ is even (because x is odd), $x(x + 3)$ is even. So, we cannot determine whether x is even or odd. Therefore, Statement (1) alone is not sufficient.

From Statement (2) alone, we have that $x^2 + 4x + 3$ is an odd number. Hence,

$x^2 + 4x$ = (an odd number) – 3 = an even number. So, $x^2 + 4x = x(x + 4)$ is an even number

The product of two positive integers is even when at least one of them is even. So, at least one of the two factors x and $x + 4$ must be even. But, if x is even, $x + 4$ is even; and if $x + 4$ is even, x is even. Hence, Statement (2) alone is sufficient. The answer to the question is "No. x is even."

So, the answer is (B): Statement (2) alone is sufficient, and Statement (1) is not sufficient.

8. Let $x + y = t$. Then $y = t - x$. Substituting this in the question changes it to

"What is the value of t?"

(1) $2x + 3(t - x) = 11$ or $3t - x = 11$
(2) $3x + 2(t - x) = 9$ or $2t + x = 9$

From Statement (1) alone, we have $3t - x = 11$. Solving the equation for t yields $t = (11 + x)/3$. Hence, the value of t is dependent on x (which is still unknown). Hence, Statement (1) alone is not sufficient to evaluate t.

Similarly, from Statement (2) alone, we have $2t + x = 9$. Solving the equation for t yields $t = (9 - x)/2$. Hence, the value of t is dependent on x (which is still unknown). Hence, Statement (2) alone is not sufficient to evaluate t.

Next, from statements (1) and (2) together, we have $3t - x = 11$ and $2t + x = 9$. Summing the two equations yields $5t = 20$; $t = 20/5 = 4$. Hence, the statements together answer the question. The answer is (C).

---

9. First, let's convert all the measurements to feet. There are 12 inches in a foot, so 2 inches equals $2/12 = 1/6$ feet, and 4 inches equals $4/12 = 1/3$ feet.

Hence, 3 feet 2 inches equals 3 1/6 feet, and 2 feet 4 inches equals 2 1/3 feet.

Now, the area of a rectangle is length × width. Hence,

$$\text{Area} = 3\ 1/6 \times 2\ 1/3 = 19/6 \times 7/3 = 133/18 = 7\ 7/18$$

The answer is (E).

---

10. Dividing both sides of the equation in Statement (1) by 2 yields $x = y + 1/2$. Reading the equation yields "x is 1/2 unit greater than y." Hence, Statement (1) alone is sufficient.

Subtracting y from both sides of the inequality yields $x - y > 0$. Hence, the question can be changed to "Is $x - y > 0$?" or "Is $x - y$ positive?"

Let's derive an expression for $x - y$ from Statement (2) alone. The equation in the statement is $3x = 4y - 1$. Subtracting $3y$ from both sides of the equation yields $3x - 3y = y - 1$. Dividing both sides by 3 yields $x - y = (y - 1)/3$. Now, the value of $(y - 1)/3$ is less than 0 (when $y = -1$) and greater than 0 (when $y = 2$). Hence, Statement (2) alone is not sufficient to answer the question.

Hence, the answer is (A).

---

11. The question is "Is x positive?" In other words, "Is $x > 0$?"

From Statement (1) alone, we have that $x + 3$ is positive. Expressing this as an inequality yields $x + 3 > 0$. Subtracting 3 from both sides yields $x > -3$. Hence, x may have a negative value, such as -2 or -0.5, or a positive value, such as 1 or 2. Hence, we have a double case, and Statement (1) alone is not sufficient.

From Statement (2) alone, we have that $x - 3$ is positive. Expressing this as an inequality yields $x - 3 > 0$. Adding 3 to both sides of the inequality yields $x > 3$. Hence, x is positive. Hence, Statement (2) alone is sufficient to answer the question. The answer is "Yes. $x > 0$ is true."

Hence, the answer is (B).

12. $2 \times 10^1 + 3 \times 10^0 + 4 \times 10^{-1} + 5 \times 10^{-2} = 20 + 3 + 0.4 + 0.05 = 23.45$.

The answer is (C).

---

13. We are given that $p = q + r$. Now, let's create the expression $q - r$ by subtracting $2r$ from both sides of this equation:

$$p - 2r = q + r - 2r$$

or

$$p - 2r = q - r$$

The answer is (C).

---

14. From Statement (1) alone, we have that $4p \neq 6q$. Dividing both sides by 2 yields $2p \neq 3q$. Subtracting $3q$ from both sides yields $2p - 3q \neq 0$. Hence, Statement (1) alone is sufficient to answer the question.

From Statement (2) alone, we have $p \neq q$. Multiplying both sides by 2 yields $2p \neq 2q$. Subtracting $3q$ from both sides yields $2p - 3q \neq -q$. Now, if q equals 0, then $2p - 3q$ does not equal 0. But if q does not equal 0, then $2p - 3q$ may equal 0 [For example, when, say, $p = 3$ and $q = 2$, then $2p - 3q = 2(3) - 3(2) = 0$]. Hence, we have a double case, and Statement (2) alone is not sufficient.

Since Statement (1) alone is sufficient, the answer is (A).

---

15. From Statement (1) alone, we have $m = 3n + 1$. Hence, $m + 2n$ equals $(3n + 1) + 2n = 5n + 1$.

If n is even, then $5n$ is even and $5n + 1$ is odd.

If n is odd, then $5n$ is odd and $5n + 1$ is even.

Hence, we have a double case, and Statement (1) alone is not sufficient. Also, in either case, only one of the two numbers m and n is even. Hence, Statement (2) is a derivation of Statement (1). Hence, we can use the same two cases in Statement (1) to determine that Statement (2) alone is not sufficient.

Also, since Statement (2) is a derivation of Statement (1), the same two cases in Statement (1) can be used to determine that the statements together are not sufficient to answer the question. Hence, the answer is (E).

16. Let the three numbers be x, y, and z. We are given that

$$\frac{x+y}{2} = 2$$

$$\frac{y+z}{2} = 3$$

$$\frac{x+z}{2} = 4$$

Summing the three equations yields

$$\frac{x+y}{2} + \frac{y+z}{2} + \frac{x+z}{2} = 2+3+4$$

$$\frac{x}{2} + \frac{y}{2} + \frac{y}{2} + \frac{z}{2} + \frac{x}{2} + \frac{z}{2} = 9$$

$$x+y+z = 9$$

The average of the three numbers is $(x + y + z)/3 = 9/3 = 3$. The answer is (C).

---

17. Joining the midpoints of the opposite sides of the rectangle $ABCD$ yields the following figure:

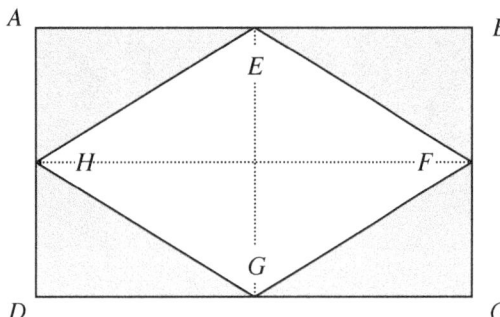

In the given figure, the bigger rectangle $ABCD$ contains four small rectangles, each one divided by a diagonal. Since diagonals cut a rectangle into two triangles of equal area, in each of the small rectangles, the regions to either side (shaded and un-shaded) have equal area. Hence, even in the bigger rectangle, the area of the shaded and un-shaded regions are equal, so the required ratio is 1 : 1. The answer is (A).

Test 4—Answers and Solutions

18. $\left(7^{\frac{1}{x-y}}\right)^{\frac{1}{x}-\frac{1}{y}} =$

$\left(7^{\frac{1}{x-y}}\right)^{\frac{y-x}{xy}} =$

$7^{\frac{1}{x-y} \cdot \frac{y-x}{xy}} =$

$7^{\frac{-1}{y-x} \cdot \frac{y-x}{xy}} =$

$7^{\frac{-1}{xy}} =$

$7^{\frac{-1}{1}} =$ since $xy = 1$

$7^{-1} =$

$\dfrac{1}{7}$

The answer is (B).

---

19. Solving the equation $2x + 1 = 10$ in Statement (1) for x yields $x = 9/2$. Hence, Statement (1) alone is sufficient.

From Statement (2) alone, we have that $(2x + 1)^2 = 100$. Square rooting both sides yields two equations: $2x + 1 = 10$ and $2x + 1 = -10$. Solving the first equation for x yields $x = 9/2$, and solving the second equation for x yields $x = -11/2$. Hence, we have a double case, and Statement (2) alone is not sufficient to answer the question.

Hence, the answer is (A).

---

20. Applying the Difference of Squares Formula $a^2 - b^2 = (a + b)(a - b)$ to the given expression yields

$\dfrac{a^2 - b^2}{a - b} - \dfrac{a^2 - b^2}{a + b} =$

$\dfrac{(a+b)(a-b)}{a-b} - \dfrac{(a+b)(a-b)}{a+b} =$

$a + b - (a - b) =$

$a + b - a + b =$

$2b =$

$2(59) =$

118

The answer is (E).

21. Start by factoring 2 from the numerators of each fraction:

$$\frac{2(x^2-36)}{x-6} - \frac{2(x^2-9)}{x-3}$$

Next, apply the Difference of Squares Formula $a^2 - b^2 = (a + b)(a - b)$ to both fractions in the expression:

$$\frac{2(x+6)(x-6)}{x-6} - \frac{2(x+3)(x-3)}{x-3}$$

Next, cancel the term $x - 6$ from the first fraction and $x - 3$ from the second fraction:

$$2(x + 6) - 2(x + 3) = 2x + 12 - 2x - 6 = 6$$

Hence, the answer is (B).

---

22. 60% of $m = (60/100)m = 3m/5 = p$.

$3/5$ of $m = 3m/5 = q$.

So, $p = q$, and therefore $p - q = 0$.

The answer is (A).

---

23. Refer to the graph CEE Exam Difficulty Level. The graph starts at 0 for each exam and ends at 10 for the most difficult exam, CEE 2000. So, the difficulty actually increases with 'D-level' value. The second highest value corresponds to the Exam CEE 2001. The answer is (B).

---

24. From the graph, the number of questions in CEE 2000 is 55. The number in CEE 2006 is 40. Hence, the percent drop is $\frac{55-40}{55} \times 100 = \frac{15}{55} \times 100 = \frac{3}{11} \times 100 = 27.27$. Since the nearest choice is (C), the answer is (C).

---

25. The time given can be evaluated as (Number of Questions) × (Time Per Question).

Both the number of questions and the time given per question are the least in 2006. Hence, their product should be minimum in that year.

Hence, the total time given is the least in 2006. The answer is (E).

---

26. The Pressure Factor in 2006 equals Difficulty level divided by Average Time given per question = 5/40 seconds or 5/(2/3 minutes) = 15/2 per minute. The answer is (A).

Test 4—Answers and Solutions

27. The Stress Factor equals

$$(\text{The difficulty level}) \times \left(\frac{\text{Number of questions}}{\text{Time given per question}}\right) =$$

$$6 \times \frac{42}{42 \text{ seconds per question}} =$$

6 per second

The answer is (D).

28. From Statement (1), we have the rule for the general term $a_m = 2m + 1$. Using this formula to evaluate the 5th and 6th terms yields

$a_5 = 2(5) + 1 = 11$
$a_6 = 2(6) + 1 = 13$

Forming the difference $a_6 - a_5$ yields

$a_6 - a_5 = 13 - 11 = 2$

Hence, Statement (1) alone is sufficient to answer the question.

Statement (2) gives the value of the 6th term but does not provide a way to evaluate the 5th term of the series. Hence, Statement (2) alone is not sufficient to answer the question.

Since only Statement (1) alone is sufficient, the answer is (A).

29. From Statement (1) alone, we have that x is 50% more than y. Now, 50% of y is $\frac{50}{100}y = \frac{y}{2}$. Hence, $x = y + \frac{y}{2} = \frac{3y}{2}$. Subtracting y from both sides yields $x - y = y/2$. Hence, the value of $x - y$ depends on the value of y, which is unknown. Hence, Statement (1) alone is not sufficient.

From Statement (2) alone, we have that x is the sum of y and 20. Hence, we have the equation $x = y + 20$. Subtracting y from both sides yields $x - y = 20$. Hence, Statement (2) alone is sufficient to answer the question.

Hence, the answer is (B).

30. Multiplying the inequality $x/15 > y/25$ by 15 yields $x > (15/25)y$ or $x > 3y/5$.

Subtracting $2y + 3x$ from both sides of the inequality in Statement (1) yields

$$3y > 5x$$

Rewriting with the variable x on the left and y on the right yields (note that the meaning of the inequality does not change, just the way it is written)

$$5x < 3y$$

Dividing by 5 yields

$$x < 3y/5$$

Hence, Statement (1) alone is sufficient. The answer to the question is "No. x is not greater than $3y/5$."

Now, subtracting $3y + 5x$ from both sides of the inequality in Statement (2) yields

$$3y > 5x$$

Rewriting with the variable x on the left and y on the right yields (note that the meaning of the inequality does not change, just the way it is written)

$$5x < 3y$$

Dividing by 5 yields

$$x < 3y/5$$

Hence, Statement (2) alone is sufficient. The answer to the question is "No. x is not greater than $3y/5$."

Since either statement alone is sufficient, the answer is (D).

---

31. Let x and y be the numbers of gold coins the two sons received. Since we are given that the difference between the squares of the two numbers is 36 times the difference between the two numbers, we have the equation

$x^2 - y^2 = 36(x - y)$

$(x - y)(x + y) = 36(x - y)$ by the Difference of Squares formula $a^2 - b^2 = (a - b)(a + b)$

$x + y = 36$ by canceling $(x - y)$ from both sides

Hence, the total number of gold coins the old man had, namely $x + y$, equals 36. The answer is (D).

Test 4—Answers and Solutions

32. From Statement (1), we have $\frac{a+b}{2} = 25$.

From Statement (2), we have $\sqrt{ab} = 25$, or by squaring $ab = 25^2$.

Solving the equation $\frac{a+b}{2} = 25$ for b yields $b = 50 - a$. Substituting this into the equation $ab = 25^2$ yields

$$a(50 - a) = 25^2$$
$$a^2 - 50a + 25^2 = 0$$
$$a^2 - 25a - 25a + 25^2 = 0$$
$$a(a - 25) - 25(a - 25) = 0$$
$$(a - 25)(a - 25) = 0$$
$$(a - 25)^2 = 0$$
$$a - 25 = 0$$
$$a = 25$$

Now, $b = 50 - a = 50 - 25 = 25$. Hence, $a = b$ and the statement "$a > b$" is false. Hence, the statements together are sufficient, and the answer is (C).

33. (The sum of the first n terms of a series) = (The sum of the first $n - 1$ terms) + (The nth term).

Substituting the given values in the equation yields $31 = 20 + n$th term. Hence, the nth term is $31 - 20 = 11$. The answer is (B).

34. By the Difference of Squares Formula, we have $x^2 - y^2 = (x - y)(x + y)$.

From Statement (1) alone, we have $x + y = 12$. But we do not have the value of $x - y$, so $x^2 - y^2$ cannot be evaluated.

For example, suppose $x = 6$ and $y = 6$, then $x + y = 12$ and $x^2 - y^2 = 6^2 - 6^2 = 36 - 36 = 0$.

Now, suppose $x = 12$ and $y = 0$. Then $x + y = 12$, and $x^2 - y^2 = 12^2 - 0^2 = 144 - 0 = 144$. Thus, we have a double case, and Statement (1) alone is not sufficient.

From Statement (2) alone, we have the value of $xy = 35$. But again, we do not have the value of $x^2 - y^2$, so $x^2 - y^2$ cannot be evaluated.

For example, suppose $x = 5$ and $y = 7$, then $xy = 35$, and $x^2 - y^2 = 7^2 - 5^2 = 49 - 25 = 24$.

But suppose $x = 35$ and $y = 1$. Then $xy = 35$, and $x^2 - y^2 = 35^2 - 1^2 = 1225 - 1 = 1224$.

Thus, we have a double case and therefore Statement (2) alone is not sufficient.

With the statements together, we have that $x + y = 12$ and $xy = 35$. Squaring both sides of the first equation $x + y = 12$ yields $(x + y)^2 = 12^2 = 144$. Multiplying the second equation $xy = 35$ by 4 yields $4xy = 140$. Subtracting this equation from the equation $(x + y)^2 = 144$ yields

$$(x + y)^2 - 4xy = 144 - 140$$
$$x^2 + y^2 + 2xy - 4xy = 4$$
$$x^2 + y^2 - 2xy = 4$$
$$(x - y)^2 = 4$$
$$x - y = \pm 2$$

Since $x - y$ is either 2 or –2, we still do not have a unique value for $x - y$. Hence, the two statements together are still not sufficient. The answer is (E).

119

35. Let the number of female children Emma has be n. Since Anna herself is one of them, she has $n - 1$ sisters. Hence, as given, she must have the same number ($= n - 1$) of brothers. Hence, the number of male children Emma has is $n - 1$. Since Andrew is one of them, Andrew has $(n - 1) - 1 = n - 2$ brothers. Now, the number of sisters Andrew has (includes Anna) is n (= the number of female children). Since Andrew has twice as many sisters as brothers, we have the equation $n = 2(n - 2)$. Solving the equation for n yields $n = 4$. Hence, Emma has 4 female children, and the number of male children she has is $n - 1 = 4 - 1 = 3$. Hence, the total number of children Emma has is $4 + 3 = 7$. The answer is (D).

36. $\dfrac{a+b}{\sqrt{ab}} = \dfrac{a}{\sqrt{ab}} + \dfrac{b}{\sqrt{ab}} = \dfrac{\sqrt{a^2}}{\sqrt{ab}} + \dfrac{\sqrt{b^2}}{\sqrt{ab}} = \sqrt{\dfrac{a^2}{ab}} + \sqrt{\dfrac{b^2}{ab}} = \sqrt{\dfrac{a}{b}} + \sqrt{\dfrac{b}{a}} = \sqrt{\dfrac{a}{b}} + \dfrac{1}{\sqrt{\dfrac{a}{b}}}$. Hence, we need only the value of a/b to evaluate the expression.

From Statement (1) alone, we have that a is 4 times b. Hence, $a = 4b$, or $a/b = 4$. Since we can derive the value of a/b from Statement (1) alone, the statement is sufficient.

From Statement (2) alone, we have that b is one-fourth of a. Hence, we have $b = a/4$. Multiplying both sides by $4/b$ yields $4 = a/b$. Since we can derive the value of a/b from Statement (2) alone, the statement is sufficient.

The answer is (D).

37. If p is not divisible by 9 and q is not divisible by 10, then $p/9$ results in a non-terminating decimal and $q/10$ results in a terminating decimal and the sum of the two would not result in an integer. [Because (a terminating decimal) + (a non-terminating decimal) is always a non-terminating decimal, and a non-terminating decimal is not an integer.]

An example of a terminating decimal is 10.25 (= 451/44).

An example of a non-terminating decimal is 22/7 = 3.142857142857142857 ... (never ends).

Since we are given that the expression is an integer, p must be divisible by 9.

For example, if $p = 1$ and $q = 10$, the expression equals $1/9 + 10/10 = 1.11...$, not an integer.

If $p = 9$ and $q = 5$, the expression equals $9/9 + 5/10 = 1.5$, not an integer.

If $p = 9$ and $q = 10$, the expression equals $9/9 + 10/10 = 2$, an integer.

In short, p must be a positive integer divisible by 9. The answer is (C).

Test 5

<u>Questions</u>: 37
<u>Time</u>: 75 minutes

1. If $42.42 = k(14 + m/50)$, where k and m are positive integers and $m < 50$, then what is the value of $k + m$?

   (A) 6
   (B) 7
   (C) 8
   (D) 9
   (E) 10

USE THIS SPACE FOR SCRATCHWORK.

2. Which one of the following equals the product of exactly two prime numbers?

   (A) $11 \cdot 6$
   (B) $13 \cdot 22$
   (C) $14 \cdot 23$
   (D) $17 \cdot 21$
   (E) $13 \cdot 23$

USE THIS SPACE FOR SCRATCHWORK.

3. In the figure, what is the value of *a* ?

   (A) 16
   (B) 18
   (C) 36
   (D) 54
   (E) 72

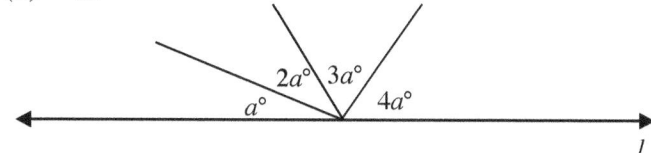

[Data Sufficiency Question]
4. Is $a + b > 0$?

   (1) The point (a, b) is in Quadrant II.
   (2) $|a| - |b| > 0$

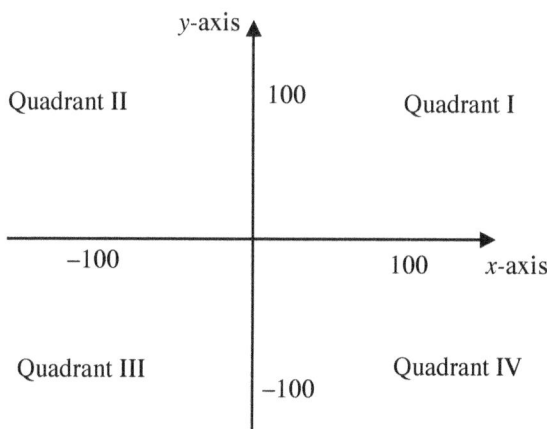

5. If $2x + 1 = 3x + 2$, then $5x + 2 =$

(A) –5
(B) –3
(C) –1
(D) 0
(E) 3

USE THIS SPACE FOR SCRATCHWORK.

6. The last digit of which one of the following results equals the last digit of the average of 3^2 and 5^2?

(A) The sum of 13 and 25
(B) The sum of 3 and 5^2
(C) The average of 13 and 25
(D) The average of 13 and 15
(E) The average of 19 and 35

USE THIS SPACE FOR SCRATCHWORK.

[Data Sufficiency Question]
7. Is the positive integer x an odd number?

(1) $x^2 + 3x + 3$ is odd.
(2) $|x| + x = 4$

USE THIS SPACE FOR SCRATCHWORK.

[Data Sufficiency Question]

8. $xy - yz =$

   (1) $yz - zx = 3$
   (2) $zx - xy = 4$

9. A certain recipe requires 3/2 cups of sugar and makes 2-dozen cookies. How many cups of sugar would be required for the same recipe to make 30 cookies?

   (A) 8/15
   (B) 5/6
   (C) 6/5
   (D) 10/7
   (E) 15/8

[Data Sufficiency Question]

10. Is $x > y$?

    (1) $x^5 > y^5$
    (2) $x^4 < y^4$

[Data Sufficiency Question]
11. In figure, ABC is a triangle. What is the length of side AB ?

   (1)   x = 50
   (2)   y = 45

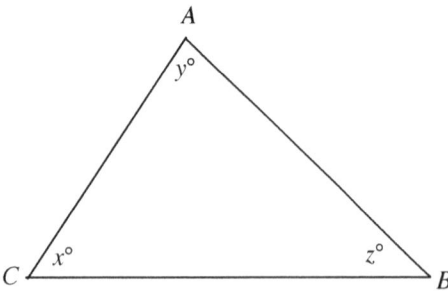

12. If $x = 10^{1.4}$, $y = 10^{0.7}$, and $x^z = y^3$, then what is the value of z ?

   (A)   0.5
   (B)   0.66
   (C)   1.5
   (D)   2
   (E)   3

13. If $x^2 - 4x + 3 = 0$, then what is the value of $(x - 2)^2$?

   (A)   −1
   (B)   0
   (C)   1
   (D)   3
   (E)   4

[Data Sufficiency Question]
14. What is the value of $ab + bc$?

   (1) $b = a + c$
   (2) $b = 3$

[Data Sufficiency Question]
15. If the value of $(x - y)(x + y)$ is 15, then what is the value of x/y ?

   (1) $x - y = 3$
   (2) $x + y = 5$

16. $\dfrac{(2x-11)(2x+11)}{4} - (x-11)(x+11) =$

   (A) 0
   (B) 4
   (C) 16
   (D) 45.5
   (E) 90.75

17. If b equals 10% of a and c equals 20% of b, then which one of the following equals 30% of c ?

(A) 0.0006% of a
(B) 0.006% of a
(C) 0.06% of a
(D) 0.6% of a
(E) 6% of a

USE THIS SPACE FOR SCRATCHWORK.

18. One ton has 2000 pounds, and one pound has 16 ounces. How many packets containing wheat weighing 16 pounds and 4 ounces each would totally fill a gunny bag of capacity 13 tons?

(A) 1600
(B) 1700
(C) 2350
(D) 2500
(E) 8000

USE THIS SPACE FOR SCRATCHWORK.

[Data Sufficiency Question]
19. What is the value of $x + y^2$?

(1) $x + y = 7$
(2) $x^2 + y^2 = 25$

USE THIS SPACE FOR SCRATCHWORK.

20. In the sequence a_n, the nth term is defined as $(a_{n-1}-1)^2$. If $a_1 = 4$, then what is the value of a_2?

    (A) 2
    (B) 3
    (C) 4
    (D) 5
    (E) 9

21. In jar A, 60% of the marbles are red and the rest are green. 40% of the red marbles are moved to an empty jar B. 60% of the green marbles are moved to an empty jar C. The marbles in both B and C are now moved to another empty jar D. What fraction of the marbles in jar A were moved to jar D?

    (A) 0.12
    (B) 0.24
    (C) 0.36
    (D) 0.48
    (E) 0.6

22. In a jar, 2/5 of the marbles are red and 1/4 are green. 1/4 of the red balls and 1/5 of the green balls are broken. If no other balls in the jar are broken, then what is the probability that a ball randomly picked from the jar is a broken one?

    (A) 3/20
    (B) 7/30
    (C) 5/16
    (D) 1/3
    (E) 2/5

Questions 23–26 refer to the following graph.

The table below provides the complete semantics of a Common Entrance Test (CET) conducted in different years.

Exam	Area	Questions	Marks per question	Total Duration (in minute)	Average time per question (in second)	Difficulty level 1 = Easy 2 = Average 3 = Difficult	Area wise Cut-off Scores	Overall cutoff mark as a percentage of maximum mark for the top five Institutes
CET – 1990	Quantitative	55	1	120	44	3	9	55
	Verbal	55	1			3	16	
	Analytical	55	1			2	12	
CET – 1991	Quantitative	50	1	120	48	2	14	65
	Verbal	50	1			1	19	
	Analytical	50	1			1	20	
CET – 1992	Quantitative	50	1	120	48	3	11	58
	Verbal	50	1			1	18	
	Analytical	50	1			3	14	
CET – 1993	Quantitative	50	1	120	48	3	10	60
	Verbal	50	1			1	18	
	Analytical	50	1			2	15	
CET – 1994	Quantitative	37	1	150	71	3	8	68
	Verbal	50	1			1	18	
	Analytical	39	1			3	9	

*The Difficulty Factor of the exam is the sum of the products of the number of questions of each type and the corresponding difficulty level. The Stress Factor is the Difficulty Factor divided by the Average Time Per Question.

23. By approximately what percent did the number of questions decrease in CET 1994 over the previous year?

    (A) 16%
    (B) 19%
    (C) 35%
    (D) 40%
    (E) 50%

24. The Difficulty Factor is the greatest for which one of the following exams?

    (A) CET 1990
    (B) CET 1991
    (C) CET 1992
    (D) CET 1993
    (E) CET 1994

25. Which one of the following exams has been marked as having the highest Stress Factor?

    (A) CET 1990
    (B) CET 1991
    (C) CET 1992
    (D) CET 1993
    (E) CET 1994

26. Which one of the following statements can be inferred from the table?

    (I)   As the Stress Factor increased, the cut off marks of the top five universities decreased
    (II)   As the Difficulty Factor of the exam decreased, the cut off marks of the top five universities increased
    (III) As the Difficulty Factor increased, the Stress Factor increased

    (A) (I) only
    (B) (II) only
    (C) (III) only
    (D) (I), and (II)
    (E) (I), and (III)

27. Goodwin has 3 different colored pants and 2 different colored shirts. In how many ways can he choose a pair of pants and a shirt?

    (A) 2
    (B) 3
    (C) 5
    (D) 6
    (E) 12

[Data Sufficiency Question]
28. Is $a > b$?

    (1) The arithmetic mean of a and b is 25.
    (2) The geometric mean of a and b is 24.

[Data Sufficiency Question]

29. Is $\dfrac{j}{m} + \dfrac{k}{n} = 2$?

   (1) $\dfrac{jk}{mn} = 1$

   (2) $\dfrac{jn}{mk} = 1$

[Data Sufficiency Question]

30. If $x - 4y = 1$, what is the value of x ?

   (1) $x = 4y + 1$
   (2) $y = x/2 + 1$

31. The functions f and g are defined as $f(x, y) = 2x + y$ and $g(x, y) = x + 2y$. What is the value of $f(3, 4) + g(3, 4)$?

   (A) 6
   (B) 8
   (C) 10
   (D) 14
   (E) 21

[Data Sufficiency Question]
32. Is $(x-2)(x-3) > 0$?

(1) $x > 2$
(2) $x < 3$

USE THIS SPACE FOR SCRATCHWORK.

33. Which one of the following is the solution of the system of equations given?

$$x + 2y = 7$$
$$x + y = 4$$

(A) $x = 3, y = 2$
(B) $x = 2, y = 3$
(C) $x = 1, y = 3$
(D) $x = 3, y = 1$
(E) $x = 7, y = 1$

USE THIS SPACE FOR SCRATCHWORK.

[Data Sufficiency Question]
34. If $x > y$, then is $1/x < 1/y$?

(1) x is negative.
(2) y is negative.

USE THIS SPACE FOR SCRATCHWORK.

35. The number 3 divides *a* with a result of *b* and a remainder of 2. The number 3 divides *b* with a result of 2 and a remainder of 1. What is the value of *a*?
    (A) 13
    (B) 17
    (C) 21
    (D) 23
    (E) 27

[Data Sufficiency Question]
36. A rectangular field is 3.2 yards long. What is the area of the field in square yards?

    (1) A fence marking the boundary is 11.2 yards in length.
    (2) The distance between the diagonally opposite corners of the rectangular field is 4 yards.

37. In the figure, *AD* and *BC* are lines intersecting at *O*. What is the value of *a*?
    (A) 15
    (B) 30
    (C) 45
    (D) 60
    (E) 135

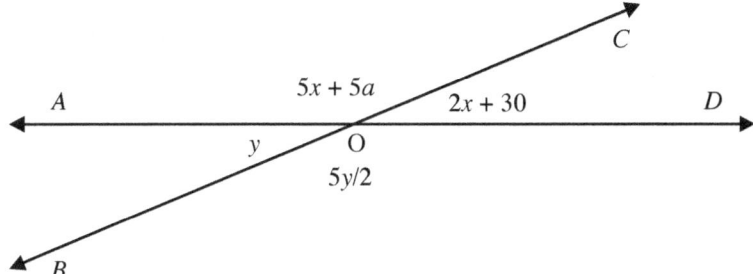

Answers and Solutions Test 5:

1. E	11. E	21. D	31. E
2. E	12. C	22. A	32. C
3. B	13. C	23. A	33. C
4. C	14. E	24. A	34. A
5. B	15. D	25. A	35. D
6. E	16. E	26. A	36. D
7. B	17. D	27. D	37. A
8. C	18. A	28. E	
9. E	19. E	29. E	
10. A	20. E	30. B	

---

1. We are given that k is a positive integer and m is a positive integer less than 50. We are also given that $42.42 = k(14 + m/50)$.

Suppose $k = 1$. Then $k(14 + m/50) = 14 + m/50 = 42.42$. Solving for m yields $m = 50(42.42 - 14) = 50 \times 28.42$, which is not less than 50. Hence, $k \neq 1$.

Now, suppose $k = 2$. Then $k(14 + m/50) = 2(14 + m/50) = 42.42$, or $(14 + m/50) = 21.21$. Solving for m yields $m = 50(21.21 - 14) = 50 \times 7.21$, which is not less than 50. Hence, $k \neq 2$.

Now, suppose $k = 3$. Then $k(14 + m/50) = 3(14 + m/50) = 42.42$, or $(14 + m/50) = 14.14$. Solving for m yields $m = 50(14.14 - 14) = 50 \times 0.14 = 7$, which is less than 50. Hence, $k = 3$ and $m = 7$ and $k + m = 3 + 7 = 10$.

The answer is (E).

---

2. Choice (A): $11 \cdot 6$ can be factored as $11 \cdot 2 \cdot 3$. The product of more than two primes. Reject.

Choice (B): $13 \cdot 22$ can be factored as $13 \cdot 2 \cdot 11$. The product of more than two primes. Reject.

Choice (C): $14 \cdot 23$ can be factored as $7 \cdot 2 \cdot 23$. The product of more than two primes. Reject.

Choice (D): $17 \cdot 21$ can be factored as $17 \cdot 3 \cdot 7$. The product of more than two primes. Reject.

Choice (E): $13 \cdot 23$ cannot be further factored and is itself the product of two primes. Accept.

The answer is (E).

---

3. The angle made by a line is 180°. Hence, from the figure, we have

$$a + 2a + 3a + 4a = 180$$
$$10a = 180$$
$$a = 18$$

The answer is (B).

Test 5—Answers and Solutions

4. From Statement (1) alone, we have that the point (a, b) is in Quadrant II. Hence, a is negative and b is positive. Since $|a|$ is the positive value of a and a is negative, a can be expressed as $-|a|$. Also, $|b|$ is the positive value of b; and since b is positive, b can be expressed as $|b|$. Hence, $a + b = -|a| + |b|$. Now, if $|b|$ is greater than $|a|$, $a + b$ is greater than 0. Otherwise, $a + b$ is not greater than 0. Hence, we have a double case, and Statement (1) alone is not sufficient.

From Statement (2) alone, we have that $|a| - |b| > 0$. Adding $|b|$ to both sides yields $|a| > |b|$. Now, suppose a equals 3 and b equals 2. Then $a + b = 5$, a positive number. Now, suppose a is -3 and b is 2. Then $a + b = -1$, a negative number. Hence, we have a double case, and even Statement (2) alone is not sufficient.

Combining the results from the two statements, $a + b = -|a| + |b|$ and $-|a| + |b| < 0$, yields $a + b < 0$. Hence, the statements together determine that $a + b$ is not greater than 0. Hence, the answer is (C).

5. Subtracting $2x + 2$ from both sides of the equation $2x + 1 = 3x + 2$ yields $-1 = x$. Now, $5x + 2 = 5(-1) + 2 = -5 + 2 = -3$. The answer is (B).

6. 3^2 equals 9 and 5^2 equals 25, and the average of the two is $(9 + 25)/2 = 34/2 = 17$, which ends with 7. Hence, select the answer-choice the result of which ends with 7.

Choice (A): The sum of 13 and 25 is 38, which does not end with 7. Reject.

Choice (B): The sum of 3 and 5^2 is $3 + 25 = 28$, which does not end with 7. Reject.

Choice (C): The average of 13 and 25 is $(13 + 25)/2 = 19$, which does not end with 7. Reject.

Choice (D): The average of 13 and 15 is $(13 + 15)/2 = 14$, which does not end with 7. Reject.

Choice (E): The average of 19 and 35 = $(19 + 35)/2 = 54/2 = 27$, which ends with 7. Accept the choice.

The answer is (E).

7. From Statement (1) alone, we have that $x^2 + 3x + 3$ is an odd number. Hence,

$$x^2 + 3x = (\text{an odd number}) - 3 = \text{an even number}$$

So, $x^2 + 3x$, which equals $x(x + 3)$, must be even. The product of the two positive integers x and $x + 3$ is even when at least one of them is even. Now, if $x + 3$ is even, x is odd; and if $x + 3$ is odd, x is even. So, x may or may not be odd. Statement (1) alone is not sufficient.

From Statement (2) alone, we have that $|x| + x = 4$. For positive numbers, $|x|$ equals x. Hence,

$$x + x = 4;\ 2x = 4;\ x = 4/2 = 2, \text{an even number}$$

Hence, Statement (2) alone is sufficient. The answer to the question is "No. x is even."

The answer is (B).

8. Adding the equation $yz - zx = 3$ from Statement (1) and the equation $zx - xy = 4$ from Statement (2) yields

$$(yz - zx) + (zx - xy) = 3 + 4$$

$$yz - zx + zx - xy = 7$$

$$yz - xy = 7$$

$$xy - yz = -7 \qquad \text{multiplying both sides by } -1$$

Hence, the statements together are sufficient to answer the question.

The answer is (C).

9. This problem can be solved by setting up a proportion between the number of cookies and the number of cups of sugar required to make the corresponding number of cookies. Since there are 12 items in a dozen, 2-dozen cookies is $2 \times 12 = 24$ cookies. Since 3/2 cups are required to make the 24 cookies, we have the proportion

$$\frac{24 \text{ cookies}}{3/2 \text{ cookies}} = \frac{30 \text{ cookies}}{x \text{ cups}}$$

$$24x = 30 \cdot 3/2 = 45 \qquad \text{by cross-multiplying}$$

$$x = 45/24 = 15/8$$

The answer is (E).

10. Statement (1) alone, says that $x^5 > y^5$. In the case of odd exponents (here 5), we can drop the exponents from both sides and conclude that $x > y$. Hence, Statement (1) alone is sufficient.

Statement (2) alone, says that $x^4 < y^4$. We cannot drop even exponents from both sides. Hence, Statement (2) alone is not sufficient.

For example, suppose $x = 1$ and $y = 2$. Here, $x < y$ and $x^4 < y^4$.

Now, Suppose $x = 1$ and $y = -2$. Here, $x > y$ and $x^4 < y^4$.

We have a double case. Hence, Statement (2) alone is not sufficient.

The answer is (A).

11. Since with the statements together we have only two of the three angles and no side length, statements (1) and (2) together are not sufficient. The answer is (E). For example, the triangle shown below satisfies statements (1) and (2), but has a greater length for side *AB* than in the original figure.

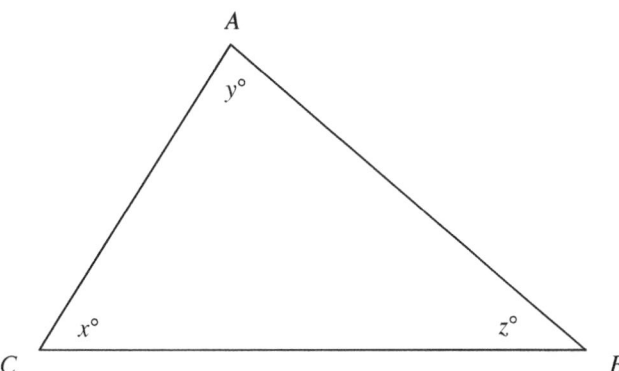

12. We are given that $x = 10^{1.4}$ and $y = 10^{0.7}$. Substituting these values in the given equation $x^z = y^3$ yields

$$(10^{1.4})^z = (10^{0.7})^3$$

$$10^{1.4z} = 10^{0.7 \cdot 3}$$

$$10^{1.4z} = 10^{2.1}$$

$$1.4z = 2.1 \qquad \text{since the bases are the same, the exponents must be equal}$$

$$z = 2.1/1.4 = 3/2$$

The answer is (C).

13. Adding 1 to both sides of the given equation $x^2 - 4x + 3 = 0$ yields $x^2 - 4x + 4 = 1$. Expanding $(x - 2)^2$ by the Perfect Square Trinomial formula $(a - b)^2 = a^2 - 2ab + b^2$ yields

$$x^2 - 4x + 2^2 = x^2 - 4x + 4 = 1$$

Hence, $(x - 2)^2 = 1$, and the answer is (C).

14. Let the rectangular box be as shown in the figure:

The surface area of the box is $lw + 2lh + 2hw$, and the volume is lwh.

From Statement (1), we have that the area of the base, which equals lw, is 23.

From Statement (2), we have that the volume of the box, which equals lwh, is 23.

Dividing the value in Statement (2) by the value in Statement (1) yields

$$\frac{lwh}{lw} = h = \frac{23}{23} = 1$$

So, we have the height of the box. Since we have the values of only h and lw, there is not enough information to determine the value of the expression $lw + 2lh + 2hw$, which has to be evaluated.

Hence, the statements together are insufficient to answer the question.

The answer is (E).

15. We are given that $(x - y)(x + y) = 15$ ...(A)

From Statement (1), we have $x - y = 3$. Squaring both sides yields $(x - y)^2 = 3^2 = 9$. Dividing equation (A) by this equation yields $\frac{(x-y)(x+y)}{(x-y)^2} = \frac{15}{9}$, or $\frac{x+y}{x-y} = \frac{15}{9}$.

Since we are looking for the ratio x/y, let's divide every variable on the left-hand side of the equation by y, thereby creating the ratio x/y:

$$\frac{\frac{x}{y} + \frac{y}{y}}{\frac{x}{y} - \frac{y}{y}} = \frac{15}{9}$$

$$\frac{\frac{x}{y} + 1}{\frac{x}{y} - 1} = \frac{15}{9}$$

$$9\left(\frac{x}{y} + 1\right) = 15\left(\frac{x}{y} - 1\right)$$

$$9\frac{x}{y} + 9 = 15\frac{x}{y} - 15$$

$$6\frac{x}{y} = 24$$

$$\frac{x}{y} = 4$$

Hence, Statement (1) alone is sufficient.

From Statement (2), we have $x + y = 5$. Squaring both sides yields $(x + y)^2 = 5^2 = 25$. Dividing equation (A) by this equation yields

$$\frac{(x-y)(x+y)}{(x+y)^2} = \frac{15}{25}$$

or

$$\frac{x-y}{x+y} = \frac{15}{25}$$

Solving the equation for x/y as above yields $x/y = 4$. Hence, Statement (2) alone is sufficient.

Since either statement is sufficient, the answer is (D).

16. Applying the Difference of Squares formula $(a + b)(a - b) = a^2 - b^2$ to the given expressions yields

$$\frac{(2x)^2 - 11^2}{4} - (x^2 - 11^2) = \frac{4x^2 - 121}{4} - (x^2 - 121) = x^2 - \frac{121}{4} - x^2 + 121 = -\frac{121}{4} + 121 = 121 \cdot \frac{3}{4} = 90.75.$$

(You can guess the suitable choice here instead of calculating). The answer is (E).

17. $b = 10\%$ of $a = (10/100)a = 0.1a$.

$c = 20\%$ of $b = (20/100)b = 0.2b = (0.2)(0.1a)$

Now, 30% of $c = (30/100)c = 0.3c = (0.3)(0.2)(0.1a) = 0.006a = 0.6\%a$.

The answer is (D).

18. One ton has 2000 pounds. The capacity of the gunny bag is 13 tons. Hence, its capacity in pounds would equal 13×2000 pounds.

One pound has 16 ounces. We are given the capacity of each packet is 16 pounds and 4 ounces. Converting it into pounds yields 16 pounds + 4/16 ounces = 16 1/4 pounds = $(16 \times 4 + 1)/4 = 65/4$ pounds.

Hence, the number of packets required to fill the gunny bag equals

(Capacity of the gunny bag) ÷ (Capacity of the each packet) =
13×2000 pounds ÷ $(65/4)$ pounds =
$13 \times 2000 \times 4/65$ =
$2000 \times 4/5$ =
1600

The answer is (A).

19. The two given statements form the following system:

$$x + y = 7$$
$$x^2 + y^2 = 25$$

Solving the top equation for y yields $y = 7 - x$. Substituting this into the bottom equation yields

$$x^2 + (7 - x)^2 = 25$$
$$x^2 + 49 - 14x + x^2 = 25$$
$$2x^2 - 14x + 24 = 0$$
$$x^2 - 7x + 12 = 0$$
$$(x - 3)(x - 4) = 0$$
$$x - 3 = 0 \text{ or } x - 4 = 0$$
$$x = 3 \text{ or } x = 4$$

Now, if $x = 3$, then $y = 7 - 3 = 4$ and $x + y^2 = 3 + 4^2$; and if $x = 4$, then $y = 7 - 4 = 3$ and $x + y^2 = 4 + 3^2$, which does not equal $3 + 4^2$. This is a double case, so the statements together are *not* sufficient. Hence, the statements individually are clearly *not* sufficient. The answer is (E).

---

20. Replacing n with 2 in the given formula $a_n = (a_{n-1} - 1)^2$ yields $a_2 = (a_{2-1} - 1)^2 = (a_1 - 1)^2$. We are given that $a_1 = 4$. Putting this in the formula $a_2 = (a_1 - 1)^2$ yields $a_2 = (4 - 1)^2 = 3^2 = 9$. The answer is (E).

---

21. Let j be the total number of marbles in the jar A. Then $60\%j$ must be red (given), and the remaining $40\%j$ must be green (given). Now,

Number of marbles moved to empty jar B = 40% of the red marbles = $40\%(60\%j) = .40(.60j) = .24j$.

Number of marbles moved to empty jar C = 60% of the green marbles = $60\%(40\%j) = .60(.40j) = .24j$.

Since the marbles in the jars B and C are now moved to the jar D, jar D should have $.24j + .24j = .48j$ marbles.

Hence, the fraction of the marbles that were moved to jar D is $.48j/j = 0.48$. The answer is (D).

---

22. Let there be j balls in the jar.

As given, $2j/5$ are red and $j/4$ are green.

Also, 1/4 of the red balls are broken. 1/4 of $2j/5 = (1/4)(2j/5) = 2j/20$.

Also, 1/5 of the green balls are broken. 1/5 of $j/4 = (1/5)(j/4) = j/20$.

So, the total number of balls broken is $2j/20 + j/20 = 3j/20$. Hence, 3/20 of the balls in the jar are broken. So, the probability of selecting a broken ball is 3/20. The answer is (A).

Test 5—Answers and Solutions

23. CET 1993 asks 50 quantitative, 50 verbal, and 50 Analytical.

The total is 50 + 50 + 50 = 150.

CET 1994 asks 37 quantitative, 50 verbal, and 39 Analytical.

The total is 37 + 50 + 39 = 126.

The decrease percent is $\frac{150-126}{150} \times 100 = \frac{24}{150} \times 100 = 16\%$.

The answer is (A).

---

24. The Difficulty Factor of the exam is the sum of the products of the number of questions of each type and the corresponding difficulty level.

Let's calculate the Difficulty Factor for each exam and pick the answer-choice that has greatest value:

Choice (A): In CET 1990, the Difficulty Factor is (3 × 55 + 3 × 55 + 2 × 55) = 165 + 165 + 110 = 440.

Choice (B): In CET 1991, the Difficulty Factor is (2 × 50 + 1 × 50 + 1 × 50) = 100 + 50 + 50 = 200 < Choice (A). Reject the current choice.

Choice (C): In CET 1992, the Difficulty Factor is (3 × 50 + 1 × 50 + 3 × 50) = 350 < Choice (A). Reject the current choice.

Choice (D): In CET 1993, the Difficulty Factor is (3 × 50 + 1 × 50 + 2 × 50) = 300 < Choice (A). Reject the current choice.

Choice (E): In CET 1994, the Difficulty Factor is (3 × 37 + 1 × 50 + 3 × 39) = 111 + 50 + 117 = 278 < Choice (A). Reject the current choice.

The answer is (A).

---

25. The Difficulty Factor of the exam is the sum of the products of the number of questions of each type and the corresponding difficulty level.

Then

The Stress Factor = the Difficulty Factor divided by the average time per question.

Let's calculate the Stress Factor for each answer-choice and choose the one that has the highest value:

Choice (A): In CET 1990,
The Difficulty Factor is (3 × 55 + 3 × 55 + 2 × 55) = 165 + 165 + 110 = 440
The Stress Factor is 440/44 = 10.

Choice (B): In CET 1991,
Difficulty Factor is (2 × 50 + 1 × 50 + 1 × 50) = 100 + 50 + 50 = 200.
The Stress Factor is 200/48 < Choice (A). Reject.

Choice (C): In CET 1992,
Difficulty Factor is (3 × 50 + 1 × 50 + 3 × 50) = 350.

The Stress Factor is 350/48 < Choice (A). Reject.

Choice (D): In CET 1993,
Difficulty Factor is $(3 \times 50 + 1 \times 50 + 2 \times 50) = 300$.
The Stress Factor is 300/48 < Choice (A). Reject.

Choice (E): In CET 1994,
Difficulty Factor is $(3 \times 37 + 1 \times 50 + 3 \times 39) = 111 + 50 + 117 = 278$.
The Stress Factor is 278/71 < Choice (A). Reject.

Hence, the answer is (A).

---

26. The increasing order of the Difficulty Factor is

CET 1991 (200) < CET 1994 (278) < CET 1993 (300) < CET 1992 (350) < CET 1990 (440).

The increasing order of the Stress Factor is

CET 1994 (278/71 = 3.92) < CET 1991 (200/48 = 4.16) < CET 1993 (300/48 = 6.25) < CET 1992 (350/48 = 7.29) < CET 1990 (440/44 = 10).

The decreasing order of the cut off marks is

CET 1994 (68) > CET 1991 (65) > CET 1993 (60) > CET 1992 (58) > CET 1990 (55).

The decreasing order of the cut off marks matches the increasing order of the Stress Factor.

The decreasing order of the cut off marks does *not* match the increasing order of the Difficulty Factor.

As the Difficulty Factor increased, the Stress Factor *did not* increase. Hence, III is false. The answer is (A), only I is true.

---

27. The pants can be selected in 3 ways and the shirt in 2 ways. Hence, the pair can be selected in $3 \cdot 2 = 6$ ways. The answer is (D).

---

28. From Statement (1), we have $\dfrac{a+b}{2} = 25$.
From Statement (2), we have $\sqrt{ab} = 24$.

The above two equations are symmetric with respect to a and b in the sense that if $a = p$ and $b = q$ is a solution [So, $\dfrac{p+q}{2} = 25$ and $\sqrt{pq} = 24$], then $a = q$ and $b = p$ (swapping) is also a solution. Now, in the case $p > q$, the first case ($a = p$ and $b = q$) yields $a > b$ and the second case ($a = q$ and $b = p$) yields $b > a$. Hence, we have a double case, and the statements together are not sufficient. The answer is (E).

29. From Statement (1) alone, we have that $jk/mn = 1$. Solving for j yields $j = mn/k$. Hence, the expression $\frac{j}{m} + \frac{k}{n}$ equals $\frac{mn/k}{m} + \frac{k}{n} = \frac{n}{k} + \frac{k}{n}$. Since we still do not have the ratio k/n, Statement (1) alone is not sufficient.

From Statement (2) alone, we have that $jn/mk = 1$. Solving for j yields $j = mk/n$. Hence, the expression $\frac{j}{m} + \frac{k}{n}n$ equals $\frac{mk/n}{m} + \frac{k}{n} = \frac{k}{n} + \frac{k}{n} = \frac{2k}{n}$. Since we still do not have the ratio k/n, Statement (2) alone is also not sufficient.

Now, equating the results of the expression from the two statements yields $\frac{n}{k} + \frac{k}{n} = \frac{2k}{n}$. Subtracting $\frac{k}{n}$ from both sides yields $\frac{n}{k} = \frac{k}{n}$. Multiplying both sides by $\frac{k}{n}$ yields $\left(\frac{k}{n}\right)^2 = 1$; $\frac{k}{n} = +1$ or -1. Hence, $\frac{2k}{n}$ equals $2(-1) = -2$ or $2(1) = 2$. Hence, we have a double case, and even the statements together do not answer the question. Hence, the answer is (E).

30. We are given the linear equation $x - 4y = 1$. Adding $4y$ to both sides yields $x = 4y + 1$. So far, we have only one equation in two unknowns.

From Statement (1) alone, we have the equation $x = 4y + 1$, which is same as the given equation. Hence, effectively, we still have only one equation in two unknowns, x and y. So, Statement (1) alone is not sufficient to determine the value of x.

From Statement (2) alone, we have that $y = x/2 + 1$. This is a different linear equation in the same two unknowns. Hence, together with the given equation $x = 4y + 1$, we are able to determine a unique value for x. The answer is (B). Solving the equations yields $x = -5$ and $y = -3/2$.

31. We are given the function rules $f(x, y) = 2x + y$ and $g(x, y) = x + 2y$.

$$f(3, 4) + g(3, 4) =$$

$$(2 \cdot 3 + 4) + (3 + 2 \cdot 4) =$$

$$10 + 11 = 21$$

The answer is (E).

32. From Statement (1) alone, we have the inequality $x > 2$.

Now, suppose $x = 2.5$. Then $x - 2 = 2.5 - 2 = 0.5$, and $x - 3 = 2.5 - 3 = -0.5$. Hence,

$$(x - 2)(x - 3) = (0.5)(-0.5) = -0.25$$

So, $(x - 2)(x - 3)$ is negative.

Now, suppose $x = 4$. Then $x - 2 = 4 - 2 = 2$, and $x - 3 = 4 - 3 = 1$. Hence,

$$(x - 2)(x - 3) = 2 \cdot 1 = 2$$

So, $(x - 2)(x - 3)$ is positive.

Hence, we have a double case, and Statement (1) alone is not sufficient.

From Statement (2) alone, we have the inequality $x < 3$.

Now, suppose $x = 2.5$. Then $x - 2 = 2.5 - 2 = 0.5$ and $x - 3 = 2.5 - 3 = -0.5$. Hence,

$$(x - 2)(x - 3) = (0.5)(-0.5) = -0.25$$

So, $(x - 2)(x - 3)$ is negative.

Now, suppose $x = 1$. Then $x - 2 = 1 - 2 = -1$ and $x - 3 = 1 - 3 = -2$. Hence,

$$(x - 2)(x - 3) = (-1)(-2) = 2$$

So, $(x - 2)(x - 3)$ is positive.

Hence, we have a double case, and Statement (2) alone is not sufficient.

Now, with statements (1) and (2) together, we have $x > 2$ and $x < 3$. Subtracting 2 from both sides of first inequality and 3 from both sides of the second inequality yields $x - 2 > 0$ and $x - 3 < 0$. Hence, $x - 2$ is positive, and $x - 3$ is negative. Since the product of a positive and a negative number is always negative, we have $(x - 2)(x - 3)$ is negative and therefore less than 0. Hence, $(x - 2)(x - 3)$ is not greater than 0, and the answer to the question is "No. $(x - 2)(x - 3)$ is less than 0."

Since both statements were required, the answer is (C).

33. The given system of equations is $x + 2y = 7$ and $x + y = 4$. Now, just substitute each answer-choice into the two equations and see which one works (start checking with the easier equation, $x + y = 4$):

Choice (A): $x = 3$, $y = 2$: Here, $x + y = 3 + 2 = 5 \neq 4$. Reject.

Choice (B): $x = 2$, $y = 3$: Here, $x + y = 2 + 3 = 5 \neq 4$. Reject.

Choice (C): $x = 1$, $y = 3$: Here, $x + y = 1 + 3 = 4 = 4$, and $x + 2y = 1 + 2(3) = 7$. Correct.

Choice (D): $x = 3$, $y = 1$: Here, $x + y = 3 + 1 = 4$, but $x + 2y = 3 + 2(1) = 5 \neq 7$. Reject.

Choice (E): $x = 7$, $y = 1$: Here, $x + y = 7 + 1 = 8 \neq 4$. Reject.

The answer is (C).

Test 5—Answers and Solutions

---

34. If you divided the inequality $x > y$ by xy (positive with the two statements together) and derived that $1/x > 1/y$ and therefore answered (C), you are mistaken. There is an deeper study to make.

From Statement (1) alone, we have x is negative. Since $x > y$, y must also be negative. Hence, xy, the product of two negative numbers, must be positive. Dividing the inequality by the positive expression xy yields $x/xy > y/xy$, or $1/y > 1/x$. Rearranging yields $1/x < 1/y$. Hence, Statement (1) alone is sufficient. The answer to the question is "Yes, $1/x < 1/y$."

From Statement (2) alone, we have y is negative. The only restriction on x is $x > y$ (given), so x may be negative, zero, or positive.

In case x is positive and since y is negative, xy is negative. Dividing the given inequality $x > y$ by xy (a negative value) and flipping the direction of inequality yields $1/y < 1/x$.

In case both x and y are negative, xy is positive and here we can divide the inequality $x > y$ by xy without flipping the direction of inequality. Thus, here we get $1/y > 1/x$.

Hence, we have a double case with Statement (2) alone.

Since Statement (1) alone is sufficient and Statement (2) alone is *not*, the answer is (A).

---

35. Since 3 divides b with a result of 2 and a remainder of 1, $b = 3 \cdot 2 + 1 = 7$. Since number 3 divides a with a result of b (which we now know equals 7) and a remainder of 2, $a = 3 \cdot b + 2 = 3 \cdot 7 + 2 = 23$. The answer is (D).

---

36. Let l be the length of the rectangle. Then $l = 3.2$ yards. The formula for the area of a rectangle is *length* × *width*. Hence, the area of the rectangle is $lw = 3.2w$. So, to evaluate the area, we need only the value of w. Hence, the question can be modified as "Width of rectangle = ?"

From Statement (1) alone, we have the length of fence required (perimeter) for the field is 11.2 yards. The formula for the perimeter of a rectangle is 2(*length* + *width*). Hence, the perimeter of the field is $2(l + w) = 11.2$, or $2(3.2 + w) = 11.2$. Solving for w yields $w = 5.6 - 3.2 = 2.4$. Hence, Statement (1) alone is sufficient.

From Statement (2) alone, we have that the distance between the diagonally opposite corners (diagonal length) of the rectangle field is 4 yards. A diagonal of a rectangle forms a hypotenuse with the length and width of the rectangle. Hence, by The Pythagorean Theorem, $l^2 + w^2 = $ (diagonal length)$^2 = 4^2$, or $3.2^2 + w^2 = 4^2$. Solving this equation for w yields $w = \sqrt{4^2 - 3.2^2} = 2.4$. Hence, Statement (2) alone is also sufficient.

The answer is (D).

---

37. Equating vertical angles $\angle AOB$ and $\angle COD$ in the figure yields $y = 2x + 30$. Also, equating vertical angles $\angle AOC$ and $\angle BOD$ yields $5y/2 = 5x + 5a$. Multiplying this equation by 2/5 yields $y = 2x + 2a$. Subtracting this equation from the equation $y = 2x + 30$ yields $2a = 30$. Hence, $a = 30/2 = 15$, and the answer is (A).

Test 6

Questions: 37
Time: 75 minutes

1. If $x^2 + 4x + 3$ is odd, then which one of the following could be the value of x?

    (A) 3
    (B) 5
    (C) 9
    (D) 13
    (E) 16

2. Which one of the following equals the product of the smallest prime number greater than 21 and the largest prime number less than 16?

    (A) $13 \cdot 16$
    (B) $13 \cdot 29$
    (C) $13 \cdot 23$
    (D) $15 \cdot 23$
    (E) $16 \cdot 21$

3. From the figure, which one of the following must be true?

    (A) $y = z$
    (B) $y < z$
    (C) $y \leq z$
    (D) $y > z$
    (E) $y \geq z$

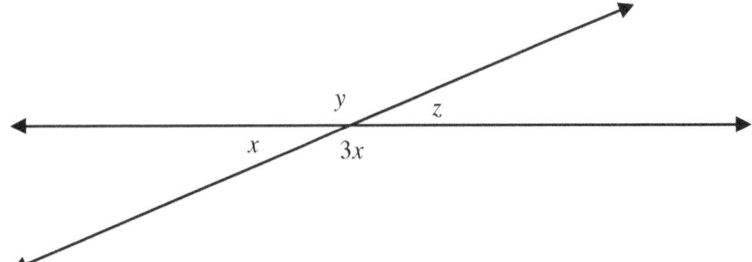

[Data Sufficiency Question]
4. Is $N/2$ an odd integer?

   (1) $2N$ is even.
   (2) N is even.

5. If $7x + 3y = 12$ and $3x + 7y = 8$, then $x - y =$

   (A) 1
   (B) 3
   (C) 7
   (D) 8
   (E) 12

6. The monthly rainfall for the first eight months of 2008 in inches was 2, 4, 4, 5, 7, 9, 10, 11. Which one of the following equals the mean monthly rainfall for the 8 months and the median of the rainfall for the 8 months, respectively?

   (A) 6.5, 6
   (B) 6, 7.5
   (C) 7, 8
   (D) 8, 9
   (E) 8.5, 9.5

[Data Sufficiency Question]
7. Is $a/b > 0$?

   (1) $ab > 0$
   (2) $a - b > 0$

[Data Sufficiency Question]
8. Is $\sqrt{m+n}$ an integer?

   (1) $\sqrt{m}$ is an integer.
   (2) $\sqrt{n}$ is an integer.

9. The ratio of x to y is $3 : 4$, and the ratio of $x + 7$ to $y + 7$ is $4 : 5$. What is the ratio of $x + 14$ to $y + 14$?

   (A) $3 : 4$
   (B) $4 : 5$
   (C) $5 : 6$
   (D) $5 : 7$
   (E) $6 : 7$

[Data Sufficiency Question]
10. How much is 20 percent of a certain number a ?

    (1) 20 is 20 percent of the number a.
    (2) 80 percent of the number a is 80.

[Data Sufficiency Question]
11. In the figure, lines l and m are parallel. What is the value of x ?

    (1) $z + t = 120$
    (2) $y - z = 60$

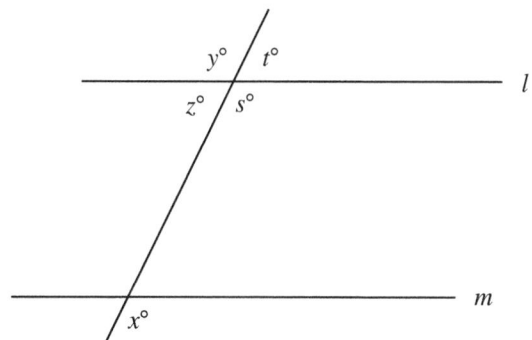

12. If x is not equal to 0, $\dfrac{x(x^2)^4}{(x^3)^3} =$

    (A)   8/9
    (B)   1
    (C)   9/8
    (D)   2
    (E) x

13. $\left(\sqrt{12.5} + \sqrt{12.5}\right)^2 - \left(\sqrt{25}\right)^2 =$

    (A)   0
    (B)   5
    (C)   12.5
    (D)   25
    (E)   50

[Data Sufficiency Question]

14. If r and s are two positive numbers, what is the value of the ratio r/s ?

    (1) r is 25% greater than s.
    (2) r is 25 units greater than s.

[Data Sufficiency Question]
15. Is it true that $x - z > y - z$?

(1) $xz > yz$
(2) $x + z > y + z$

USE THIS SPACE FOR SCRATCHWORK.

16. If $\frac{1}{x} + \frac{1}{y} = \frac{1}{3}$, then $\frac{xy}{x+y} =$

(A) 1/5
(B) 1/3
(C) 1
(D) 3
(E) 5

USE THIS SPACE FOR SCRATCHWORK.

17. If 500% of a equals $500b$, then $a =$

(A) $b/100$
(B) $b/10$
(C) b
(D) $10b$
(E) $100b$

USE THIS SPACE FOR SCRATCHWORK.

18. Patrick purchased 80 pencils and sold them at a loss equal to the selling price of 20 pencils. The cost of 80 pencils is how many times the selling price of 80 pencils?

(A) 0.75
(B) 0.8
(C) 1
(D) 1.2
(E) 1.25

USE THIS SPACE FOR SCRATCHWORK.

[Data Sufficiency Question]
19. Is the product of two numbers x and y a prime number?

(1) x and y are two prime numbers.
(2) x and y are two odd numbers not equal to 1.

USE THIS SPACE FOR SCRATCHWORK.

20. A sequence of numbers is represented as $a_1, a_2, a_3, \ldots, a_n$. Each number in the sequence (except the first and the last) is the mean of the two adjacent numbers in the sequence. If $a_1 = 1$ and $a_5 = 3$, what is the value of a_3 ?

(A) 1/2
(B) 1
(C) 3/2
(D) 2
(E) 5/2

USE THIS SPACE FOR SCRATCHWORK.

21. For how many positive integers n is it true that the sum of $13/n$, $18/n$, and $29/n$ is an integer?

   (A) 6
   (B) 60
   (C) Greatest common factor of 13, 18, and 29
   (D) Least common multiple of 13, 18, and 29
   (E) 12

22. A man walks at a rate of 10 mph. After every ten miles, he rests for 6 minutes. How much time does he take to walk 50 miles?

   (A) 300
   (B) 318
   (C) 322
   (D) 324
   (E) 330

23. The minimum temperatures from Monday through Sunday in the first week of July in southern Iceland are observed to be −2°C, 4°C, 4°C, 5°C, 7°C, 9°C, 10°C. What is the range of the temperatures?

   (A) −10°C
   (B) −8°C
   (C) 8°C
   (D) 10°C
   (E) 12°C

Questions 24–27 refer to the following table.

2007 Composition of Maryland Employment by Industry
(Annual Average by Place of Work)

Industry Groups and Totals	Number of Establishments	Employment	Percent of Total Employment
Federal Government	4,564	455,492	8.12%
State Government	849	1,121,712	19.99%
Local Government	345	96,972	1.73%
Total Government Sector	5,758	1,674,176	9.20%
Natural Resources and Mining	23,449	331,590	5.91%
Construction	749	6,836	0.30%
Manufacturing	19,335	188,420	3.36%
Service-Providing	14,283	136,334	2.43%
Utilities	121,238	1,041,777	31.04%
Wholesale Trade	2,320	9,711	0.17%
Retail Trade	11,342	94,997	1.69%
Transportation and Warehousing	18,593	299,648	5.34%
Information	3,998	65,765	1.17%
Financial Analysis	2,898	50,726	0.904082362
Professional and Business Services	14,828	344,565	6.14113352
Education and Health Services	36,384	347,821	6.19916475
Leisure and Hospitality	16,534	229,219	4.085337989
Other Services	13,733	87,309	1.556096024
Unclassified	1,802	1,878	0.03347133
Total Private Sector	301,486	3,936,596	70
Total Employment	307,244	5,610,772	100

24. In 2007, how many industry groups consisted of more than 1 million employees?

   (A) 0
   (B) 1
   (C) 2
   (D) 3
   (E) 4

25. Which one of the following industry groups employs the maximum number of people?

    (A) Utilities
    (B) Information
    (C) State Government
    (D) Natural Resources and Mining
    (E) Transportation and Warehousing

26. Which one of the following industry groups employs more than 10 employees per establishment on average?

    (A) Construction
    (B) Manufacturing
    (C) Wholesale Trade
    (D) Retail Trade
    (E) Transportation and Warehousing

27. Which one of the following is a valid inference?

    (I)   The State Government can be inferred as employing the highest number of Employees per Establishment only because the Percentage Employment it provides is the highest. The number of Establishments is not important.
    (II) The State Government can be inferred as employing the highest number of Employees per Establishment since it has the least number of organizations and offers the highest Employment.
    (III) The State Government can be inferred as employing the highest number of Employees per Establishment since it has the least number of organizations and offers the highest Percentage of Employment.

    (A) I only
    (B) II only
    (C) III only
    (D) I and II
    (E) II and III

159

28. There are 5 doors to a lecture room. Two are red and the others are green. In how many ways can a lecturer enter the room and leave the room from different colored doors?

   (A) 1
   (B) 3
   (C) 6
   (D) 9
   (E) 12

[Data Sufficiency Question]
29. Is $(x-2)(x-3) > 0$?

   (1) $x < 2$
   (2) $x < 3$

[Data Sufficiency Question]
30. What is the average score of the test takers on a test?

   (1) Exactly half the test takers scored above 500.
   (2) The lowest and the highest test scores are 200 and 800, respectively.

[Data Sufficiency Question]
31. What is the value of $2p + q$?

    (1) $3p + 2q = 5$
    (2) $6p + 4q = 10$

32. If $(2x + 1)^2 = 100$, then which one of the following COULD equal x ?

    (A) $-11/2$
    (B) $-9/2$
    (C) $11/2$
    (D) $13/2$
    (E) $17/2$

[Data Sufficiency Question]
33. If $a < b$, is $(a - b) + (c - b)$ positive?

    (1) $c < a$
    (2) $c < b$

34. If *m* and *n* are two different prime numbers, then the least common multiple of the two numbers must equal which one of the following?

    (A) *mn*
    (B) *m* + *n*
    (C) *m* − *n*
    (D) *m* + *mn*
    (E) *mn* + *n*

[Data Sufficiency Question]

35. If $H = 3$, then is $\sqrt{H^2 - 2H}$ equal to $\dfrac{T\sqrt{1-R^2}}{k\sqrt{1-g^k}}$?

    (1) $T = 3, R = 1/2$
    (2) $k = 1, g = 7/16$

[Data Sufficiency Question]

36. How many families in the town of Windsor have exactly one car?

    (1) 250 families have at least one car.
    (2) 60 families have at least two cars.

Test 6—Questions

37. In the figure, O is the center of the circle. What is average of the numbers $a, b, c,$ and d?

    (A) 45
    (B) 60
    (C) 90
    (D) 180
    (E) 360

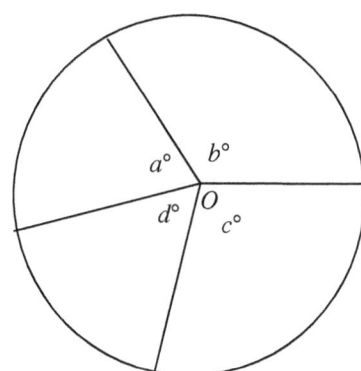

Answers and Solutions Test 6:

1.	E	11.	D	21.	E	31.	E
2.	C	12.	B	22.	D	32.	A
3.	D	13.	D	23.	E	33.	D
4.	E	14.	B	24.	C	34.	A
5.	A	15.	B	25.	C	35.	C
6.	A	16.	D	26.	E	36.	C
7.	A	17.	E	27.	E	37.	C
8.	E	18.	E	28.	E		
9.	C	19.	D	29.	A		
10.	D	20.	D	30.	E		

1. Let's substitute the given choices for x in the expression $x^2 + 4x + 3$ and find out which one results in an odd number.

Choice (A): $x = 3$. $x^2 + 4x + 3 = 3^2 + 4(3) + 3 = 9 + 12 + 3 = 24$, an even number. Reject.
Choice (B): $x = 5$. $x^2 + 4x + 3 = 5^2 + 4(5) + 3 = 25 + 20 + 3 = 48$, an even number. Reject.
Choice (C): $x = 9$. $x^2 + 4x + 3 = 9^2 + 4(9) + 3 = 81 + 36 + 3 = 120$, an even number. Reject.
Choice (D): $x = 13$. $x^2 + 4x + 3 = 13^2 + 4(13) + 3 = 169 + 52 + 3 = 224$, an even number. Reject.
Choice (E): $x = 16$. $x^2 + 4x + 3 = 16^2 + 4(16) + 3 = 256 + 64 + 3 = 323$, an odd number. Correct.

The answer is (E).

Method II (without substitution):

$x^2 + 4x + 3 =$ An Odd Number
$x^2 + 4x =$ An Odd Number – 3
$x^2 + 4x =$ An Even Number
$x(x + 4) =$ An Even Number. This happens only when x is even. If x is odd, $x(x + 4)$ is not even.
Hence, x must be even. Since 16 is the only even answer-choice, the answer is (E).

2. The smallest prime number greater than 21 is 23, and the largest prime number less than 16 is 13. The product of the two is $13 \cdot 23$, which is listed in choice (C). The answer is (C).

3. Equating the two pairs of vertical angles in the figure yields $y = 3x$ and $x = z$. Replacing x in first equation with z yields $y = 3z$. This equation says that y is 3 times as large as z. Hence, $y > z$. The answer is (D).

4. Suppose $N/2$ is odd. Then $N = 2 \times$ (an odd number) = even. Also, $2N = 2 \times$ (even number) = even. Hence, both statements (1) and (2) are satisfied.

If $N/2$ is even, then $N = 2 \times$ (an even number) = even, and $2N = 2 \times$ (an even number) = an even number. Here, both statements (1) and (2) are satisfied.

Hence, the two statements are valid both when $N/2$ is odd and when $N/2$ is even. Hence, the statements together are not sufficient to answer the question. The answer is (E).

Test 6—Answers and Solutions

5. We are given the two equations:

$$7x + 3y = 12$$
$$3x + 7y = 8$$

Subtracting the bottom equation from the top equation yields

$$(7x + 3y) - (3x + 7y) = 12 - 8$$
$$7x + 3y - 3x - 7y = 4$$
$$4x - 4y = 4$$
$$4(x - y) = 4$$
$$x - y = 1$$

The answer is (A).

6. The mean rainfall for the 8 months is the sum of the eight rainfall measurements divided by 8:

$$(2 + 4 + 4 + 5 + 7 + 9 + 10 + 11)/8 = 6.5$$

When a set of numbers is arranged in order of size, the *median* is the middle number. If a set contains an even number of elements, then the median is the average of the two middle elements. The average of 5 and 7 is 6, which is the median of the set.
Hence, the answer is (A).

7. Dividing the inequality $ab > 0$ by b^2, a positive value, yields $a/b > 0$. Hence, Statement (1) alone is sufficient.

Now, $a - b$ is positive when a is greater than b. When both a and b are positive, a/b is positive. When a is positive and b is negative, a/b is negative. Hence, we have a double case, and Statement (2) alone is not sufficient.

Hence, the answer is (A): Statement (1) alone is sufficient, and Statement (2) alone is not sufficient.

8. Let $m = 9$ and $n = 16$. Then $\sqrt{m} = 3$ is an integer, and $\sqrt{n} = 4$ is also an integer. Now, $\sqrt{m+n} = \sqrt{19+16} = \sqrt{25} = 5$ is also an integer.

Now, let $m = 4$ and $n = 9$. Then $\sqrt{m} = 2$ is an integer, and $\sqrt{n} = 3$ is also an integer. But here, $\sqrt{m+n} = \sqrt{4+9} = \sqrt{13}$, not an integer.

Hence, we have a double case. The answer is (E): the two choices together are insufficient to answer the question.

9. Forming the two ratios yields $\frac{x}{y} = \frac{3}{4}$ and $\frac{x+7}{y+7} = \frac{4}{5}$. Let's solve this system of equations by the substitution method. Multiplying the first equation by y yields $x = 3y/4$. Substituting this into the second equation yields $\frac{\frac{3y}{4}+7}{y+7} = \frac{4}{5}$. Cross-multiplying yields

$$5(3y/4 + 7) = 4(y + 7)$$
$$15y/4 + 35 = 4y + 28$$
$$15y/4 - 4y = 28 - 35$$
$$-y/4 = -7$$
$$y = 28$$

and $x = 3y/4 = (3 \cdot 28)/4 = 3 \cdot 7 = 21$.

Plugging the values for x and y into the requested ratio $\frac{x+14}{y+14}$ yields

$$\frac{21+14}{28+14} =$$
$$\frac{35}{42} =$$
$$\frac{5}{6}$$

The answer is (C).

---

10. From Statement (1) alone, we have that 20 is 20 percent of a. Hence, we have $20/100 \times a = 20$. Solving this equation for a yields $a = 100/20 \times 20 = 100$. Hence, Statement (1) alone is sufficient.

Now, from Statement (2) alone, we have that 80 is 80 percent of a. Now, 80 percent of a is $80/100 \times a$. Equating this to 80 yields $80/100 \times a = 80$. Solving this equation for a yields $a = 100/80 \times 80 = 100$. Hence, Statement (2) alone is sufficient.

The answer is (D).

Test 6—Answers and Solutions

11. Equating vertical angles in the figure yields $y = s$ and $z = t$.

Since lines l and m are parallel, the corresponding angles must be equal. So, $x = s$. Hence, the question is equivalent to "What is the value of s?"

Also, since a line has 180°, summing the angles z and s, which make the line l, yields $z + s = 180$. Solving for s yields $s = 180 - z$. From this equation, s is a dependent variable that depends only on z. Hence, if we know the value of z, we can determine the value of s, which answers the question. Hence, the question is equivalent to "What is the value of z?"

Now, from Statement (1) alone, we have that $z + t = 120$. Since $z = t$, we have $z + z = 120$, or $2z = 120$, or $z = 120/2 = 60$. Hence, Statement (1) alone determines z.

Now, from Statement (2) alone, we have that $y - z = 60$. Adding z to both sides yields $y = z + 60$. Now, a straight angle has 180°. Hence, we have

$$y + z = 180$$
$$(z + 60) + z = 180$$
$$2z = 180 - 60 = 120$$
$$z = 120/2 = 60$$

Hence, Statement (2) alone also determines z. Hence, the answer is (D).

12. Numerator: $x(x^2)^4 = x \cdot x^{2 \cdot 4} = x^1 \cdot x^8 = x^{1+8} = x^9$.

Denominator: $(x^3)^3 = x^{3 \cdot 3} = x^9$.

Hence, $\dfrac{x(x^2)^4}{(x^3)^3} = \dfrac{x^9}{x^9} = 1$.

The answer is (B).

13. $\left(\sqrt{12.5} + \sqrt{12.5}\right)^2 - \left(\sqrt{25}\right)^2 =$
$\left(12.5 + 12.5 + 2\sqrt{12.5}\sqrt{12.5}\right) - 25 =$
$12.5 + 12.5 + 2(12.5) - 25 =$
25

The answer is (D).

14. From Statement (1) alone, we have that r is 25% greater than s. Hence, $r = (1 + 25/100)s$. Hence, $r/s = 1 + 25/100 = 1.25$. Hence, Statement (1) alone is sufficient.

From Statement (2) alone, we have that r is 25 units greater than s. Hence, we have the equation $r = s + 25$. Dividing the equation by s yields $r/s = s/s + 25/s = 1 + 25/s$. Since s is unknown, $1 + 25/s$ cannot be calculated. Hence, Statement (2) alone is not sufficient.

Hence, the answer is (A).

15. Canceling z from both sides of the inequality $x - z > y - z$ yields $x > y$. Hence, $x - z$ is greater than $y - z$ when $x > y$. So, the question reduces to "Is $x > y$?"

From Statement (1) alone, we have the inequality $xz > yz$.

Suppose z is positive. Then we can divide the inequality $xz > yz$ by z without flipping the direction of the inequality, and we get $x > y$.

Suppose z is negative. Then we can divide the inequality $xz > yz$ by z while flipping the direction of inequality, and we get $x < y$.

We have a double case, and therefore Statement (1) alone is not sufficient.

From Statement (2) alone, we have that $x + z > y + z$. Subtracting z from both sides yields $x > y$. Hence, Statement (2) alone is sufficient to answer the question.

The answer is (B).

---

16. Multiplying the given equation $\frac{1}{x} + \frac{1}{y} = \frac{1}{3}$ by xy yields $y + x = xy/3$, or $x + y = xy/3$. Multiplying both sides of the equation $x + y = xy/3$ by $\frac{3}{x+y}$ yields $\frac{xy}{x+y} = 3$. The answer is (D).

---

17. We are given that 500% of a equals $500b$. Since 500% of a is $\frac{500}{100}a = 5a$, we have $5a = 500b$. Dividing the equation by 5 yields $a = 100b$. The answer is (E).

---

18. Let c be the cost of each pencil and s be the selling price of each pencil. Then the loss incurred by Patrick on each pencil is $c - s$. The net loss on 80 pencils is $80(c - s)$. Since we are given that the loss incurred on the 80 pencils equaled the selling price of 20 pencils which is $20s$, we have the equation:

$80(c - s) = 20s$
$80c - 80s = 20s$
$80c = 100s$
$(80/100)c = s$

The cost of 80 pencils is $80c$.

The selling price of 80 pencils is $80s = 80(80/100)c = 64c$. Hence, the cost of 80 pencils is $80c/64c = 5/4 = 1.25$ times the selling price. The answer is (E).

Test 6—Answers and Solutions

---

19. An integer is called prime if the only positive integers that divide it evenly are 1 and the number itself.

From Statement (1), we have that x and y are two prime numbers. So, xy does not equal x or y. Now, xy divided by x equals y (an integer), and xy divided by y equals x (an integer). Hence, xy has two more factors other than 1 and xy itself. So, by the definition of a prime number, xy is *not* prime. Hence, Statement (1) alone is sufficient to answer the question.

From Statement (2), we have that x and y are two odd numbers not equal to 1. So, xy does not equal x or y. Now, xy divided by x equals y (an integer), and xy divided by y equals x (an integer). Hence, xy has at least two more factors other than 1 and xy itself. So, by the definition of a prime number, xy is *not* prime. Hence, Statement (2) alone is sufficient to answer the question.

The answer is (D).

---

20. Since each number in the sequence (except the first and the last) is the mean of the adjacent two numbers in the sequence, we have

$a_2 = (a_1 + a_3)/2$
$a_3 = (a_2 + a_4)/2$
$a_4 = (a_3 + a_5)/2$

Substituting the given values $a_1 = 1$ and $a_5 = 3$ yields

$a_2 = (1 + a_3)/2$
$a_3 = (a_2 + a_4)/2$
$a_4 = (a_3 + 3)/2$

Substituting the top and the bottom equations into the middle one yields

$$a_3 = \frac{a_2 + a_4}{2}$$

$$a_3 = \frac{\frac{1+a_3}{2} + \frac{a_3+3}{2}}{2}$$

$$a_3 = \frac{\frac{1}{2} + \frac{a_3}{2} + \frac{a_3}{2} + \frac{3}{2}}{2}$$

$$a_3 = \frac{a_3 + 2}{2}$$

Subtracting $a_3/2$ from both sides yields $a_3/2 = 1$, or $a_3 = 2$. The answer is (D).

---

21. The sum of $13/n$, $18/n$, and $29/n$ is $\frac{13+18+29}{n} = \frac{60}{n}$. Now, if $60/n$ is to be an integer, n must be a factor of 60. Since the factors of 60 are 1, 2, 3, 4, 5, 6, 10, 12, 15, 20, 30, and 60, there are 12 possible values for n. The answer is (E).

22. Remember that *Time = Distance ÷ Speed*. Hence, the time taken by the man to walk 10 miles is 10 miles/10 mph = 1 hour.

Since the man walks 50 miles in five installments of 10 miles each, each installment should take him 1 hour. Hence, the total time for which he walked equals 5 · 1 hr = 5 hr = 5 · 60 mins = 300 mins.

Since he takes a break after each installment (until reaching the 50 mile point: one after 10 miles; one after 20 miles; one after 30 miles; final one after 40 miles, as the 50 mile point is his destination), he takes four breaks; and since each break lasts 6 minutes, the total time spent in the breaks is 4 · 6 mins = 24 mins.

Hence, the total time taken to reach the destination is 300 + 24 = 324 mins. The answer is (D).

---

23. The *range* is the greatest measurement minus the smallest measurement. The greatest of the seven temperature measurements is 10°C, and the smallest is –2°C. Hence, the required range is 10 – (–2) = 12°C. The answer is (E).

---

24. From the chart, the employment is greater than 1 million in the industry groups State Government and Utilities. Hence, the answer is 2, which is in choice (C).

---

25. From the table, the State Government employs the maximum number. The number is 1,121,712. The answer is (C).

---

26. The correct choice is the industry that employs more than 10 employees per establishment in an average. Hence, the industry with the criterion: The Number of Establishments · 10 < the Number of Employees would be the correct choice.

Choice (A): Construction.
The number of establishments = 749.
The Number of Establishments × 10 = 7490.
The number of Employees = 6,836.
Here, The Number of Establishments × 10 is not less than The number of Employees.
Reject the choice.

Choice (B): Manufacturing.
The number of Establishments = 19,335.
The Number of Establishments × 10 = 193,350.
The number of Employees = 188,420.
Here, The Number of Establishments × 10 is not less than The number of Employees.
Reject the choice.

Choice (C): Wholesale Trade.
The number of Establishments = 2,320.
The Number of Establishments × 10 = 23,200.
The number of Employees = 9,711.
Here, The Number of Establishments × 10 is not less than The number of Employees.
Reject the choice.

Choice (D): Retail Trading.
The number of Establishments = 11,342.
The Number of Establishments × 10 = 113,420.

Test 6—Answers and Solutions

The number of Employees = 94,997.
Here, The Number of Establishments × 10 is not less than The number of Employees.
Reject the choice.

Choice (E): Transportation and Warehousing.
The number of Establishments = 18,593.
The Number of Establishments × 10 =.185,930.
The number of Employees = 299,648.
Here, The Number of Establishments × 10 is less than The number of Employees.
Accept.

The answer is (E).

---

27. The Employment per establishment is given as The Number of Employees/The Number of Establishments. The ratio is greatest when the numerator has the greatest positive value, and the denominator has the smallest positive value. Hence, II is true.

The highest employment can also be directly understood by the highest percentage employment. Hence, just as Statement II is true because of the highest employment, Statement III is also true because of the highest percentage employment.

Hence, II and III are correct and the answer is (E).

---

28. There are 2 red and 3 green doors. We have two cases:

The room can be entered from a red door (2 red doors, so 2 ways) and can be left from a green door (3 green doors, so 3 ways): $2 \cdot 3 = 6$.

The room can be entered from a green door (3 green doors, so 3 ways) and can be left from a red door (2 red doors, so 2 ways): $3 \cdot 2 = 6$.

Hence, the total number of ways is

$$2 \cdot 3 + 3 \cdot 2 = 6 + 6 = 12$$

The answer is (E).

---

29. From Statement (1) alone, we have the inequality $x < 2$. So, $x - 2$ is negative. So, $x - 3 = x - 2 - 1 =$ a Negative Number $- 1 =$ a Negative Number. So, $(x - 2)(x - 3) =$ a Negative Number × a Negative Number $=$ a Positive Number. Hence, Statement (1) alone is sufficient.

From Statement (2) alone, we have the inequality $x < 3$.

Now, suppose $x = 2.5$. Then $x - 2 = 2.5 - 2 = 0.5$ and $x - 3$ equals $2.5 - 3 = -0.5$. Hence, $(x - 2)(x - 3) = (0.5)(-0.5) = -0.25$. So, $(x - 2)(x - 3)$ is negative.

Now, suppose $x = 1$. Then $x - 2 = 1 - 2 = -1$, and $x - 3 = 1 - 3 = -2$. Hence, $(x - 2)(x - 3) = (-1)(-2) = 2$. So, $(x - 2)(x - 3)$ is positive.

Hence, we have a double case, and Statement (2) alone is *not* sufficient.

The answer is (A), Statement (1) alone sufficient and Statement (2) alone *not* sufficient.

30. To calculate an average, we need exact quantities such as the distribution of the numbers, the averages across sections, etc. But from statements (1) and (2) together, we have only the ranges: Half of the test takers scored above 500, and the lowest and the highest scores on the test are 200 and 800. These are not exact quantities and therefore do not help us evaluate an exact quantity such as an average. Hence, the statements together are not sufficient. The answer is (E).

31. Dividing the equation $6p + 4q = 10$ in Statement (2) by 2 yields $3p + 2q = 5$; this is the same equation in Statement (1). Hence, Statement (1) here is the same as Statement (2) put in another form. Now, if a solution is possible, it should be possible by either statement alone. Otherwise, it is not possible with the statements together. Hence, the possible answers are (D) and (E).

Now, multiplying the equation $3p + 2q = 5$ by 2/3 yields $2p + 4q/3 = 10/3$. Subtracting $q/3$ from both sides yields $2p + q = 10/3 - q/3$. Since q is unknown, $2p + q$ cannot be evaluated. Hence, the statements together are not sufficient. The answer is (E).

32. Choice (A): $(2x+1)^2 = \left(2\left[\dfrac{-11}{2}\right]+1\right)^2 = (-11+1)^2 = (-10)^2 = 100$. Since this value of x satisfies the equation, the answer is (A).

Method II (without substitution):
Square rooting both sides of the given equation $(2x + 1)^2 = 100$ yields two equations:

$$2x + 1 = 10 \text{ and } 2x + 1 = -10$$

Solving the first equation for x yields $x = 9/2$, and solving the second equation for x yields $x = -11/2$. We have the second solution in choice (A), so the answer is (A).

33. We are given the inequality $a < b$.

From statement (1) alone, we have $c < a$. Combining this with the inequality $a < b$ yields $c < a < b$. Picking the first and the last parts we have the inequality $c < b$ [Same as Statement (2)]. We will use this inequality to see whether the given expression is positive. Adding the inequality to the known inequality $a < b$ yields $a + c < 2b$. Subtracting $2b$ from both sides yields $a + c - 2b < 0$. Hence, $(a - b) + (c - b) = a + c - 2b$ is less than 0 and is *not* positive. Hence, Statement (2) alone, derived from Statement (1), is also sufficient. The answer is (D).

34. Prime numbers do not have common factors. Hence, the least common multiple of a set of such numbers equals the product of the numbers. For example, the LCM of 11 and 23 is 11 • 23. The answer is (A).

Test 6—Answers and Solutions

35. We are asked to determine whether the equation $\sqrt{H^2 - 2H} = \dfrac{T\sqrt{1-R^2}}{k\sqrt{1-g^k}}$ is true.

We are given that $H = 3$. Hence, we can evaluate the left-hand side.

There are four unknowns in the right-hand side: T, R, k, and g. If we know the values of these unknowns, then the right-hand side can also be evaluated and we can determine whether the equation is true. We need both statements to know the values of the four unknowns. Hence, the statements together are sufficient to answer the problem. The answer is (C).

36. Let A be the set of families having exactly one car. Then the question is how many families are there in set A.

Next, let B be the set of families having exactly two cars, and let C be the set of families having more than two cars.

Then the set of families having at least one car is the collection of the three sets A, B, and C. Since Statement (1) gives only the total number of families in the three sets, the statement is not sufficient.

Next, the set of families having at least two cars is the collection of the two sets B and C. Since Statement (2) does not have any information about set A, Statement (2) alone is not sufficient.

Now, from the statements together we have that

The number of families in all the three sets A, B, and C together = 250 [from Statement (1)]

and

The number of families in the two sets B and C together = 60 [from Statement (2)]

Since set A is the difference between a set containing the three families of A, B, and C and a set of families of B and C only, The number of families in set A =

The number of families in sets A, B, and C together – the number of families in sets B and C =

250 – 60 =

190

Hence, both statements are required to answer the question, and the answer is (C).

37. Since the angle around a point has 360°, the sum of the four angles a, b, c, and d is 360 and their average is 360/4 = 90. The answer is (C).

Test 7

GMAT Math Tests

Questions: 37
Time: 75 minutes

1. Which one of the following is the first number greater than 200 that is a multiple of both 6 and 8?

   (A) 200
   (B) 208
   (C) 212
   (D) 216
   (E) 224

2. A, B, C, and D are points on a line such that point B bisects line AC and point A bisects line CD. What is the ratio of AB to CD?

   (A) 1/4
   (B) 1/3
   (C) 1/2
   (D) 2/3
   (E) 3/4

3. Which one of the following must equal $p + q$, if $x - y = p$ and $2x + 3y = q$?

   (A) $x + y$
   (B) $3x - 2y$
   (C) $2x - 3y$
   (D) $2x + 3y$
   (E) $3x + 2y$

[Data Sufficiency Question]

4. If p is the circumference of the circle Q, what is the value of p ?

(1) The radius of circle Q is 5.
(2) The area of circle Q is 25π.

USE THIS SPACE FOR SCRATCHWORK.

5. If $|x| \neq 1/2$, then $\frac{4x^2-1}{2x+1}-\frac{4x^2-1}{2x-1}=$

(A) –2
(B) –1
(C) 0
(D) 2
(E) 4

USE THIS SPACE FOR SCRATCHWORK.

6. If n equals $10^5 + (2 \times 10^3) + 10^6$, then the number of zeros in the number n is

(A) 2
(B) 3
(C) 4
(D) 5
(E) 6

USE THIS SPACE FOR SCRATCHWORK.

GMAT Math Tests

[Data Sufficiency Question]
7. What is the value of x?

    (1) x is the sum of all prime numbers greater than 49 and less than 24,632.
    (2) x is the sum of all odd prime numbers greater than 50 and less than 24,650.

[Data Sufficiency Question]
8. In the figure shown, AB is a diameter of the circle and O is the center of the circle. What is the value of circumference of the circle?

    (1) $A = (3, 4)$
    (2) The diameter of the circle is 10.

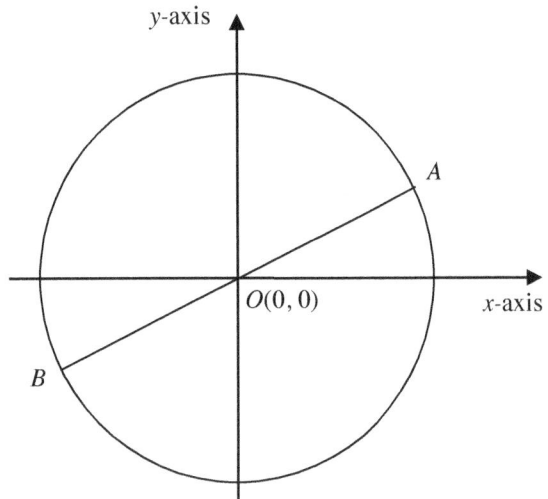

9. What is the maximum possible difference between two three-digit numbers each of which is made up of all the digits 1, 2, and 3?

    (A) 156
    (B) 168
    (C) 176
    (D) 196
    (E) 198

Test 7—Questions

[Data Sufficiency Question]
10. Station Q is to the East of Station T. At 12 noon, a train starts from Station Q and travels at a constant speed of *x* mph towards Station T. At 12 noon of the same day, another train starts from Station T and travels at a constant speed of *y* mph towards Station Q. At what time will the trains meet?

   (1) $y = 4x/3$
   (2) $x = 100$ mph

[Data Sufficiency Question]
11. In the figure, the area of the first rectangle is 100. What is the area of the second rectangle?

   (1) $x = 5$
   (2) $y = 20$

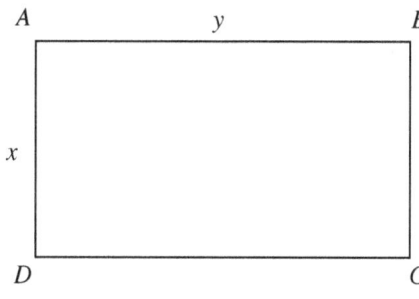

First Rectangle

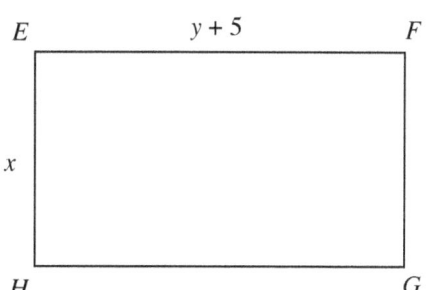

Second Rectangle

179

12. In a zoo, the ratio of the number of cheetahs to the number of pandas is 1 : 3 and was the same five years ago. If the increase in the number of cheetahs in the zoo since then is 5, then what is the increase in the number of pandas?

    (A) 2
    (B) 3
    (C) 5
    (D) 10
    (E) 15

13. If $x = 2$ and $y = -1$, which one of the following expressions is greatest?

    (A) $x + y$
    (B) xy
    (C) $-x + y$
    (D) $x - y - 1$
    (E) $-x - y$

[Data Sufficiency Question]
14. Does the positive integer n have at least 3 positive prime factors?

    (1) $n/10$ is an integer.
    (2) $n/30$ is an integer.

[Data Sufficiency Question]
15. The savings from a person's income is the difference between his or her income and expenditure. What is the ratio of Mr. Kelvin's savings in the year 1998 to the year 1999?

   (1) The ratio of his income in the years 1998 to 1999 is 3 : 4.
   (2) The ratio of his expenditure in the years 1998 to 1999 is 5 : 6.

16. If $(a + 2)(a - 3)(a + 4) = 0$ and $a > 0$, then $a =$

   (A) 1
   (B) 2
   (C) 3
   (D) 4
   (E) 5

17. In January, the value of a stock increased by 25%; and in February, it decreased by 20%. In March, it increased by 50%; and in April, it decreased by 40%. If Jack invested $80 in the stock on January 1 and sold it at the end of April, what was the percentage change in the price of the stock?

   (A) 0%
   (B) 5%
   (C) 10%
   (D) 40%
   (E) 50%

18. A project has three test cases. Three teams are formed to study the three different test cases. James is assigned to all three teams. Except for James, each researcher is assigned to exactly one team. If each team has exactly 6 members, then what is the exact number of researchers required?

    (A) 10
    (B) 12
    (C) 14
    (D) 15
    (E) 16

[Data Sufficiency Question]
19. The population of the town of Paxton continuously increased in the two decades 1960 through 1969 and 1970 through 1979. Was the percentage increase greater in the first decade than in the second decade?

    (1) The population increase in the first decade was 10,082.
    (2) The population increased by the same amount in both decades.

20. A group of 30 employees of Cadre A has a mean age of 27. A different group of 70 employees of Cadre B has a mean age of 23. What is the mean age of the employees of the two groups together?

    (A) 23
    (B) 24.2
    (C) 25
    (D) 26.8
    (E) 27

21. In the figure, if $AB = 8$, $BC = 6$, $AC = 10$ and $CD = 9$, then $AD =$

    (A) 12
    (B) 13
    (C) 15
    (D) 17
    (E) 24

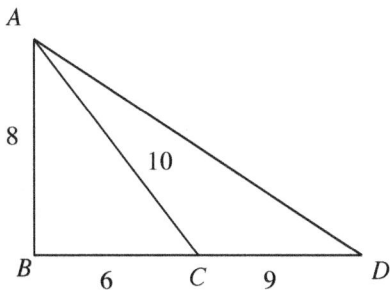

22. The digits of a two-digit number differ by 4 and their squares differ by 40. Which one of the following could be the number?

    (A) 15
    (B) 26
    (C) 40
    (D) 59
    (E) 73

Questions 23–26 refer to the following graphs.

SALES AND EARNINGS OF CONSOLIDATED CONGLOMERATE

Sales
(in millions of dollars)

Earnings
(in millions of dollars)

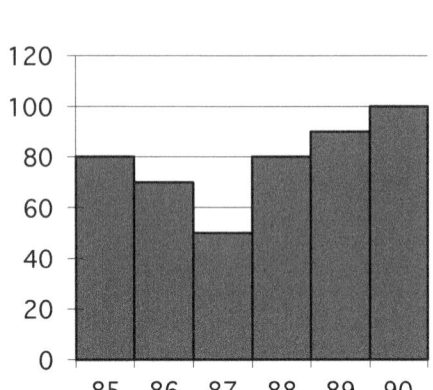
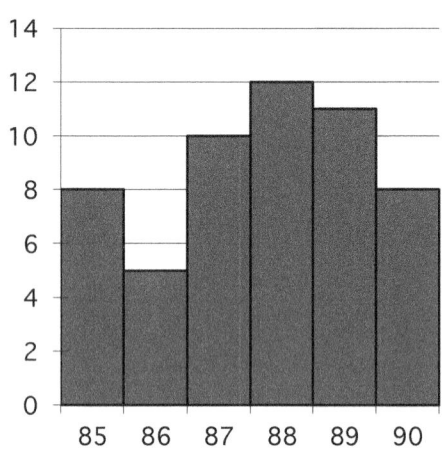

Note: Figure drawn to scale.

23. During which year was the company's earnings 10 percent of its sales?

   (A) 85
   (B) 86
   (C) 87
   (D) 88
   (E) 90

24. During the years 1986 through 1988, what were the average earnings per year?

   (A) 6 million
   (B) 7.5 million
   (C) 9 million
   (D) 10 million
   (E) 27 million

25. In which year did sales increase by the greatest percentage over the previous year?

(A) 86
(B) 87
(C) 88
(D) 89
(E) 90

USE THIS SPACE FOR SCRATCHWORK.

26. If Consolidated Conglomerate's earnings are less than or equal to 10 percent of sales during a year, then the stockholders must take a dividend cut at the end of the year. In how many years did the stockholders of Consolidated Conglomerate suffer a dividend cut?

(A) None
(B) One
(C) Two
(D) Three
(E) Four

USE THIS SPACE FOR SCRATCHWORK.

27. The combined salaries of three brothers is $90,000. Mr. Big earns twice what Mr. Small earns, and Mr. Middle earns 1 1/2 times what Mr. Small earns. What is the smallest salary of the three brothers?

(A) 20,000
(B) 22,000
(C) 25,000
(D) 30,000
(E) 40,000

USE THIS SPACE FOR SCRATCHWORK.

[Data Sufficiency Question]

28. If $a, b,$ and c are three different numbers, then what is the value of $ax + by + cz$?

   (1) $x/(b-c) = y/(c-a) = z/(a-b)$
   (2) $ax : by : cz = 1 : 2 : -3$

[Data Sufficiency Question]

29. In the figure, O is the center of the circle of radius 3, and $ABCD$ is a square. If $\angle AOP = x$ and the side BC of the square is tangent to the circle, then what is the area of the square $ABCD$?

   (1) $PC = 3$
   (2) $x = 60$

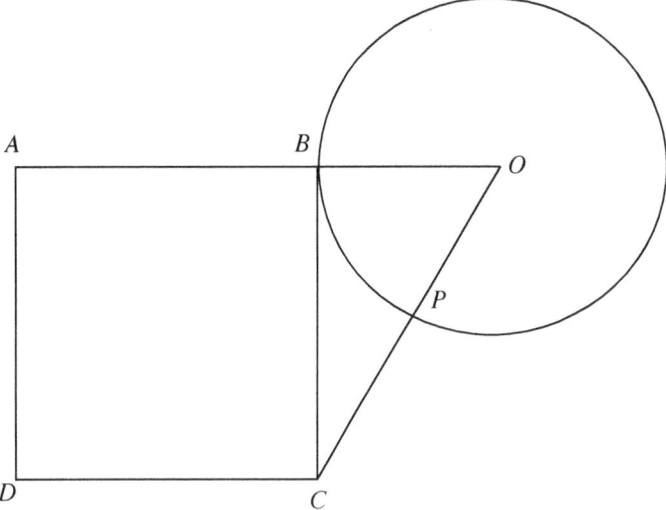

[Data Sufficiency Question]
30. What is the area of quadrilateral ABCD ?

    (1) $AB = CD = 3$
    (2) $AD = BC = 4$

31. A trainer on a Project Planning Module conducts batches of soft skill training for different companies. The trainer sets the batch size (the number of participants) of any batch such that he can make groups of equal numbers without leaving out any of the participants. For a particular batch he decides that he should be able to make teams of 3 participants each, teams of 5 participants each, and teams of 6 participants each, successfully without leaving out anyone in the batch. Which one of the following best describes the batch size (number of participants) that he chooses for the program?

    (A) Exactly 30 participants.
    (B) At least 30 participants.
    (C) Less than 30 participants.
    (D) More than 30 participants.
    (E) Participants in groups of 30 or its multiples.

[Data Sufficiency Question]
32. Is x greater than zero?

    (1) $x^6 > x^2$
    (2) $x^5 < x^2$

33. A menu offers 2 entrees, 3 main courses, and 3 desserts. How many different combinations of dinner can be made? (A dinner must contain an entrée, a main course, and a dessert.)

(A) 12
(B) 15
(C) 18
(D) 21
(E) 24

USE THIS SPACE FOR SCRATCHWORK.

[Data Sufficiency Question]
34. What is the value of $x^3 + y^3$?

(1) $x + y = 7$
(2) $x^2 + y^2 = 25$

USE THIS SPACE FOR SCRATCHWORK.

35. Which one of the following equals the number of multiples of 3 between 102 and 210, inclusive?

(A) 32
(B) 33
(C) 36
(D) 37
(E) 38

USE THIS SPACE FOR SCRATCHWORK.

[Data Sufficiency Question]
36. If *x* equals one of the numbers 1/54, 1/23, or 1/12, then

    (1)   1/55 < *x* < 1/22
    (2)   1/33 < *x* < 1/11

37. If *m* and *n* are two positive integers such that 5*m* + 7*n* = 46, then what is the value of *mn* ?

    (A)   15
    (B)   21
    (C)   24
    (D)   27
    (E)   35

Answers and Solutions Test 7:

1.	D	11.	E	21.	D	31.	E
2.	A	12.	A	22.	E	32.	C
3.	E	13.	D	23.	A	33.	C
4.	D	14.	B	24.	C	34.	C
5.	A	15.	E	25.	C	35.	D
6.	C	16.	C	26.	D	36.	C
7.	D	17.	C	27.	A	37.	A
8.	D	18.	E	28.	D		
9.	E	19.	B	29.	D		
10.	E	20.	B	30.	E		

1. A multiple of 6 and 8 must be a multiple of the least common multiple of the two, which is 24. Now,

$$200/24 = 192/24 + 8/24 = 8 + 8/24$$

So, the first multiple of 24 that is smaller than 200 is 192 (= 8 × 24), and the first multiple of 24 that is greater than 200 is 216 (= 24 × [8 + 1] = 24 × 9). The answer is (D).

2. Drawing the figure given in the question, we get

D   A   B   C

$AB = BC$
$CA = DA$

Suppose AB equal 1 unit. Since point B bisects line segment AC, AB equals half AC. Hence, AC equals twice $AB = 2(AB) = 2(1 \text{ unit}) = 2$ units. Again, since point A bisects line segment DC, DC equals twice $AC = 2(AC) = 2(2 \text{ units}) = 4$ units. Hence, $AB/DC = 1 \text{ unit}/4 \text{ units} = 1/4$. The answer is (A).

3. We are given the equations $x - y = p$ and $2x + 3y = q$. Adding the two equations yields

$(x - y) + (2x + 3y) = p + q$
$x - y + 2x + 3y = p + q$
$3x + 2y = p + q$.

Hence, $p + q = 3x + 2y$. The answer is (E).

4. If we know the radius of the circle, we can draw a unique circle with the radius and can then measure the circumference. So, Statement (1) alone is sufficient.

Now, the area of the circle Q equals $\pi \times radius^2 = 25\pi$. Solving the equation for the radius yields $radius = \sqrt{\frac{25\pi}{\pi}} = 5$. Hence, we have the radius from Statement (2) alone, and therefore Statement (2) alone is sufficient. The answer is (D).

Test 7—Answers and Solutions

---

5. Applying the Difference of Squares Formula $a^2 - b^2 = (a + b)(a - b)$ to the given expression yields

$$\frac{4x^2 - 1}{2x + 1} - \frac{4x^2 - 1}{2x - 1} =$$

$$\frac{(2x + 1)(2x - 1)}{2x + 1} - \frac{(2x + 1)(2x - 1)}{2x - 1} =$$

$$2x - 1 - (2x + 1) =$$

$$-2$$

The answer is (A).

---

6. $n = 10^5 + (2 \times 10^3) + 10^6 = 100{,}000 + 2{,}000 + 1{,}000{,}000 = 1{,}102{,}000$. Since the result has 4 zeroes, the answer is (C).

---

7. The number of primes greater than 49 and less than 24,632 is fixed and therefore can be summed and the question can be answered. Hence, Statement (1) alone is sufficient.

The number of odd primes that are greater than 50 and less than 24,650 is fixed and therefore can be summed and the question can be answered. Hence, Statement (2) alone is sufficient.

Since either Statement alone is sufficient, the answer is (D). This question merely tests your understanding of the Data Sufficiency format.

---

8. The formula for the circumference of a circle is $2\pi \times radius$. Hence, if we know the radius, then the circumference of the circle can be calculated.

The point $A(3, 4)$ is on the circle, and $O(0, 0)$ is the center of the circle. Hence, AO is a *radius*. Since the points can be located (because we have the coordinates of the two end points of the line segment), the distance between them AO (= *radius*) can be calculated and therefore Statement (1) alone is also sufficient.

The radius is half the diameter. The diameter is given in Statement (2), so the statement is sufficient.

The answer is (D).

---

9. The difference between two numbers is maximum when one of the numbers takes the largest possible value and the other one takes the smallest possible value.

The maximum possible three-digit number that can be formed using all three digits 1, 2, and 3 is 321 (Here, we assigned the higher numbers to the higher significant digits).

The minimum possible three-digit number that can be formed from all three digits 1, 2, and 3 is 123 (Here, we assigned the lower numbers to the higher significant digits).

The difference between the two numbers is $321 - 123 = 198$. The answer is (E).

10. The time at which the trains meet depends on the distance between the stations. So, from the speeds alone, we cannot evaluate the time taken. Hence, statements (1) and (2) together are not sufficient to answer the question. The answer is (E).

11. The area of a rectangle is *length* × *width*. Hence, the area of the first rectangle is $xy = 100$ (given that the area is 100).

The area of the second rectangle is $x(y + 5) = xy + 5x = 100 + 5x$ (since $xy = 100$). Hence, the value of x is sufficient to answer the question. Hence, Statement (1) alone is sufficient.

Now, if we have the value of y, we can evaluate x as follows: Since $xy = 100$, $x = 100/y$. Hence, Statement (2) alone is sufficient.

Since either statement is sufficient, the answer is (D).

12. Let k and $3k$ be the number of cheetahs and pandas five years ago. Let d and $3d$ be the corresponding numbers now.

The increase in the number of cheetahs is $d - k = 5$ (given).

The increase in the number of pandas is $3d - 3k = 3(d - k) = 3 \times 5 = 15$. The answer is (E).

M7. We are given that $p : q : r = 3 : 5 : -8$. Now, let $p = 3t$, $q = 5t$, and $r = -8t$ (such that $p : q : r = 3 : 5 : -8$). Then $p + q + r = 3t + 5t - 8t = 0$. The answer is (A).

13. Choice (A): $x + y = 2 + (-1) = 1$.
     Choice (B): $xy = 2(-1) = -2$.
     Choice (C): $-x + y = -2 + (-1) = -3$.
     Choice (D): $x - y - 1 = 2 - (-1) - 1 = 2$.
     Choice (E): $-x - y = -2 - (-1) = -1$.

The greatest result is Choice (D). The answer is (D).

14. From Statement (1) alone, we have that $n/10$ is an integer. Hence, n is either equal to 10 or a multiple of 10.

Suppose $n = 10$. The number 10 factors into the primes $2 \cdot 5$. Hence, n has exactly 2 (not at least 3) prime factors. Here, n does not even have 3 prime factors.

Now, suppose $n = 30$. Then $n/10$ equals 3 an integer. Now, n factors into the primes $2 \cdot 3 \cdot 5$ and has exactly 3 prime factors.

Hence, we have a double case, and Statement (1) alone is not sufficient to answer the question.

From Statement (2) alone, we have that $n/30$ is an integer. Hence, n is equal to either 30 or a multiple of 30. The number 30 factors into the primes $2 \cdot 3 \cdot 5$, and multiples of 30 may have even more prime factors. Hence, n has at least 3 prime factors 2, 3, and 5. So, Statement (2) alone is sufficient to answer the question.

The answer is (B).

15. Savings (in the current context) equals Income – Expenditure.

Statement (1) has information only about income, and Statement (2) has information only about expenditure. Hence, neither statement alone is sufficient to answer the question.

From the statements together, suppose Kelvin's income is $9 in 1998 and $12 in 1999 [the incomes are in accordance with the ratio in Statement (1)]. Also suppose his expenditure is $5 in 1998 and $6 in 1999 [the expenditures are in accordance with the ratio in Statement (2)]. Then the ratio of his savings in the year 1998 to 1999 would be

$$(\$9 - \$5) : (\$12 - \$6) = \$4 : \$6 = 2 : 3$$

In another case, suppose Kelvin's income is $12 in 1998 and $16 in 1999 [the incomes are in accordance with the ratio in Statement (1)]. Also suppose his expenditure is $10 in 1998 and $12 in 1999 [the expenditures are in accordance with the ratio in Statement (2)]. Then the ratio of his savings in 1998 to 1999 would be ($12 – $10) : ($16 – $12) = $2 : $4 = 1 : 2. We have a different savings ratio here. Hence, we already have a double case and therefore the two statements together do not determine a unique ratio for savings.

Hence, the answer is (E).

---

16. We are given that $a > 0$ and $(a + 2)(a - 3)(a + 4) = 0$. Hence, the possible solutions are

$a + 2 = 0$; $a = -2$, a is not greater than 0, so reject.
$a - 3 = 0$; $a = 3$, a is greater than 0, so accept.
$a + 4 = 0$; $a = -4$, a is not greater than 0, so reject.

The answer is (C).

---

17. At the end of January, the value of the stock is $80 + 25%($80) = $80 + $20 = $100.

At the end of February, the value of the stock is $100 – 20%($100) = $100 – $20 = $80.

At the end of March, the value of the stock is $80 + 50%($80) = $80 + $40 = $120.

At the end of April, the value of the stock is $120 – 40%($120) = $120 – $48 = $72.

Now, the percentage change in price is

$$\frac{\text{change in price}}{\text{original price}} = \frac{80 - 72}{80} = \frac{8}{80} = \frac{1}{10} = 10\%$$

The answer is (C).

---

18. Since James is common to all three teams, he occupies one of six positions in each team. Since any member but James is with exactly one team, 5 different researchers are required for each team. Hence, apart from James, the number of researchers required is $5 \cdot 3 = 15$. Including James, there are $15 + 1 = 16$ researchers. The answer is (E).

19. Let p be the population of Paxton in 1960.

Then from Statement (1) alone, the population increased by 10,082 in the first decade. So, the new population is $p + 10{,}082$. Hence, the percentage increase in the population is $10{,}082/p \times 100$. Since we do not know the population increase in the second decade, we cannot calculate the percentage increase and therefore Statement (1) alone is not sufficient.

From Statement (2) alone, we have that the population increase was the same (say, i) in each decade. Hence, the population should be $p + i$ at the end of the year 1969 and $(p + i) + i = p + 2i$ at the end of the second decade. So, the percentage increase in population in the first decade equals

$$\frac{\text{Increase in population in the first decade}}{\text{The population in 1960}} \times 100 = \frac{i}{p} \times 100$$

Also, the percentage increase in population in the second decade equals

$$\frac{\text{Increase in population in the second decade}}{\text{The population in 1970}} \times 100 = \frac{i}{p+i} \times 100$$

Now, since both p and i are positive, $\frac{i}{p}$ is greater than $\frac{i}{p+i}$ since the numerator is the same in both fractions and the denominator is lesser and positive. Hence, Statement (2) alone answers the question. The answer to the question is "Yes. Percentage increase was greater in first decade than in second decade."

The answer is (B).

20. Cadre A has 30 employees whose mean age is 27. Hence, the sum of their ages is $30 \times 27 = 810$. Cadre B has 70 employees whose mean age is 23. Hence, the sum of their ages is $23 \times 70 = 1610$. Now, the total sum of the ages of the 100 (= 30 + 70) employees is $810 + 1610 = 2420$. Hence, the average age is

The sum of the ages divided by the number of employees =

2420/100 =

24.2

The answer is (B).

21. The lengths of the three sides of $\triangle ABC$ are $AB = 8$, $BC = 6$, $AC = 10$. The three sides satisfy The Pythagorean Theorem: $AC^2 = BC^2 + AB^2$ ($10^2 = 6^2 + 8^2$). Hence, triangle ABC is right angled and $\angle B$, the angle opposite the longest side AC (hypotenuse), is a right angle. Now, from the figure, this angle is part of $\triangle ADB$, so $\triangle ADB$ is also right angled. Applying The Pythagorean Theorem to the triangle yields

$$\begin{aligned}
AD^2 &= AB^2 + BD^2 \\
&= AB^2 + (BC + CD)^2 &&\text{from the figure, } BD = BC + CD \\
&= 8^2 + (6 + 9)^2 \\
&= 8^2 + 15^2 \\
&= 289 \\
&= 17^2 \\
AD &= 17 &&\text{by square rooting}
\end{aligned}$$

The answer is (D).

22. Since the digits differ by 4, let a and $a + 4$ be the digits. The difference of their squares, which is $(a + 4)^2 - a^2$, equals 40 (given). Hence, we have

$$(a + 4)^2 - a^2 = 40$$
$$a^2 + 8a + 16 - a^2 = 40$$
$$8a + 16 = 40$$
$$8a = 24$$
$$a = 3$$

The other digit is $a + 4 = 3 + 4 = 7$. Hence, 37 and 73 are the two possible answers. The answer is (E).

23. Reading from the graph, we see that in 1985 the company's earnings were $8 million and its sales were $80 million. This gives

$$\frac{8}{10} = \frac{1}{10} = \frac{10}{100} = 10\%$$

The answer is (A).

24. The graph yields the following information:

Year	Earnings
1986	$5 million
1987	$10 million
1988	$12 million

Forming the average yields $\frac{5 + 10 + 12}{3} = \frac{27}{3} = 9$. The answer is (C).

25. To find the percentage increase (or decrease), divide the numerical change by the original amount. This yields

Year	Percentage increase
86	$\frac{70 - 80}{80} = \frac{-10}{80} = \frac{-1}{8} = -12.5\%$
87	$\frac{50 - 70}{70} = \frac{-20}{70} = \frac{-2}{7} \approx -29\%$
88	$\frac{80 - 50}{50} = \frac{30}{50} = \frac{3}{5} = 60\%$
89	$\frac{90 - 80}{80} = \frac{10}{80} = \frac{1}{8} = 12.5\%$
90	$\frac{100 - 90}{90} = \frac{10}{90} = \frac{1}{9} \approx 11\%$

The largest number in the right-hand column, 60%, corresponds to the year 1988. The answer is (C).

26. Calculating 10 percent of the sales for each year yields

Year	10% of Sales (millions)	Earnings (millions)
85	.10 × 80 = 8	8
86	.10 × 70 = 7	5
87	.10 × 50 = 5	10
88	.10 × 80 = 8	12
89	.10 × 90 = 9	11
90	.10 × 100 = 10	8

Comparing the right columns shows that earnings were 10 percent or less of sales in 1985, 1986, and 1990. The answer is (D).

27. Let s be the salary of Mr. Small. Since Mr. Big earns twice what Mr. Small earns, the salary of Mr. Big is $2s$; and since Mr. Middle earns 1 1/2 times what Mr. Small earns, the salary of Mr. Middle equals $(1\ 1/2)s = 3s/2$. Since $s < 3s/2$ and $s < 2s$, Mr. Small earns the smallest salary. Summing the salaries to 90,000 (given) yields

$$2s + 3s/2 + s = 90,000$$

$$9s/2 = 90,000$$

$$s = 90,000 \cdot 2/9 = 20,000$$

The answer is (A).

28. Let each expression in Statement (1) equal k. Then we have the equation $\dfrac{x}{b-c} = \dfrac{y}{c-a} = \dfrac{z}{a-b} = k$. This reduces to

$$x = (b-c)k, y = (c-a)k, z = (a-b)k$$

Now, $ax + by + cz$ equals

$$a(b-c)k + b(c-a)k + c(a-b)k =$$
$$k(ab - ac + bc - ba + ca - cb) =$$
$$k \times 0 =$$
$$0$$

Hence, Statement (1) alone determines the value of the given expression.

Now, from Statement (2) alone, we have $ax : by : cz = 1 : 2 : -3$. Let $ax = t$, $by = 2t$, and $cz = -3t$ (such that $ax : by : cz = 1 : 2 : -3$). Then $ax + by + cz = t + 2t - 3t = 0$. Hence, Statement (2) alone is also sufficient.

Since both statements are individually sufficient, the answer is (D).

Test 7—Answers and Solutions

29. We are given that the radius of the circle is 3 units and *BC*, which is tangent to the circle, is a side of the square *ABCD*. Now, let's test if we will be able to construct a figure with unique dimensions for the problem, using the statements.

From Statement (1) alone, we have that *PC* = 3. From the figure, *OC* equals

[*OP* (radius of circle)] + [*PC* (= 3 units, given)] =

radius + 3 =

3 + 3 =

6

Now, draw a circle with radius *OB* of length 3 units (given that the radius is 3 units). Then draw a perpendicular (tangent) to the line from the point *B*. Then locate a point on this line that is 6 units from the center *O* of the circle. The point thus formed is *C*, and the side length of the square is *BC*. We can measure this and calculate the area as BC^2. The result is the answer of the question. Hence, Statement (1) alone is sufficient to answer the question.

From Statement (2) alone, we have that *x* = 60. Hence, draw a circle with radius *OB* and radius 3. Then draw a perpendicular to *OB* from the point *B*. Then draw a line making 60° to meet the tangent. Name the point of intersection *C*. Now, *BC* is the side length of the square *ABCD* and BC^2, the area. Hence, calculate *BC* and then evaluate the area. The result is the answer. Hence, Statement (2) alone is also sufficient to answer the question.

Hence, the answer is (D).

30. From Statement (1), we have that sides *AB* and *CD* (the two sides are opposite in the quadrilateral *ABCD* since the two do not have a common vertex) are both equal to 3. Also, from Statement (2), we have that sides *AD* and *BC* (the two sides are opposite in the quadrilateral *ABCD* since the two do not have a common vertex) are both equal to 4.

Clearly, the statements individually cannot determine the area. So, the answer is not (A), or (B), or (D).

Such a figure, in which pairs of opposite sides are equal, must be a parallelogram, as shown in the figure below. To evaluate the area of the parallelogram, we also need the inclination of the parallelogram with respect to its base. For example, in the figure shown below, even if *AD* equals *ED*, *AB* equals *EF*, and *BC* equals *FC*, the area of the parallelogram *ABCD* is greater than area of the parallelogram *EFCD* since the inclination of *ABCD*, with common base *CD*, is greater than that of *EFCD*, with common base *CD*. The answer is (E).

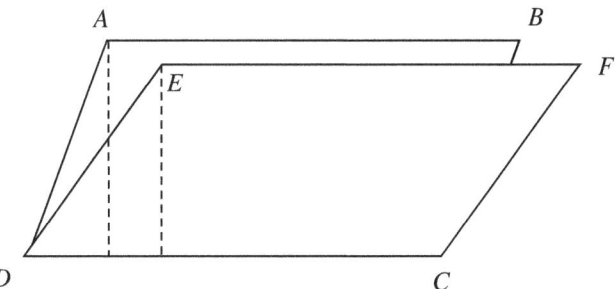

31. The trainer wants to make teams of either 3 participants each or 5 participants each or 6 participants each successfully without leaving out any one of the participants in the batch. Hence, the batch size must be a multiple of all three numbers 3, 5, and 6. Hence, the batch size must be a multiple of the least common multiple of 3, 5, and 6, which is 30. The answer is (E).

32. x is not equal to 0 because the statements are not satisfied with the value of 0.

Dividing the inequality in Statement (1) by x^2 yields $x^4 > 1$. Now, whether x is positive or negative, x^4 is positive. Hence, we cannot determine whether x is positive or negative from this inequality alone. So, we have a double case with Statement (1) alone and therefore Statement (1) alone is not sufficient to answer the question: Is x greater than 0.

Now, dividing the inequality in Statement (2) by the positive value x^2 yields $x^3 < 1$. Hence, the range of x is, x is less than 1 (not including 0). There are numbers greater than 0 and less than 0 in the range. So, we have a double case and Statement (2) alone is not sufficient.

From Statement (1) alone, we have $x^4 > 1$. Hence, x must be either greater than 1 or less than –1. From Statement (2), we have $x^3 < 1$. Hence, x must be less than 1 not including 0. The common range that can be derived from the two statements is $x < -1$. Any such number is negative. Hence, the statements together answer the question. The answer is (C).

33. The problem is a mix of 3 combinational problems. The goal is to choose 1 of 2 entrees, then 1 of 3 main courses, then 1 of 3 desserts. The choices can be made in 2, 3, and 3 ways, respectively. Hence, the total number of ways of selecting the combinations is $2 \cdot 3 \cdot 3 = 18$. The answer is (C).

We can also count the combinations by the Fundamental Principle of Counting:

		Dessert 1
	Main Course 1	Dessert 2
		Dessert 3
		Dessert 1
Entrée 1	Main Course 2	Dessert 2
		Dessert 3
		Dessert 1
	Main Course 3	Dessert 2
		Dessert 3
		Dessert 1
	Main Course 1	Dessert 2
		Dessert 3
		Dessert 1
Entrée 2	Main Course 2	Dessert 2
		Dessert 3
		Dessert 1
	Main Course 3	Dessert 2
		Dessert 3
		Total 18

Test 7—Answers and Solutions

The Fundamental Principle of Counting states:

The total number of possible outcomes of a series of decisions, making selections from various categories, is found by multiplying the number of choices for each decision.

Counting the number of choices in the final column above yields 18.

---

34. Statements (1) and (2) individually are not sufficient to determine the value of $x^3 + y^3$ because in each case there are two variables but only one equation.

Together the statements form the following system:

$$x + y = 7$$
$$x^2 + y^2 = 25$$

Solving the top equation for y yields $y = 7 - x$. Substituting this into the bottom equation yields

$$x^2 + (7 - x)^2 = 25$$
$$x^2 + 49 - 14x + x^2 = 25$$
$$2x^2 - 14x + 24 = 0$$
$$x^2 - 7x + 12 = 0$$
$$(x - 3)(x - 4) = 0$$
$$x - 3 = 0 \text{ or } x - 4 = 0$$
$$x = 3 \text{ or } x = 4$$

Now, if $x = 3$, then $y = 7 - 3 = 4$; and if $x = 4$, then $y = 7 - 4 = 3$. In either case, $x^3 + y^3$ equals $3^3 + 4^3$ ($= 4^3 + 3^3$). Hence, statements (1) and (2) together are sufficient to answer the question. The answer is (C).

---

35. The numbers 102 and 210 are themselves multiples of 3. Also, a multiple of 3 exists once in every three consecutive integers. Counting the multiples of 3 starting with 1 for 102, 2 [= 1 + (105 − 102)/3 = 1 + 1 = 2] for 105, 3 [= 1 + (108 − 102)/3 = 1 + 2 = 3] for 108, and so on, the count we get for 210 equals 1 + (210 − 102)/3 = 1 + 36 = 37. Hence, the answer is (D).

---

36. x is one of the numbers in the set 1/54, 1/23, and 1/12.

From Statement (1) alone, we have the inequality $1/55 < x < 1/22$. Since the numbers 23 and 54 lie between 22 and 55, the reciprocals 1/23 and 1/54 lie between 1/55 to 1/22. Hence, x could be either 1/23 or 1/54. Hence, Statement (1) alone is not sufficient.

From Statement (2) alone, we have the inequality $1/33 < x < 1/11$. Since the numbers 12 and 23 lie between the numbers 11 and 33, the reciprocals 1/12 and 1/23 lie in the range 1/33 to 1/11. Hence, x could be either 1/11 or 1/23. Hence, Statement (2) alone is not sufficient.

Now, from statements (1) and (2) together, we have $1/55 < x < 1/22$ and $1/33 < x < 1/11$. Combining the two inequalities yields $1/33 < x < 1/22$. Since among the three numbers 12, 23, and 54, the number 23 is the only one between 22 and 33, only the number 1/23 (among the three numbers 1/54, 1/23, and 1/12) lies between 1/23 and 1/54. Hence, $x = 1/23$. Since the statements together determine the value of x, the answer is (C).

37. Usually, an equation such as $5m + 7n = 46$ alone will not have a unique solution. But if we attach a constraint into the system such as an inequality or some other information (Here, m and n are constrained to take positive integers values only), we might have a unique solution.

Since m is a positive integer, $5m$ is a positive integer; and since n is a positive integer, $7n$ is a positive integer. Let $p = 5m$ and $q = 7n$. So, p is multiple of 5 and q is multiple of 7 and $p + q = 46$. Subtracting q from both sides yields

$$p = 46 - q \text{ [(a positive multiple of 5) equals 46} - \text{(a positive multiple of 7)]}$$

Let's seek such solution for p and q:

If $q = 7$, $p = 46 - 7 = 39$, not a multiple of 5. Reject.

If $q = 14$, $p = 46 - 14 = 32$, not a multiple of 5. Reject.

If $q = 21$, $p = 46 - 21 = 25$, a multiple of 5. Acceptable. So, $n = q/7 = 3$ and $m = p/5 = 5$.

The checks below are not required since we already have an acceptable solution.

If $q = 28$, $p = 46 - 28 = 18$, not a multiple of 5. Reject.

If $q = 35$, $p = 46 - 35 = 11$, not a multiple of 5. Reject.

If $q = 42$, $p = 46 - 42 = 4$, not a multiple of 5. Reject.

If $q \geq 49$, $p \leq 46 - 49 = -3$, not positive either. Reject.

So, we have only one acceptable assumption and that is $n = 3$ and therefore $m = 5$. Hence, $mn = 3 \cdot 5 = 15$. The answer is (A).

Test 8

Questions: 37
Time: 75 minutes

1. If n is an even integer, which one of the following is an odd integer?

(A) n^2
(B) $\frac{n+1}{2}$
(C) $-2n-4$
(D) $2n^2-3$
(E) $\sqrt{n^2+2}$

USE THIS SPACE FOR SCRATCHWORK.

2. The remainder when the positive integer m is divided by 7 is x. The remainder when m is divided by 14 is $x + 7$. Which one of the following could m equal?

(A) 45
(B) 53
(C) 72
(D) 85
(E) 100

USE THIS SPACE FOR SCRATCHWORK.

3. The following are the measures of the sides of five different triangles. Which one of them represents a right triangle?

(A) $\sqrt{3}$, $\sqrt{4}$, $\sqrt{5}$
(B) 1, 5, 4
(C) 7, 3, 4
(D) $\sqrt{3}$, $\sqrt{7}$, $\sqrt{4}$
(E) 4, 8, 10

USE THIS SPACE FOR SCRATCHWORK.

[Data Sufficiency Question]
4. Is *x* equal to –1?

   (1) $|2x - 2| + |2x + 2| = 4$
   (2) $|3x - 2| + |3x + 2| = 6$

5. The average length of the sides of $\triangle ABC$ is 12. What is the perimeter of $\triangle ABC$?

   (A) 4
   (B) 6
   (C) 12
   (D) 24
   (E) 36

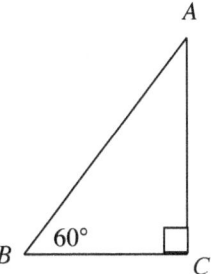

6. If $(x - 2y)(x + 2y) = 5$ and $(2x - y)(2x + y) = 35$, then $\dfrac{x^2 - y^2}{x^2 + y^2} =$

   (A) –8/5
   (B) –4/5
   (C) 0
   (D) 4/5
   (E) 7/5

GMAT Math Tests

[Data Sufficiency Question]
7. What is the average speed of the car during its entire trip?

   (1) The car traveled at 75 mph for the first half (by time) of the trip and at 40 mph for the second half of the trip.
   (2) The car would have taken 5 hrs. to complete the trip if it traveled at 75 mph for the entire trip.

[Data Sufficiency Question]
8. Is x equal to 1?

   (1) $(3x - 2) + (3x + 2) = 6$
   (2) $x^2 + 2x = 3$

9. Which one of the following points in the figure is the median of the points $M, P, Q, R,$ and S?

   (A) M
   (B) P
   (C) Q
   (D) R
   (E) S

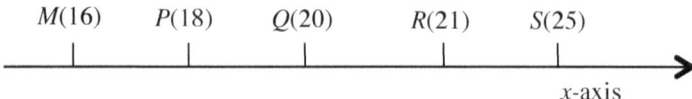

The figure is not drawn to scale.

[Data Sufficiency Question]
10. If *s* and *t* are positive integers, then what is the remainder when *s* is divided by *t* ?

 (1) $s/t = 39.13$
 (2) $s = 17{,}731$ and $t = 429$

[Data Sufficiency Question]
11. Does *a* equal *b*?

 (1) *a* and *b* are positive integers.
 (2) *a* plus *b* equals 3.

12. If *p*, *q*, and *r* are three different numbers and $p : q : r = 3 : 5 : -8$, then what is the value of $p + q + r$?

 (A) 0
 (B) 3/8
 (C) 5/8
 (D) 3/5
 (E) 1

13. How many positive five-digit numbers can be formed with the digits 0, 3, and 5?

    (A) 14
    (B) 15
    (C) 108
    (D) 162
    (E) 243

[Data Sufficiency Question]
14. In the figure, l, m, and k are straight lines. Are the lines l and m parallel?

    (1) $x = q$
    (2) $y = p$

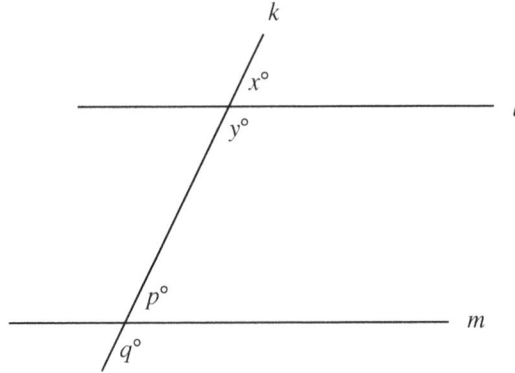

[Data Sufficiency Question]
15. What does the number x equal?

    (1) The quotient when the number is divided by 7 is 52.
    (2) The remainder when the number is divided by 7 is 2.

16. A perfect square is a positive integer that is the result of squaring a positive integer. If $N = 3^4 \cdot 5^3 \cdot 7$, then what is the biggest perfect square that is a factor of N ?

(A) 3^2
(B) 5^2
(C) 9^2
(D) $(9 \cdot 5)^2$
(E) $(3 \cdot 5 \cdot 7)^2$

USE THIS SPACE FOR SCRATCHWORK.

17. If a is positive and b is one-fourth of a, then what is the value of $\frac{a+b}{\sqrt{ab}}$?

(A) 1/5
(B) 1/3
(C) 1/2
(D) 1 ½
(E) 2 ½

USE THIS SPACE FOR SCRATCHWORK.

18. If $a/2$ is 25% of 30 and a is c% of 50, then which one of the following is the value of c ?

(A) 5
(B) 10
(C) 15
(D) 20
(E) 30

USE THIS SPACE FOR SCRATCHWORK.

[Data Sufficiency Question]

19. In which quadrant does the point (a, b) lie if $ab \neq 0$?

    (1) (b, a) lies in Quadrant III.
    (2) $a/b > 0$

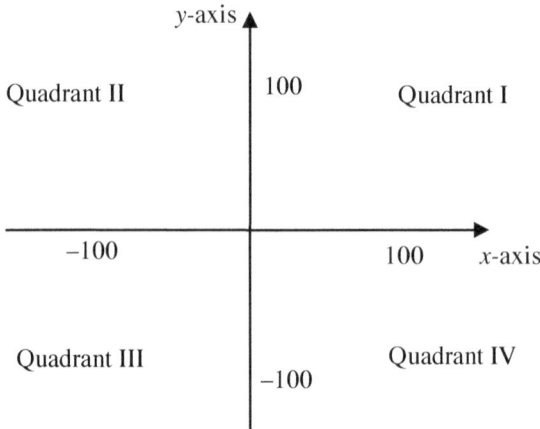

20. When the price of oranges is lowered by 40%, 4 more oranges can be purchased for $12 than can be purchased for the original price. How many oranges can be purchased for 24 dollars at the original price?

    (A) 8
    (B) 12
    (C) 16
    (D) 20
    (E) 24

21. Kelvin takes 3 minutes to inspect a car, and John takes 4 minutes to inspect a car. If they both start inspecting different cars at 8:30 AM, what would be the ratio of the number of cars inspected by Kelvin and John by 8:54 AM of the same day?

    (A) 1 : 3
    (B) 1 : 4
    (C) 3 : 4
    (D) 4 : 3
    (E) 7 : 4

22. In the figure, lines l and k are parallel. Which one of the following must be true?

    (A) $a < b$
    (B) $a \leq b$
    (C) $a = b$
    (D) $a \geq b$
    (E) $a > b$

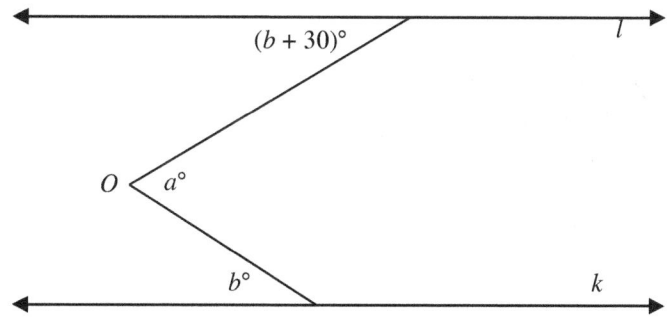

Questions 23–27 refer to the following graphs.

PROFIT AND REVENUE DISTRIBUTION FOR ZIPPY PRINTING, 1990–1993, COPYING AND PRINTING.

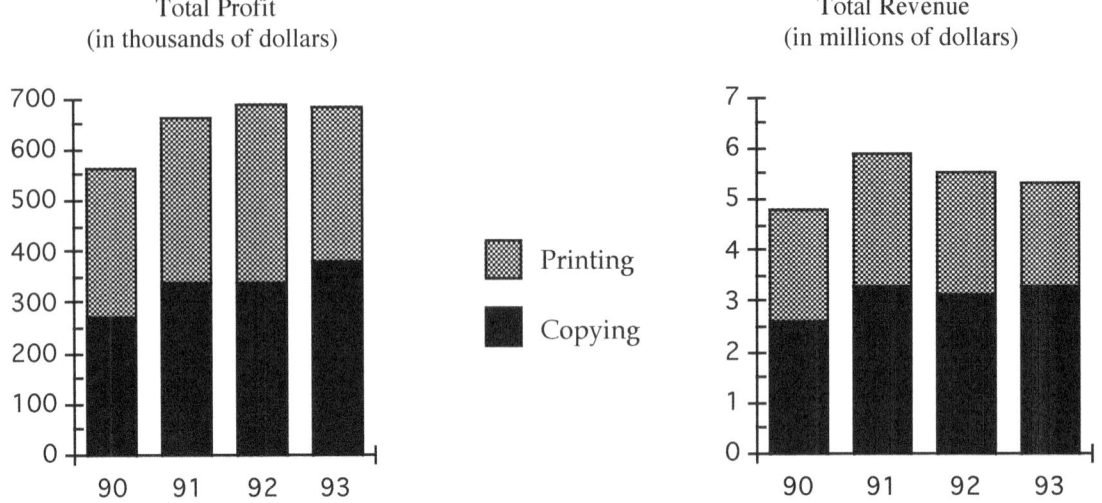

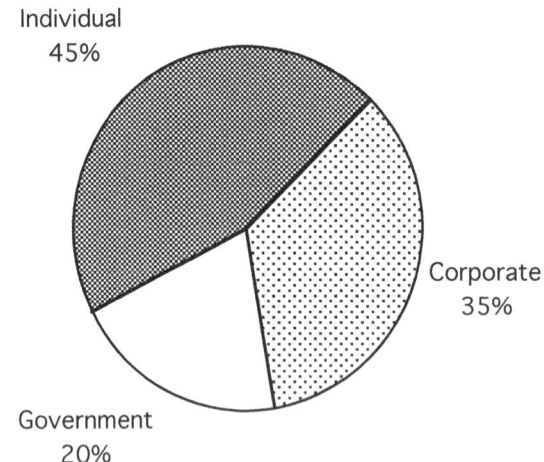

Distribution of Profit from Copying, 1992
(in thousands of dollars)

23. In 1993, the total profit was approximately how much greater than the total profit in 1990?

   (A) 50 thousand
   (B) 75 thousand
   (C) 120 thousand
   (D) 200 thousand
   (E) 350 thousand

24. In 1990, the profit from copying was approximately what percent of the revenue from copying?

(A) 2%
(B) 10%
(C) 20%
(D) 35%
(E) 50%

USE THIS SPACE FOR SCRATCHWORK.

25. In 1992, the profit from copying for corporate customers was approximately how much greater than the profit from copying for government customers?

(A) 50 thousand
(B) 80 thousand
(C) 105 thousand
(D) 190 thousand
(E) 260 thousand

USE THIS SPACE FOR SCRATCHWORK.

26. During the two years in which total profit was most nearly equal, the combined revenue from printing was closest to

(A) 1 million
(B) 2 million
(C) 4.5 million
(D) 6 million
(E) 6.5 million

USE THIS SPACE FOR SCRATCHWORK.

27. The amount of profit made from government copy sales in 1992 was
    (A) 70 thousand
    (B) 100 thousand
    (C) 150 thousand
    (D) 200 thousand
    (E) 350 thousand

[Data Sufficiency Question]
28. Is $x + y > 6$?

    (1) $x + 2y > 8$
    (2) $2x + y > 8$

[Data Sufficiency Question]
29. What is the area of the equilateral triangle shown in the figure?

    (1) The base $BC = 6$.
    (2) The altitude $AD = 3\sqrt{3}$.

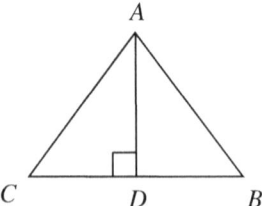

[Data Sufficiency Question]
30. The cost of production of a certain instrument increases with the number of units produced. What is the cost of production for 270 units?

    (1) The cost of production for 300 units is $300.
    (2) The cost of production is directly proportional to the number of units produced.

31. A series has three numbers a, ar, and ar^2. In the series, the first term is twice the second term. What is the ratio of the sum of the first two terms to the sum of the last two terms in the series?

    (A) 1 : 1
    (B) 1 : 2
    (C) 1 : 4
    (D) 2 : 1
    (E) 4 : 1

[Data Sufficiency Question]
32. Is $\dfrac{(a-b)+(c-b)}{d} > 0$?

    (1) $a + c < 2b$
    (2) $d < 0$

33. How many 3-digit numbers do not have an even digit or a zero?

    (A) 20
    (B) 30
    (C) 60
    (D) 80
    (E) 125

[Data Sufficiency Question]

34. $a - b =$

    (1) $a + 3a$ is 4 less than $b + 3b$.
    (2) $a + 3b$ is two times more than $b + 3a$.

35. In a multi-voting system, voters can vote for more than one candidate. Two candidates A and B are contesting the election. 100 voters voted for A. Fifty out of 250 voters voted for both candidates. If each voter voted for at least one of the two candidates, then how many candidates voted only for B?

    (A) 50
    (B) 100
    (C) 150
    (D) 200
    (E) 250

[Data Sufficiency Question]
36. Is $x > y$?

(1) $(x-y)^3 > (x-y)^2$
(2) $(x-y)^4 > (x-y)^3$

37. In the figure, *ABC* and *ADC* are right triangles. Which of the following could be the lengths of *AD* and *DC*, respectively?

(I) $\sqrt{3}$ and $\sqrt{4}$
(II) 4 and 6
(III) 1 and $\sqrt{24}$
(IV) 1 and $\sqrt{26}$

(A) I and II only
(B) II and III only
(C) III and IV only
(D) IV and I only
(E) I, II and III only

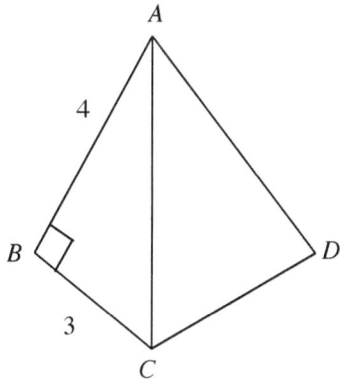

Figure not drawn to scale

Answers and Solutions Test 8:

1. D	11. C	21. D	31. D
2. B	12. A	22. E	32. C
3. D	13. D	23. C	33. E
4. E	14. E	24. B	34. A
5. E	15. C	25. A	35. C
6. D	16. D	26. C	36. A
7. A	17. E	27. A	37. C
8. A	18. E	28. E	
9. C	19. A	29. D	
10. B	20. B	30. C	

---

1. We are told that n is an even integer. So, choose an even integer for n, say, 2 and substitute it into each answer-choice. Now, n^2 becomes $2^2 = 4$, which is not an odd integer. So eliminate (A). Next, $\frac{n+1}{2} = \frac{2+1}{2} = \frac{3}{2}$ is not an odd integer—eliminate (B). Next, $-2n - 4 = -2 \cdot 2 - 4 = -4 - 4 = -8$ is not an odd integer—eliminate (C). Next, $2n^2 - 3 = 2(2)^2 - 3 = 2(4) - 3 = 8 - 3 = 5$ is odd and hence the answer is possibly (D). Finally, $\sqrt{n^2 + 2} = \sqrt{2^2 + 2} = \sqrt{4+2} = \sqrt{6}$, which is not odd—eliminate (E). The answer is (D).

---

2. Choice (A): 45/7 = 6 + 3/7, so x = 3. Now, 45/14 = 3 + 3/14. The remainder is 3, not $x + 7$ (= 10). Reject.

Choice (B): 53/7 = 7 + 4/7, so x = 4. Now, 53/14 = 3 + 11/14. The remainder is 11, and equals $x + 7$ (= 11). Accept the choice.

Choice (C): 72/7 = 10 + 2/7, so x = 2. Now, 72/14 = 5 + 2/14. The remainder is 2, not $x + 7$ (= 9). Reject.

Choice (D): 85/7 = 12 + 1/7, so x = 1. Now, 85/14 = 6 + 1/14. The remainder is 1, not $x + 7$ (= 8). Reject.

Choice (E): 100/7 = 14 + 2/7, so x = 2. Now, 100/14 = 7 + 2/14. The remainder is 2, not $x + 7$ (= 9). Reject.

The answer is (B).

---

3. A right triangle must satisfy The Pythagorean Theorem: the square of the longest side of the triangle is equal to the sum of the squares of the other two sides. Hence, we look for the answer-choice that satisfies this theorem:

Choice (A): $\left(\sqrt{5}\right)^2 \neq \left(\sqrt{3}\right)^2 + \left(\sqrt{4}\right)^2$. Reject.
Choice (B): $5^2 \neq 1^2 + 4^2$. Reject.
Choice (C): $7^2 \neq 3^2 + 4^2$. Reject.
Choice (D): $\left(\sqrt{7}\right)^2 = \left(\sqrt{3}\right)^2 + \left(\sqrt{4}\right)^2$. Correct.
Choice (E): $10^2 \neq 8^2 + 4^2$. Reject.

The answer is (D).

Test 8—Answers and Solutions

---

4. Substitution A:

Both statements are satisfied when $x = -1$.

$|2(-1) - 2| + |2(-1) + 2| = |-2 - 2| + |-2 + 2| = |-4| + |0| = 4 + 0 = 4$.

$|3x - 2| + |3x + 2| = |3(-1) - 2| + |3(-1) + 2| = |-3 - 2| + |-3 + 2| = |-5| + |-1| = 5 + 1 = 6$.

Substitution B:

Both statements are also satisfied when $x = 1$.

$|2(1) - 2| + |2(1) + 2| = |2 - 2| + |2 + 2| = |0| + |4| = 0 + 4 = 4$.

$|3x - 2| + |3x + 2| = |3(1) - 2| + |3(1) + 2| = |3 - 2| + |3 + 2| = |1| + |5| = 1 + 5 = 6$.

Hence, we have a double case with the statements taken together.

The answer is (E).

---

5. The perimeter of a triangle equals the sum of the lengths of the sides of the triangle.

The average length of the sides of the triangle equals 1/3 × (the sum of the lengths of the three sides).

Hence, the perimeter of a triangle equals three times the average length of the sides of the triangle.

Now, we are given that the average length of the triangle is 12. Hence, the perimeter of the triangle equals $3 \times 12 = 36$. The answer is (E).

---

6. We are given the two equations:

$$(x - 2y)(x + 2y) = 5$$
$$(2x - y)(2x + y) = 35$$

Applying the Difference of Squares formula, $(a + b)(a - b) = a^2 - b^2$, to the left-hand sides of each equation yields

$$x^2 - (2y)^2 = 5$$
$$(2x)^2 - y^2 = 35$$

Simplifying these two equations yields

$$x^2 - 4y^2 = 5$$
$$4x^2 - y^2 = 35$$

Subtracting the bottom equation from the top one yields

$$(x^2 - 4y^2) - (4x^2 - y^2) = 5 - 35$$
$$-3x^2 - 3y^2 = -30$$
$$-3(x^2 + y^2) = -30$$
$$x^2 + y^2 = -30/-3 = 10$$

Instead, adding the two equations yields

$$x^2 - 4y^2 + 4x^2 - y^2 = 5 + 35$$
$$5x^2 - 5y^2 = 40$$
$$x^2 - y^2 = 40/5 = 8$$

Now, $(x^2 - y^2)/(x^2 + y^2) = 8/10 = 4/5$. The answer is (D).

7. Let t be the entire time of the trip.

Then from Statement (1) alone, we have that the car traveled at 75 mph for $t/2$ hours and at 40 mph for the remaining $t/2$ hours. Remember that *Distance = Speed × Time*. Hence, the net distance traveled during the two periods equals $75 \times t/2 + 40 \times t/2$. Now, remember that

$$\text{Average Speed} =$$
$$\text{Net Distance} / \text{Time Taken} =$$
$$\frac{75 \times t/2 + 40 \times t/2}{t} =$$
$$75 \times 1/2 + 40 \times 1/2$$

Hence, Statement (1) alone is sufficient.

Now, from Statement (2) alone, we have that if the car had constantly traveled at 75 mph, it would have needed 5 hrs. to complete the trip. But, we do not know how much time it has actually taken to complete the trip. Hence, we cannot find the average speed. So, Statement (2) alone is not sufficient.

The answer is (A).

---

8. Both statements satisfy the question (more precisely they are compatible with the question). The problem model in Statement (1) is a linear equation in x, so degree is 1. Hence, we expect a single solution, and $x = 1$ must be it.

Since the problem model in Statement (2) is a quadratic equation in x, the degree of the equation is 2 and we expect two solutions.[*] The solutions are either equal (here, data sufficient) or unequal (here, data insufficient because there is one more solution other than $x = 1$). Solutions are equal when the equation taken to the left side or right side yields a perfect square trinomial such as $x^2 + 2ax + a^2 = 0$ or $x^2 - 2ax + a^2 = 0$. But, subtracting 3 from both sides of $x^2 + 2x = 3$ yields

$$x^2 + 2x - 3 = 0$$

This is not same as the corresponding perfect square trinomial form, which is $x^2 + 2x + 1 = (x + 1)^2$, and therefore we say there are two different solutions and therefore the statement is *not* sufficient.

The answer is (A).

---

9. The definition of *median* is "When a set of numbers is arranged in order of size, the *median* is the middle number. If a set contains an even number of elements, then the median is the average of the two middle elements."

From the number line $M = 16$, $P = 18$, $Q = 20$, $R = 21$, and $S = 25$. The numbers arranged in order are 16, 18, 20, 21, and 25. The median is 20. Since $Q = 20$, the answer is (C).

---

[*] For math experts: We have two real solutions, one real solution, or two imaginary ones.

10. From Statement (1) alone, we have that $s/t = 39.13$. But, 39.13 is the result of one of the ratios: $\frac{3913}{100}$, $\frac{2 \times 3913}{2 \times 100}$, $\frac{3 \times 3913}{3 \times 100}$, ..., and so on.

The first fraction $\frac{3913}{100}$ equals $\frac{3900}{100} + \frac{13}{100}$, so 13 is the remainder.

The second fraction $\frac{7826}{200}$ equals $\frac{7800}{200} + \frac{26}{200}$, so the remainder is 26.

Hence, we have do not have a unique value for the remainder. Hence, Statement (1) alone is not sufficient.

From Statement (2) alone, we have that $s = 17{,}731$ and $t = 429$. Since we have the values of the dividend and the divisor, we can find the quotient and the remainder. Hence, Statement (2) alone is sufficient. Calculating the remainder is not necessary.

The answer is (B).

---

11. If two positive integers sum to 3, then the numbers must be 1 and 2. Clearly, the two numbers are not equal. Hence, the statements together are sufficient. The answer is (C).

---

12. We are given that $p : q : r = 3 : 5 : -8$. Now, let $p = 3t$, $q = 5t$, and $r = -8t$ (such that $p : q : r = 3 : 5 : -8$). Then $p + q + r = 3t + 5t - 8t = 0$. The answer is (A).

---

13. Let the digits of the five-digit positive number be represented by 5 compartments:

Each of the last four compartments can be filled in 3 ways (with any one of the numbers 0, 3 and 5).

The first compartment can be filled in only 2 ways (with only 3 and 5, not with 0, because placing 0 in the first compartment would yield a number with fewer than 5 digits).

3	0	0	0	0
5	3	3	3	3
	5	5	5	5

Hence, the total number of ways the five compartments can be filled in is $2 \cdot 3 \cdot 3 \cdot 3 \cdot 3 = 162$. The answer is (D).

14. In the figure below, statements (1) $x = q$ and (2) $y = p$ are satisfied. Still, lines l and m intersect and therefore are not parallel.

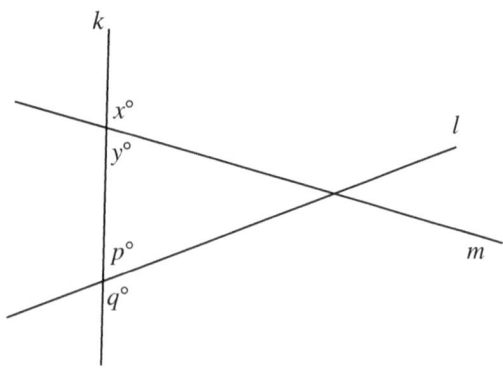

Now, consider the figure below, where each of the angles $x, y, p,$ and q equals 90°. Here, the statements are satisfied and lines l and m are parallel.

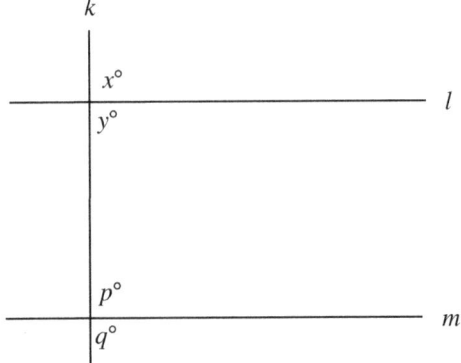

Since we have a double case, the statements together are *not* sufficient. Hence, the answer is (E).

---

15. The number equals the Quotient × 7 + the Remainder = 52 [from Statement (1)] × 7 + 2 [from Statement (2)] = 364 + 2 = 366. The statements are together sufficient. With Statement (1) alone, we do not have the remainder; and with Statement (2) alone, we do not have the quotient. Hence, neither statement is sufficient alone. The answer is (C).

---

16. Every positive integer can be uniquely factored into powers of primes. When the integer is squared, all powers of these primes are doubled. Hence, a perfect square has only even powers of the primes in its factorization, and clearly any positive integer whose prime factorization has only even powers of primes is a perfect square. Any factor of N is the product of some or all of the primes contained in $3^4 \cdot 5^3 \cdot 7$; the largest such product containing only even powers of is $3^4 \cdot 5^2 = (9 \cdot 5)^2$. The answer is (D).

Test 8—Answers and Solutions

---

17. We are given that b is $1/4$ of a. Hence, we have the equation $b = a/4$. Multiplying both sides of this equation by $4/b$ yields $4 = a/b$. Now,

$$\frac{a+b}{\sqrt{ab}} =$$

$$\frac{a}{\sqrt{ab}} + \frac{b}{\sqrt{ab}} =$$

$$\frac{\sqrt{a^2}}{\sqrt{ab}} + \frac{\sqrt{b^2}}{\sqrt{ab}} =$$

$$\sqrt{\frac{a^2}{ab}} + \sqrt{\frac{b^2}{ab}} =$$

$$\sqrt{\frac{a}{b}} + \sqrt{\frac{b}{a}} =$$

$$\sqrt{4} + \sqrt{\frac{1}{4}} =$$

$$2 + \frac{1}{2} =$$

$$2\frac{1}{2}$$

The answer is (E).

---

18. We are given that $a/2$ is 25% of 30. Now, 25% of 30 is $\frac{25}{100} \cdot 30 = \frac{30}{4} = \frac{15}{2}$. Hence, $\frac{a}{2} = \frac{15}{2}$. Multiplying this equation by 2 yields $a = 15$. We are also given that a is $c\%$ of 50. Now, $c\%$ of 50 is $\frac{c}{100} \cdot 50 = \frac{c}{2}$. Hence, we have $a = c/2$. Solving for c yields $c = 2a = 2 \cdot 15 = 30$. The answer is (E).

---

19. From Statement (1) alone, we have that the point (b, a) lies in the third quadrant. In the third quadrant, both x- and y-coordinates are negative. So, b and a are negative and therefore (a, b) also lies in the same quadrant (Quadrant III). Hence, Statement (1) alone is sufficient.

From Statement (2) alone, we have that a/b is greater than 0 (positive). This happens when both a and b are positive or when both a and b are negative. In the first case, (a, b) is in Quadrant I; and in the second case, (a, b) is in Quadrant III. So, we have a double case, and Statement (2) alone is not sufficient.

The answer is (A).

---

20. Let the original price of each orange be x dollars. Remember that *Quantity = Amount ÷ Rate*. Hence, we can purchase $12/x$ oranges for 12 dollars. After a 40% drop in price, the new price is $x(1 - 40/100) = 0.6x$ dollars per orange. Hence, we should be able to purchase $12/(0.6x) = 20/x$ oranges for the same 12 dollars. The excess number of oranges we get (for $12) from the lower price is $20/x - 12/x = (1/x)(20 - 12) = (1/x)(8) = 8/x = 4$ (given). Solving the equation $8/x = 4$ for x yields $x = 2$. Hence, the number of oranges that can be purchased for 24 dollars at original price x is $24/2 = 12$. The answer is (B).

21. Kelvin takes 3 minutes to inspect a car, and John takes 4 minutes to inspect a car. Hence, after t minutes, Kelvin inspects $t/3$ cars and John inspects $t/4$ cars. Hence, the ratio of the number of cars inspected by them is $t/3 : t/4 = 1/3 : 1/4 = 4 : 3$. The answer is (D).

22. Draw line m passing through O and parallel to both line l and line k.

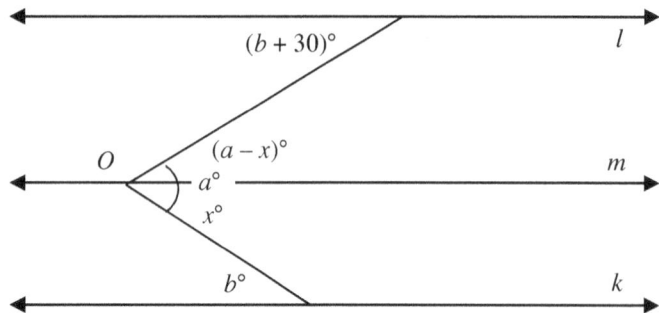

Now, observe that angle x is only part of angle a, and $x = b$ since they are alternate interior angles. Since x is only part of angle a, $a > x$ and $a > b$. The answer is (E).

23. Rarely does a graph question involve significant computation. For this question, we need merely to read the bar graph. The Total Profit graph shows that in 1993 approximately 680 thousand was earned, and in 1990 approximately 560 thousand was earned. Subtracting these numbers yields

$$680 - 560 = 120$$

The answer is (C).

24. The Total Revenue graph indicates that in 1990 the revenue from copying was about $2,600,000. The Total Profit graph shows the profit from copying in that same year was about $270,000. The profit margin is

$$\frac{\text{Profit}}{\text{Revenue}} = \frac{270,000}{2,600,000} \approx 10\%$$

The answer is (B).

25. From the chart, the profit in 1992 for copying was approximately $340,000 of which 35% x $340,000 = $119,000 was from corporate customers and 20% x $340,000 = $68,000 was from government customers. Subtracting these amounts yields

$$\$119,000 - \$68,000 = \$51,000$$

The answer is (A).

26. The Total Profit graph shows that 1992 and 1993 are clearly the two years in which total profit was most nearly equal. Turning to the Total Revenue graph, we see that in 1992 the revenue from printing sales was approximately 2.5 million, and that in 1993 the revenue from printing sales was approximately 2 million. This gives a total of 4.5 million in total printing sales revenue for the period. The answer is (C).

Test 8—Answers and Solutions

27. The Total Profit graph shows that Zippy Printing earned about $340,000 from copying in 1992. The Pie Chart indicates that 20% of this was earned from government sales. Multiplying these numbers gives

$$\$340,000 \times 20\% \approx \$70,000$$

The answer is (A).

28.
Statement (1): $x + 2y > 8$

$$x + 2y > 8$$
$$x + y > 8 - y$$

This is greater than 6 only when

$$8 - y > 6$$
$$y < 2$$

We do not have any such restriction so far, so the statement alone is *not* sufficient.

Statement (2): $2x + y > 8$

$$2x + y > 8$$
$$x + y > 8 - x$$

This is greater than 6 whenever

$$8 - x > 6 \text{ or}$$
$$x < 2$$

We do not have any such restriction again, so the statement alone is *not* sufficient.

From the two statements together, we have $x + 2y > 8$ and $2x + y > 8$. Summing the two yields

$$(x + 2y) + (2x + y) > 8 + 8$$
$$3x + 3y > 16$$
$$3(x + y) > 16$$
$$x + y > 16/3 \approx 5.33$$

So, $x + y$ might still be greater than 6 or less than 6. This is a double case. Since the statements together do not constrain the problem to a single case, the answer is (E).

29. The formula for the area of an equilateral triangle of side length a is $\frac{\sqrt{3}}{4}a^2$. Since the only unknown in the equation is the side length a, given the value, the area can be determined. Hence, Statement (1) alone, which gives the side length BC, is sufficient.

From Statement (2) alone, we have the length of an altitude of the triangle. The formula for the side length of an altitude of an equilateral triangle of side length a is $\frac{\sqrt{3}}{2}a$. So, if d is the length of the altitude, then $d = \frac{\sqrt{3}}{2}a$. Solving the equation for a yields $a = \frac{2d}{\sqrt{3}}$. Hence, even if we have just an altitude, the side length, and therefore the area of the triangle, can be evaluated. Hence, Statement (2) alone, which gives the altitude length AD, is sufficient.

Hence, the answer is (D), either statement is sufficient.

30. From Statement (1) alone, we have that the cost of production for 300 units is $300. Suppose the cost of production (in dollars) is calculated as 100 + 2/3 × quantity. Then the cost of production of 300 units equals 300 dollars, and the cost of production of 270 units equals 100 + 2/3 × 270 = 100 + 180 = 280.

Now, suppose it were calculated as 200 + 1/3 × quantity, then the cost of production for 270 units would equal 200 + 1/3 × 270 = 200 + 90 = 290 dollars.

Since we do not have a unique value, Statement (1) alone is not sufficient.

From Statement (2) alone, the cost of production is proportional to the number of units produced. Hence, we have the equation *The Cost of Production* = k × *Quantity*, where k is some constant. The *Cost of Production* of 270 units equals k × 270. But we do not know the value of k. So, Statement (2) alone is not sufficient.

Now, from the statements together, we have that 300 units cost 300 dollars. Putting this in the proportionality equation yields 300 = k × 300. Solving the equation for k yields k = 300/300 = 1. Since we now know the value of k, we can evaluate the cost of production of 270 items. Hence, the statements together answer the question. Hence, the answer is (C). The answer is the cost = k × 270 = 1 × 270 = 270 dollars.

---

31. Since "the first term in the series is twice the second term," we have $a = 2(ar)$. Canceling a from both sides of the equation yields $1 = 2r$. Hence, $r = 1/2$.

Hence, the three numbers a, ar, and ar^2 become a, $a(1/2)$, and $a(1/2)^2$, or a, $a/2$, and $a/4$.

The sum of first two terms is $a + a/2$ and the sum of the last two terms is $a/2 + a/4$. Forming their ratio yields

$$\frac{a + \frac{a}{2}}{\frac{a}{2} + \frac{a}{4}} =$$

$$\frac{\frac{2a+a}{2}}{\frac{2a+a}{4}} =$$

$$\frac{\frac{3a}{2}}{\frac{3a}{4}} =$$

$$\left(\frac{3a}{2}\right)\left(\frac{4}{3a}\right) =$$

$$2 =$$

$$\frac{2}{1} \text{ or } 2:1$$

The answer is (D).

Test 8—Answers and Solutions

32. The question is about the fraction $\dfrac{(a-b)+(c-b)}{d}$. The numerator of the fraction is $(a - b) + (c - b)$ and the denominator is d.

From Statement (1), we do not have any information about d. So, if $(a - b) + (c - b)$ is negative and d is positive, the fraction is negative; and if $(a - b) + (c - b)$ is negative and d is negative, the fraction is positive. Hence, Statement (1) alone is *not* sufficient.

From Statement (2), we do not have information about the numerator $(a - b) + (c - b)$. So, if the numerator is negative and the denominator d is negative, the fraction is positive; and if the numerator is positive and the denominator d is negative, the fraction is negative. Hence, we have a double case and Statement (2) alone is *not* sufficient.

Now, the numerator is $(a - b) + (c - b) = a + c - 2b$ and according to Statement (1) alone, we have the expression is negative (< 0). Now, from statement (2) alone, we have the denominator d is negative. So, the fraction Numerator/Denominator = (a Negative Number) ÷ (a Negative Number) = a Positive Number. So, the answer is "Yes. $\dfrac{(a-b)+(c-b)}{d} > 0$". Hence, the answer is (C), the statements together are sufficient.

---

33. There are 5 digits that are not even or zero: 1, 3, 5, 7, and 9. Now, let's count all the three-digit numbers that can be formed from these five digits. The first digit of the number can be filled in 5 ways with any one of the mentioned digits. Similarly, the second and third digits of the number can be filled in 5 ways. Hence, the total number of ways of forming the three-digit number is 125 (= 5 × 5 × 5). The answer is (E).

---

34. Statement (1): $a + 3a$ is 4 less than $b + 3b$.

Translating the sentence into an equation gives	$a + 3a = b + 3b - 4$
Combining like terms gives	$4a = 4b - 4$
Subtracting $4b$ from both sides gives	$4a - 4b = -4$
Finally, dividing by 4 gives	$a - b = -1$

Statement (1) is sufficient.

Statement (2): $a + 3b$ is two times more than $b + 3a$.

Translating the sentence into an equation gives	$a + 3b = 2(b + 3a)$
Distributing the right hand side yields	$a + 3b = 2b + 6a$
Subtracting $2b$ from both sides yields	$a + b = 6a$
Subtracting a from both sides yields	$b = 5a$
Finally,	$a - b = a - 5a = -4a$

Since we do not know the value of a, the value of $-4a$ cannot be determined. So, Statement (2) is not sufficient.

The answer is (A).

GMAT Math Tests

35. There are three kinds of voters:

   1) Voters who voted for A only. Let the count of such voters be a.
   2) Voters who voted for B only. Let the count of such voters be b.
   3) Voters who voted for both A and B. The count of such voters is 50 (given).

Since the total number of voters is 250, we have

$a + b + 50 = 250$
$a + b = 200$ (1)   By subtracting 50 from both sides

Now, we have that 100 voters voted for A. Hence, we have

(Voters who voted for A only) + (Voters who voted for both A and B) = 100

Forming this as an equation yields

$$a + 50 = 100$$
$$a = 50$$

Substituting this in equation (1) yields $50 + b = 200$. Solving for b yields $b = 150$.

The answer is (C).

36. Subtracting $(x - y)^2$ from both sides of $(x - y)^3 > (x - y)^2$ in Statement (1) yields

$$(x - y)^3 - (x - y)^2 > 0$$

Factoring out $(x - y)^2$ yields

$$(x - y)^2(x - y - 1) > 0$$

Since $(x - y)^2$ is positive (being a square), $x - y - 1$ must be positive, otherwise $(x - y)^2(x - y - 1)$ would be negative. Hence, $x - y - 1 > 0$, or $x > y + 1$. This inequality says that x is at least one unit larger than y, so $x > y$. Hence, Statement (1) alone is sufficient.

Now, dividing both sides of the inequality $(x - y)^4 > (x - y)^3$ in Statement (2) by the positive expression $(x - y)^2$ yields

$$(x - y)^2 > x - y$$

This inequality is true when either $x - y$ is negative or $x - y$ is positive and greater than 1. If $x - y$ is negative, x is less than y; and if $x - y$ is positive, x is greater than y. Hence, we have a double case, and therefore Statement (2) alone is *not* sufficient to answer the question.

The answer is (A).

37. From the figure, we have that $\angle B$ is a right angle in $\triangle ABC$. Applying The Pythagorean Theorem to the triangle yields

$$AC^2 = AB^2 + BC^2 = 4^2 + 3^2 = 25$$

Hence, $AC = \sqrt{25} = 5$.

Now, we are given that $\triangle ADC$ is a right-angled triangle. But, we are not given which one of the three angles of the triangle is right-angled. We have two possibilities: either the common side of the two triangles, AC, is the hypotenuse of the triangle, or it is not.

In the case AC is the hypotenuse of the triangle, we have by The Pythagorean Theorem,

$$AC^2 = AD^2 + DC^2$$
$$5^2 = AD^2 + DC^2$$

This equation is satisfied by III since $5^2 = 1^2 + \left(\sqrt{24}\right)^2$. Hence, III is possible.

In the case AC is not the hypotenuse of the triangle and, say, DC is the hypotenuse, then by applying The Pythagorean Theorem to the triangle, we have

$$AD^2 + AC^2 = DC^2$$
$$AD^2 + 5^2 = DC^2$$

This equation is satisfied by IV: $5^2 + 1^2 = \left(\sqrt{26}\right)^2$.

Hence, we conclude that III and IV are possible. The two are available in choice (C). Hence, the answer is (C).

Test 9

Questions: 37
Time: 75 minutes

1. If *n* is an integer, which of the following CANNOT be an integer?

    (A) $\dfrac{n-2}{2}$
    (B) $\sqrt{n}$
    (C) $\dfrac{2}{n+1}$
    (D) $\sqrt{n^2+3}$
    (E) $\sqrt{\dfrac{1}{n^2+2}}$

2. If $x * y$ represents the number of integers between x and y, then $(-2 * 8) + (2 * -8) =$

    (A) 0
    (B) 9
    (C) 10
    (D) 18
    (E) 20

3. Each of the two positive integers *a* and *b* ends with the digit 2. With which one of the following numbers does $a - b$ end?

    (A) 0
    (B) 1
    (C) 2
    (D) 3
    (E) 4

[Data Sufficiency Question]
4. What is the average of the consecutive integers m through n, inclusive?

   (1) The average of m and n is 23.5.
   (2) The average of the integers between m and n not including either is 23.5.

5. If p and q are two positive integers and $p/q = 1.15$, then p can equal which one of the following?

   (A) 15
   (B) 18
   (C) 20
   (D) 22
   (E) 23

6. From the figure, which one of the following could be the value of b?

   (A) 20
   (B) 30
   (C) 60
   (D) 75
   (E) 90

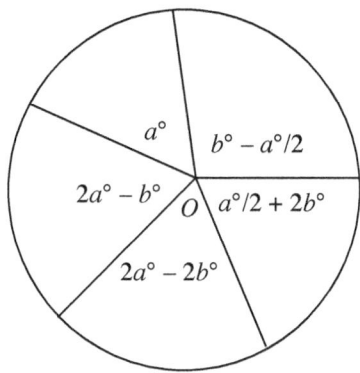

[Data Sufficiency Question]

7. If *r* and *s* are two positive numbers, what is the value of the ratio *r*/*s* ?

   (1) *r* is 25% greater than *s*.
   (2) *r* is 25 units greater than *s*.

[Data Sufficiency Question]

8. In the figure, is the quadrilateral *ABCD* a square?

   (1) $x = y = z = p$
   (2) $AB = BC = CD = DA$

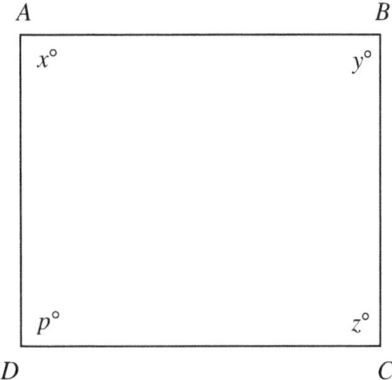

9. If $2x + 3y = 11$ and $3x + 2y = 9$, then $x + y =$

   (A) 4
   (B) 7
   (C) 8
   (D) 9
   (E) 11

[Data Sufficiency Question]
10. What is the sum of the two numbers x and y?

    (1) The ratio of the sum of the reciprocals of x and y to the product of the reciprocals of x and y is 1 : 3.
    (2) The product of x and y is 11/36 units greater than the sum of x and y.

[Data Sufficiency Question]
11. Is $x > y$?

    (1) $x^2 = 4$
    (2) $y^3 = -8$

12. The average length of all the sides of a rectangle equals twice the width of the rectangle. If the area of the rectangle is 18, what is its perimeter?

    (A) $6\sqrt{6}$
    (B) $8\sqrt{6}$
    (C) 24
    (D) 32
    (E) 48

13. In a class, 10% of the girls have blue eyes, and 20% of the boys have blue eyes. If the ratio of girls to boys in the class is 3 : 4, then what is the fraction of the students in the class having blue eyes?

   (A) 11/70
   (B) 11/45
   (C) 14/45
   (D) 12/33
   (E) 23/49

[Data Sufficiency Question]
14. In the rectangular coordinate system shown, ABCD is a quadrilateral. The coordinates of the points A, B, C, and D are (0, 2), (a, b), (a, 2), and (0, 0), respectively. Is the quadrilateral ABCD a parallelogram?

   (1) $a = 3$
   (2) $b = 5$

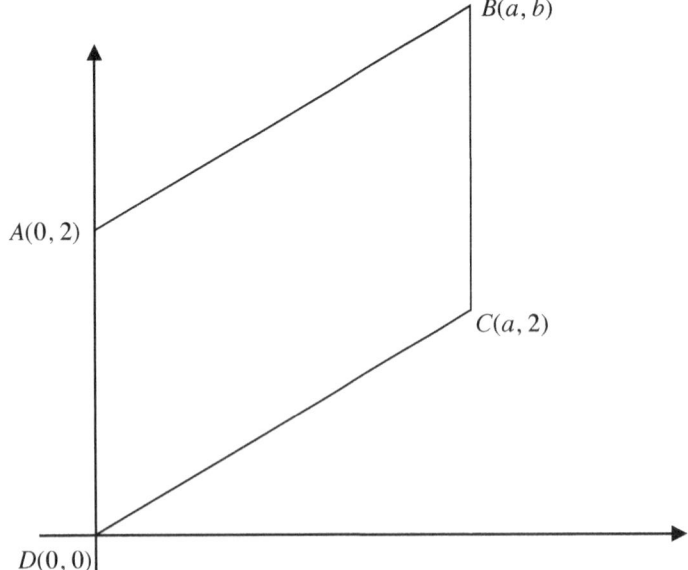

[Data Sufficiency Question]
15. Is $(x-2)(x-3) > 0$?

    (1) $x < 2$
    (2) $x < 3$

16. If $p = \dfrac{\sqrt{3}-2}{\sqrt{2}+1}$, then which one of the following equals $p - 4$?

    (A) $\sqrt{3} - 2$
    (B) $\sqrt{3} + 2$
    (C) 2
    (D) $-2\sqrt{2} + \sqrt{6} - \sqrt{3} - 2$
    (E) $-2\sqrt{2} + \sqrt{6} - \sqrt{3} + 2$

17. If $x = 1/y$, then which one of the following must $\dfrac{x^2 + x + 2}{x}$ equal?

    (A) $\dfrac{y^2 + y + 2}{y}$
    (B) $\dfrac{y^2 + 2y + 1}{y}$
    (C) $\dfrac{2y^2 + y + 1}{y}$
    (D) $\dfrac{y^2 + y + 1}{y^2}$
    (E) $\dfrac{2y^2 + y + 1}{y^2}$

235

18. 8 is 4% of a, and 4 is 8% of b. c equals b/a. What is the value of c?

   (A) 1/32
   (B) 1/4
   (C) 1
   (D) 4
   (E) 32

[Data Sufficiency Question]
19. Is the product of the three nonzero numbers a, b, and c divisible by 81?

   (1) The product of the three numbers a, b, and c is a multiple of 27.
   (2) None of the three numbers a, b, and c is divisible by 9.

20. If the least common multiple of m and n is 24, then what is the first integer larger than 3070 that is divisible by both m and n?

   (A) 3072
   (B) 3078
   (C) 3084
   (D) 3088
   (E) 3094

21. John had $42. He purchased fifty mangoes and thirty oranges with the whole amount. He then chose to return six mangoes for nine oranges as both quantities are equally priced. What is the price of each Mango?

(A) 0.4
(B) 0.45
(C) 0.5
(D) 0.55
(E) 0.6

USE THIS SPACE FOR SCRATCHWORK.

22. What is the probability that a number randomly picked from the range 1 through 1000 is divisible by both 7 and 10?

(A) 7/1000
(B) 1/100
(C) 7/500
(D) 7/100
(E) 1/10

USE THIS SPACE FOR SCRATCHWORK.

Questions 23–26 refer to the following graphs.

DISTRIBUTION OF CRIMINAL ACTIVITY BY CATEGORY OF CRIME FOR COUNTRY X IN 1990 AND PROJECTED FOR 2000.

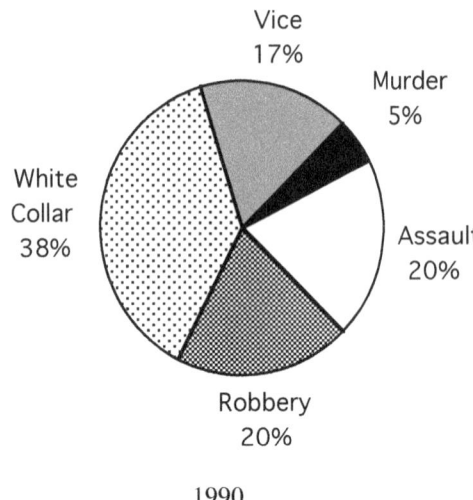
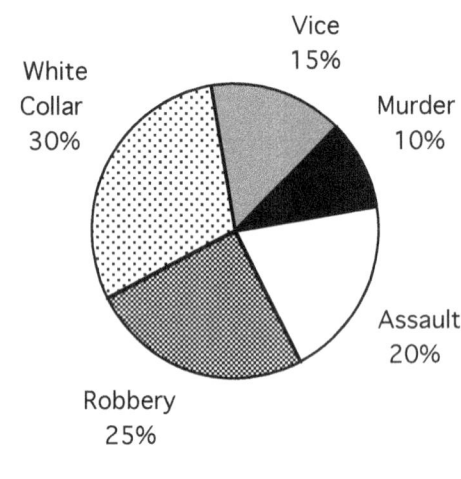

23. What is the projected number of white-collar criminals in 2000?

    (A) 1 million
    (B) 3.8 million
    (C) 6 million
    (D) 8 million
    (E) 10 million

24. The ratio of the number of robbers in 1990 to the number of projected robbers in 2000 is

    (A) 2/5
    (B) 3/5
    (C) 1
    (D) 3/2
    (E) 5/2

25. From 1990 to 2000, there is a projected decrease in the number of criminals for which of the following categories?

    I. Vice
    II. Assault
    III. White Collar

    (A) None
    (B) I only
    (C) II only
    (D) II and III only
    (E) I, II, and III

USE THIS SPACE FOR SCRATCHWORK.

26. What is the approximate projected percent increase between 1990 and 2000 in the number of criminals involved in vice?

    (A) 25%
    (B) 40%
    (C) 60%
    (D) 75%
    (E) 85%

USE THIS SPACE FOR SCRATCHWORK.

27. The sum of the positive integers from 1 through n can be calculated by the formula $n(n + 1)/2$. Which one of the following equals the sum of all the even numbers from 0 through 20, inclusive?

    (A) 50
    (B) 70
    (C) 90
    (D) 110
    (E) 140

USE THIS SPACE FOR SCRATCHWORK.

GMAT Math Tests

[Data Sufficiency Question]
28. Does the sum $p + q + r + s$ equal 1?

   (1) $(p + q)/(r + s) = 1$
   (2) $p = q$ and $r = s$

[Data Sufficiency Question]
29. Is $x = y$?

   (1) $x + y = 100$
   (2) $(x - 50)^2 = (y - 50)^2$

30. A function $f(x)$ is defined for all real numbers by the expression $(x - 1.5)(x - 2.5)(x - 3.5)(x - 4.5)$. For which one of the following values of x, represented on the number line, is $f(x)$ negative?

   (A) Point A
   (B) Point B
   (C) Point C
   (D) Point D
   (E) Point E

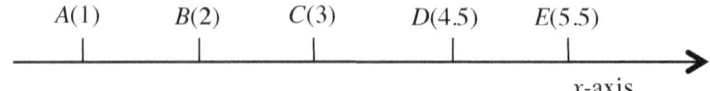

The graph is not drawn to scale.

31. Which of the following statements is true about the line segment with endpoints (–1, 1) and (1, –1)?

    (A) Crosses the *x*-axis only.
    (B) Crosses the *y*-axis only.
    (C) Crosses the *y*-axis on its positive side.
    (D) Passes through the origin (0, 0).
    (E) Crosses the *x*- and *y*-axes on their negative sides.

[Data Sufficiency Question]
32. By what percent did the company's earnings increase this year in terms of US dollars?

    (1) The company earned 18% more Canadian dollars this year.
    (2) The company earned 100,000 Canadian dollars this year.

33. A system of equations is as shown below

    $x + l = 6$
    $x - m = 5$
    $x + p = 4$
    $x - q = 3$

    What is the value of $l + m + p + q$?

    (A) 2
    (B) 3
    (C) 4
    (D) 5
    (E) 6

[Data Sufficiency Question]

34. Is $x = y$?

(1) $(x+y)\left(\dfrac{1}{x}+\dfrac{1}{y}\right) = 4$

(2) $x - 100 = y - 100$

35. In the sequence a_n, the nth term is defined as $(a_{n-1} - 1)^2$. If $a_3 = 64$, then what is the value of a_2?

(A) 2
(B) 3
(C) 4
(D) 5
(E) 9

36. Hose A can fill a tank in 5 minutes, and Hose B can fill the same tank in 6 minutes. How many tanks would Hose B fill in the time Hose A fills 6 tanks?

(A) 3
(B) 4
(C) 5
(D) 5.5
(E) 6

37. If $\dfrac{x+y}{x-y} = \dfrac{4}{3}$ and $x \neq 0$, then what percentage of $x + 3y$ is $x - 3y$?

   (A) 20%
   (B) 25%
   (C) 30%
   (D) 35%
   (E) 40%

Answers and Solutions Test 9:

1. E	11. E	21. E	31. D
2. D	12. B	22. C	32. E
3. A	13. A	23. C	33. A
4. D	14. B	24. A	34. A
5. E	15. A	25. A	35. E
6. C	16. D	26. D	36. C
7. A	17. C	27. D	37. E
8. C	18. B	28. E	
9. A	19. B	29. E	
10. A	20. A	30. B	

---

1. Choose n to be 0. Then $\frac{n-2}{2} = \frac{0-2}{2} = \frac{-2}{2} = -1$, which is an integer. So eliminate (A). Next, $\sqrt{n} = \sqrt{0} = 0$. Eliminate (B). Next, $\frac{2}{n+1} = \frac{2}{0+1} = \frac{2}{1} = 2$. Eliminate (C). Next, $\sqrt{n^2+3} = \sqrt{0^2+3} = \sqrt{0+3} = \sqrt{3}$, which is *not* an integer—it *may* be our answer. However, $\sqrt{\frac{1}{n^2+2}} = \sqrt{\frac{1}{0^2+2}} = \sqrt{\frac{1}{0+2}} = \sqrt{\frac{1}{2}}$, which is *not* an integer as well. So, we choose another number, say, 1. Then $\sqrt{n^2+3} = \sqrt{1^2+3} = \sqrt{1+3} = \sqrt{4} = 2$, which is an integer, eliminating (D). Thus, choice (E), $\sqrt{\frac{1}{n^2+2}}$, is the answer.

---

2. The integers between –2 and 8 are –1, 0, 1, 2, 3, 4, 5, 6, 7 (a total of 9). Hence, –2 * 8 = 9. The integers between –8 and 2 are: –7, –6, –5, –4, –3, –2, –1, 0, 1 (a total of 9). Hence, 2 * –8 = 9. Therefore, (–2 * 8) + (2 * –8) = 9 + 9 = 18. The answer is (D).

---

3. Since each of the two integers a and b ends with the same digit, the difference of the two numbers ends with 0. For example 642 – 182 = 460, and 460 ends with 0. Hence, the answer is (A).

4.

Statement (1): The average of m and n is 23.5.	Statement (2): The average of the integers between m and n not including either is 23.5.
The average of the consecutive integers m through n always equals the average of just the integers m and n since the elements in the sum are consecutive. Hence, Statement (1) alone answers the question.	The average of the consecutive integers between m and n not including either is the same as the average including them since the elements in the sum are consecutive. Hence, Statement (2) alone also answers the question.
For example, the average of the numbers 1 through 5 is 3, which equals (1 + 5)/2 = 6/2 = 3.	For example, the average of the numbers 1, 2, 3, 4, 5 is 3, which equals (2 + 3 + 4)/2 = 3.
For example, the average of the numbers 1 through 6 is 3.5, which equals (1 + 6)/2 = 7/2 = 3.5.	The average of the numbers 1, 2, 3, 4, 5, and 6 is 3.5, which equals (2 + 3 + 4 + 5)/4 = 3.5.
The statement is sufficient.	The statement is sufficient.

The answer is (D), either statement alone is sufficient.

Test 9—Answers and Solutions

5. We have that $p/q = 1.15$. Solving for p yields $p = 1.15q = q + 0.15q =$ (a positive integer) $+ 0.15q$. Now, p is a positive integer only when $0.15q$ is an integer. Now, $0.15q$ equals $15/100 \cdot q = 3q/20$ and would result in an integer only when the denominator of the fraction (i.e., 20) is canceled out by q. This happens only when q is a multiple of 20. Hence, $q = 20$, or 40, or 60, ... Pick the minimum value for q, which is 20. Now, $1.15q = q + 0.15q = q + 3/20 \cdot q = 20 + 3/20 \cdot 20 = 23$. For other values of q (40, 60, 80, ...), p is a multiple of 23. Only choice (E) is a multiple of 23. The answer is (E).

6. In the figure, angles $b° - a°/2$ and $2a° - 2b°$ must be positive. Hence, we have the inequalities, $b - a/2 > 0$ and $2a - 2b > 0$.

Adding $a/2$ to both sides of first inequality and $2b$ to both sides of second inequality yields the following two inequalities:

$$b > a/2$$
$$2a > 2b$$

Dividing the second inequality by 2 yields $a > b$.

Now, summing angles around point O to $360°$ yields $a + (b - a/2) + (a/2 + 2b) + (2a - 2b) + (2a - b) = 360$. Simplifying this yields $5a = 360$, and solving yields $a = 360/5 = 72$.

Substituting this value in the inequalities $b > a/2$ and $a > b$ yields

$$b > a/2 = 72/2 = 36, \text{ and } 72 > b$$

Combining the inequalities $b > 36$ and $72 > b$ yields $36 < b < 72$. The only choice in this range is (C), so the answer is (C).

7. From Statement (1) alone, we have that r is 25% greater than s. Hence, $r = (1 + 25/100)s$. Hence, $r/s = 1 + 25/100 = 1.25$. Hence, Statement (1) alone is sufficient.

From Statement (2) alone, we have that r is 25 units greater than s. Hence, we have the equation $r = s + 25$. Dividing the equation by s yields $r/s = s/s + 25/s = 1 + 25/s$. Since s is unknown, $1 + 25/s$ cannot be calculated. Hence, Statement (2) alone is not sufficient.

The answer is (A).

8. From Statement (1) alone, we have that $x = y = z = p$. Each angle in a quadrilateral is equal when the quadrilateral is a rectangle. A rectangle (only opposite sides necessarily equal) may or may not be a square (all sides equal). Hence, Statement (1) alone is not sufficient to answer the question.

From Statement (2) alone, we have that $AB = BC = CD = DA$. All the sides in a quadrilateral are equal when the quadrilateral is a rhombus. Since a rhombus (only opposite angles necessarily equal) may or may not be a square (all angles equal), Statement (2) alone is not sufficient to answer the question.

Now, from the statements together, we have that in the quadrilateral all the angles are equal and all the sides are equal. This is possible only in a square. Hence, both statements are required to answer the question. The answer is (C).

GMAT Math Tests

9. Adding the two equations $2x + 3y = 11$ and $3x + 2y = 9$ yields $5x + 5y = 20$, or $x + y = 20/5 = 4$. The answer is (A).

10. From Statement (1) alone, we have that the ratio of the sum of the reciprocals of x and y to the product of the reciprocals of x and y is 1 : 3. Writing this as an equation yields

$$\frac{\frac{1}{x} + \frac{1}{y}}{\frac{1}{x} \cdot \frac{1}{y}} = \frac{1}{3}$$

$$\frac{\frac{x+y}{xy}}{\frac{1}{xy}} = \frac{1}{3}$$

$$\frac{x+y}{xy} \cdot \frac{xy}{1} = \frac{1}{3}$$

$$x + y = \frac{1}{3} \qquad \text{by canceling } xy \text{ from the numerator and denominator}$$

Hence, Statement (1) alone is sufficient.

From Statement (2) alone, we have that the product of x and y is 11/36 units greater than the sum of x and y. Writing this as an equation yields

$$xy - (x + y) = 11/36$$
$$x + y = xy - 11/36 \qquad \text{by solving for } x + y$$

Since we do not know the value of xy, we cannot determine the value of $x + y$. Hence, Statement (2) alone is not sufficient.

The answer is (A).

11. $y^3 = -8$ yields one cube root, $y = -2$. However, $x^2 = 4$ yields two square roots, $x = \pm 2$. Now, if $x = 2$, then $x > y$; but if $x = -2$, then $x = y$. Hence, $x > y$ is not necessarily true. The answer is (E).

12. The perimeter of a rectangle is twice the sum of its length and width. Hence, if l and w are length and width, respectively, of the given rectangle, then the perimeter of the rectangle is $2(l + w)$. Also, the average side length of the rectangle is 1/4 times the sum. So, the average side length is $2(l + w)/4 = l/2 + w/2$.

Now, we are given that the average equals twice the width. Hence, we have $l/2 + w/2 = 2w$. Multiplying the equation by 2 yields $l + w = 4w$ and solving for l yields $l = 3w$.

Now, the area of the rectangle equals *length* × *width* = $l \times w = 18$ (given). Plugging $3w$ for l in the equation yields $3w \times w = 18$. Dividing the equation by 3 yields $w^2 = 6$, and square rooting both sides yields $w = \sqrt{6}$. Finally, the perimeter equals $2(l + w) = 2(3w + w) = 8w = 8\sqrt{6}$. The answer is (B).

Test 9—Answers and Solutions

13. Let the number of girls be x. Since the ratio of the girls to boys is 3 : 4, the number of boys equals $(4/3)x$. Hence, the number of students in the class equals $x + 4x/3 = 7x/3$. We are given that 10% of girls are blue eyed, and 10% of x is $10/100 \cdot x = x/10$. Also, 20% of the boys are blue eyed, and 20% of $4x/3$ is $(20/100)(4x/3) = 4x/15$.

Hence, the total number of blue-eyed students is $x/10 + 4x/15 = 11x/30$.

Hence, the required fraction is $\dfrac{\frac{11x}{30}}{\frac{7x}{3}} = \dfrac{11 \cdot 3}{30 \cdot 7} = \dfrac{11}{70}$. The answer is (A).

---

14. In the figure, points $A(0, 2)$ and $D(0, 0)$ have the same x-coordinate (which is 0). Hence, the two points must be on the same vertical line in the coordinate system.

Similarly, the x-coordinates of the points B and C are the same (both equal a). Hence, the points are on the same vertical line in the coordinate system.

Since any two vertical lines are parallel, lines AD and BC are parallel (for any value of a).

Now, if $ABCD$ is a parallelogram, then the opposite sides must also be equal. Hence, AD must equal BC.

Since AD and BC are vertical lines, AD equals the y-coordinate difference of points A and $D = 2 - 0 = 2$, and BC equals the y-coordinate difference of points B and $C = b - 2$. Now, AD equals BC when $b - 2 = 2$, or $b = 4$. This is when $ABCD$ is a parallelogram and in any other case (when $b \ne 4$), it is not a parallelogram. So, we need the value of b [value given in Statement (2)] alone and the value of a is unimportant here. So, Statement (1) is not needed. Since $b = 5$ in Statement (2) (which shows that $b \ne 4$ and therefore $ABCD$ is not parallelogram), the statement is sufficient. Hence, the answer is (B).

---

15. From Statement (1) alone, we have the inequality $x < 2$. So, $x - 2$ is negative. So,

$x - 3 = x - 2 - 1 =$ a Negative Number $- 1 =$ a Negative Number

So, $(x - 2)(x - 3) =$ a Negative Number $\times$ a Negative Number $=$ a Positive Number. Hence, Statement (1) alone is sufficient.

From Statement (2) alone, we have the inequality $x < 3$.

Now, suppose $x = 2.5$. Then $x - 2 = 2.5 - 2 = 0.5$ and $x - 3$ equals $2.5 - 3 = -0.5$. Hence, $(x - 2)(x - 3) = (0.5)(-0.5) = -0.25$. So, $(x - 2)(x - 3)$ is negative.

Now, suppose $x = 1$. Then $x - 2 = 1 - 2 = -1$, and $x - 3 = 1 - 3 = -2$. Hence, $(x - 2)(x - 3) = (-1)(-2) = 2$. So, $(x - 2)(x - 3)$ is positive.

Hence, we have a double case, and Statement (2) alone is *not* sufficient.

The answer is (A), Statement (1) alone sufficient and Statement (2) alone *not* sufficient.

16. Since none of the answers are fractions, let's rationalize the given fraction by multiplying top and bottom by the conjugate of the bottom of the fraction:

$$p = \frac{\sqrt{3}-2}{\sqrt{2}+1} \cdot \frac{\sqrt{2}-1}{\sqrt{2}-1} \qquad \text{the conjugate of } \sqrt{2}+1 \text{ is } \sqrt{2}-1$$

$$= \frac{\sqrt{3}\sqrt{2} + \sqrt{3}(-1) + (-2)\sqrt{2} + (-2)(-1)}{\left(\sqrt{2}\right)^2 - 1^2}$$

$$= \frac{\sqrt{6} - \sqrt{3} - 2\sqrt{2} + 2}{2 - 1}$$

$$= \sqrt{6} - \sqrt{3} - 2\sqrt{2} + 2$$

Now, $p - 4 = \left(\sqrt{6} - \sqrt{3} - 2\sqrt{2} + 2\right) - 4 = \sqrt{6} - \sqrt{3} - 2\sqrt{2} - 2$. The answer is (D).

---

17. $\dfrac{x^2 + x + 2}{x} =$

$\dfrac{x^2}{x} + \dfrac{x}{x} + \dfrac{2}{x} =$

$x + 1 + \dfrac{2}{x}$

Now, substituting $1/y$ for x yields

$$\frac{1}{y} + 1 + \frac{2}{1/y} =$$

$$\frac{1}{y} + 1 + 2y =$$

$$\frac{1 + y + 2y^2}{y}$$

The answer is (C).

---

18. 4% of a is $4a/100$. Since this equals 8, we have $4a/100 = 8$. Solving for a yields $a = 8 \cdot \dfrac{100}{4} = 200$.

Also, 8% of b equals $8b/100$, and this equals 4. Hence, we have $\dfrac{8b}{100} = 4$. Solving for b yields $b = 50$. Now,

$$c = b/a = 50/200 = 1/4$$

The answer is (B).

19. From Statement (1) alone, we have that the product of the three numbers a, b, and c is a multiple of 27. The number 162 (= 27 · 6) is divisible by 81, while the number 54 (= 27 · 2) is not divisible by 81. Since we have a double case, Statement (1) alone is not sufficient.

From Statement (2) alone, we have that none of the three numbers a, b, and c is divisible by 9. Now, even assuming that the three numbers a, b, and c are divisible by at least 3, though not 9, the three numbers can be represented as $3p$, $3q$, and $3r$, where none of the three supposed positive integers p, q, and r is divisible by 3. Then the product of the three numbers equals $3p \cdot 3q \cdot 3r = 27(pqr)$. None of the three numbers p, q, and r is divisible by 3. Hence, pqr is not divisible by 3. So, $27(pqr)$ is not divisible by 27 · 3, which equals 81. So, the product of abc is not divisible by 81. Hence, Statement (2) alone is sufficient to answer the question.

Hence, the answer is (B), and the answer to the question is "No. abc is not divisible by 81."

20. Any number divisible by both m and n must be a multiple of the least common multiple of the two numbers, which is given to be 24. The first multiple of 24 greater than 3070 is 3072. Hence, the answer is (A).

21. Since 6 mangoes are returnable for 9 oranges, if each mango costs m and each orange costs n, then $6m = 9n$, or $2m = 3n$. Solving for n yields, $n = 2m/3$. Now, since 50 mangoes and 30 oranges together cost 42 dollars,

$$50m + 30n = 42$$
$$50m + 30(2m/3) = 42$$
$$m(50 + 30 \cdot 2/3) = 42$$
$$m(50 + 20) = 42$$
$$70m = 42$$
$$m = 42/70 = 6/10 = 0.6$$

The answer is (E).

22. Any number divisible by both 7 and 10 is a common multiple of 7 and 10. The least common multiple of 7 and 10 is 70. There are 14 numbers, (70, 140, 210, ..., 980), divisible by 70 from 1 through 1000, and there are 1000 numbers from 1 through 1000. Hence, the required fraction is 14/1000 = 7/500. The answer is (C).

23. From the projected-crime graph, we see that the criminal population will be 20 million and of these 30 percent are projected to be involved in white-collar crime. Hence, the number of white-collar criminals is

(30%)(20 million) = (.30)(20 million) = 6 million

The answer is (C).

GMAT Math Tests

24. In 1990, there were 10 million criminals and 20% were robbers. Thus, the number of robbers in 1990 was

$$(20\%)(10 \text{ million}) = (.20)(10 \text{ million}) = 2 \text{ million}$$

In 2000, there are projected to be 20 million criminals of which 25% are projected to be robbers. Thus, the number of robbers in 2000 is projected to be

$$(25\%)(20 \text{ million}) = (.25)(20 \text{ million}) = 5 \text{ million}$$

Forming the ratio of the above numbers yields

$$\frac{\text{number of robbers in } 1990}{\text{number of robbers in } 2000} = \frac{2}{5}$$

The answer is (A).

---

25. The following table lists the number of criminals by category for 1990 and 2000 and the projected increase or decrease:

Category	Number in 1990 (millions)	Number in 2000 (millions)	Projected increase (millions)	Projected decrease (millions)
Vice	1.7	3	1.3	None
Assault	2	4	2	None
White Collar	3.8	6	2.2	None

As the table displays, there is a projected increase (not decrease) in all three categories. Hence, the answer is (A).

---

26. Remember, to calculate the percentage increase, find the absolute increase and divide it by the original number. Now, in 1990, the number of criminals in vice was 1.7 million, and in 2000 it is projected to be 3 million. The absolute increase is thus:

$$3 - 1.7 = 1.3$$

Hence the projected percent increase in the number of criminals in vice is

$$\frac{\text{absolute increase}}{\text{original number}} = \frac{1.3}{1.7} \approx 75\%.$$

The answer is (D).

---

27. The even numbers between 0 and 20, inclusive, are 0, 2, 4, 6, ..., 20. Their sum is

$$0 + 2 + 4 + 6 + \ldots + 20 =$$
$$2 \times 1 + 2 \times 2 + 2 \times 3 + \ldots + 2 \times 10 =$$
$$2 \times (1 + 2 + 3 + \ldots + 10) =$$
$$2 \times \frac{10(10+1)}{2} = 10 \times 11 = 110 \qquad \text{by the formula (sum of } n \text{ terms)} = \frac{n(n+1)}{2}$$

The answer is (D).

Test 9—Answers and Solutions

28. Substituting $p = q$ and $r = s$ from Statement (2) in Statement (1) yields

$$\frac{q+q}{s+s} = 1$$
$$\frac{2q}{2s} = 1$$
$$q = s$$

Combining this equation with the known equations $p = q$ and $r = s$ yields $p = q = s = r$. Clearly, p, q, r and s are equal, but we do not know what they are equal to. Hence, we cannot evaluate the required expression. Suppose they all equal 1. Then

$$p + q + r + s = 1 + 1 + 1 + 1 = 4$$

Now, suppose all equal 2, then

$$p + q + r + s = 2 + 2 + 2 + 2 = 8$$

The statements together are *not* sufficient. The answer is (E).

29. By square rooting the equation $(x - 50)^2 = (y - 50)^2$ in Statement (2), we have two possible solutions $x - 50 = y - 50$ and $x - 50 = -(y - 50)$. Canceling -50 from both sides of first solution yields $x = y$, and adding $y + 50$ to both sides of second solution yields $x + y = 100$ (This is given in Statement (1)). Now, freezing at the common solution of the two statements, we have $x + y = 100$. Now, suppose $x = 5$ and $y = 95$. Then $x + y = 100$, but $x \neq y$. Now, suppose $x = 50$ and $y = 50$. Then $x = y$. Hence, we have a double case, and the statements together are not sufficient. The answer is (E).

30. Choice A: The point A represents $x = 1$. Now, $f(1) = (1 - 1.5)(1 - 2.5)(1 - 3.5)(1 - 4.5) = (-0.5)(-1.5)(-2.5)(-3.5)$ = product of four (an even number of) negative numbers. The result is positive. Reject.

Choice B: The point B represents $x = 2$. Now, $f(2) = (2 - 1.5)(2 - 2.5)(2 - 3.5)(2 - 4.5) = (0.5)(-0.5)(-1.5)(-2.5)$ = product of a positive number and three (an odd number of) negative numbers. The result is negative. Hence, correct.

Choice C: The point C represents $x = 3$. Now, $f(3) = (3 - 1.5)(3 - 2.5)(3 - 3.5)(3 - 4.5) = (1.5)(0.5)(-0.5)(-1.5)$ = Product of two positive numbers and two (an even number of) negative numbers. The result is positive. Reject.

Choice D: The point D represents $x = 4.5$. Now, $f(4.5) = (4.5 - 1.5)(4.5 - 2.5)(4.5 - 3.5)(4.5 - 4.5) = 3 \times 2 \times 1 \times 0 = 0$, not a negative number. Reject.

Choice E: The point E represents $x = 5.5$. Now, $f(5.5) = (5.5 - 1.5)(5.5 - 2.5)(5.5 - 3.5)(5.5 - 4.5) = 4 \times 3 \times 2 \times 1$ = product of positive numbers. The result is positive. Reject.

The answer is (B).

31. Locating the points (–1, 1) and (1, –1) on the *xy*-plane gives

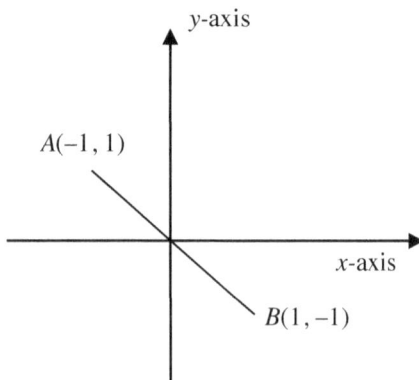

The midpoint of two points is given by

(Half the sum of the *x*-coordinates of the two points, Half the sum of the *y*-coordinates of the two points)

Hence, the midpoint of *A* and *B* is $\left(\dfrac{-1+1}{2}, \dfrac{1-1}{2}\right) = (0, 0)$.

Hence, the line-segment passes through the origin. The answer is (D).

---

32. The statements are entirely in Canadian dollars, while the question setup expects the answer in US dollars. Even with the two statements together, we are not told whether the exchange rate changed this year from last year. Hence, we cannot answer the question. The answer is (E).

---

33. The given system of equations is

$$x + l = 6$$
$$x - m = 5$$
$$x + p = 4$$
$$x - q = 3$$

Subtracting the second equation from the first one yields

$$(x + l) - (x - m) = 6 - 5$$
$$l + m = 1 \qquad \ldots (1)$$

Subtracting the fourth equation from the third one yields

$$(x + p) - (x - q) = 4 - 3$$
$$p + q = 1 \qquad \ldots (2)$$

Adding equations (1) and (2) yields

$$(l + m) + (p + q) = 1 + 1 = 2.$$
$$l + m + p + q = 2$$

The answer is (A).

Test 9—Answers and Solutions

34. From Statement (1) alone, we have

$$(x+y)\left(\frac{1}{x}+\frac{1}{y}\right) = 4$$

$$(x+y)\left(\frac{x+y}{xy}\right) = 4$$

$$(x+y)^2 = 4xy$$

$$x^2 + y^2 + 2xy = 4xy \quad \text{by the formula } (a+b)^2 = a^2 + b^2 + 2ab$$

$$x^2 + y^2 - 2xy = 0$$

$$(x-y)^2 = 0 \quad \text{by the formula } a^2 + b^2 - 2ab = (a-b)^2$$

$$x - y = 0 \quad \text{by taking the square root of both sides}$$

$$x = y$$

Hence, Statement (1) alone is sufficient. The answer to the question is "Yes, $x = y$."

---

35. Replacing n with 3 in the formula $a_n = (a_{n-1} - 1)^2$ yields

$$a_3 = (a_{3-1} - 1)^2 = (a_2 - 1)^2$$

We are given that $a_3 = 64$. Putting this in the formula $a_3 = (a_2 - 1)^2$ yields

$$64 = (a_2 - 1)^2$$

$$a_2 - 1 = \pm 8$$

$$a_2 = -7 \text{ or } 9$$

Since, we know that a_2 is the result of the square of number [$a_2 = (a_1 - 1)^2$], it cannot be negative. Hence, pick the positive value 9 for a_2. The answer is (E).

---

36. Hose A takes 5 minutes to fill one tank. To fill 6 tanks, it takes $6 \cdot 5 = 30$ minutes. Hose B takes 6 minutes to fill one tank. Hence, in the 30 minutes, it would fill $30/6 = 5$ tanks. The answer is (C).

37. Solving the equation $\dfrac{x+y}{x-y} = \dfrac{4}{3}$ for x by multiplying both sides by $3(x-y)$ yields

$$3(x+y) = 4(x-y)$$

$$3x + 3y = 4x - 4y$$

$$7y = x$$

Plugging this into the expression $\dfrac{x-3y}{x+3y}$ yields

$$\dfrac{7y-3y}{7y+3y} =$$

$$\dfrac{4y}{10y} =$$

$$\dfrac{4}{10} =$$

$$\dfrac{4}{10} \cdot \dfrac{10}{10} =$$

$$\dfrac{40}{100} =$$

$$40\%$$

The answer is (E).

Test 10

Questions: 37
Time: 75 minutes

1. What is the probability that the product of two integers (not necessarily different integers) randomly selected from the numbers 1 through 20, inclusive, is odd?

(A) 0
(B) 1/4
(C) 1/2
(D) 2/3
(E) 3/4

USE THIS SPACE FOR SCRATCHWORK.

2. If $a + 3a$ is 4 less than $b + 3b$, then $a - b =$

(A) –4
(B) –1
(C) 1/5
(D) 1/3
(E) 2

USE THIS SPACE FOR SCRATCHWORK.

3. What is the average of x, $2x$, and 6?

(A) $x/2$
(B) $2x$
(C) $\frac{x+2}{6}$
(D) $x + 2$
(E) $\frac{x+2}{3}$

USE THIS SPACE FOR SCRATCHWORK.

[Data Sufficiency Question]
4. Steve deposited $100 to open a savings account. If there are no other transactions in the account, what amount of money would the account accrue in 6 months after opening the account?

   (1) The interest rate is 4%.
   (2) Interest is compounded quarterly.

5. If $(a - b)(a + b) = 7 \times 13$, then which one of the following pairs could be the values of a and b, respectively?

   (A) 7, 13
   (B) 5, 15
   (C) 3, 10
   (D) −10, 3
   (E) −3, −10

6. For any positive integer n, $n!$ denotes the product of all the integers from 1 through n. What is the value of $3!(7 - 2)!$?

   (A) 2!
   (B) 3!
   (C) 5!
   (D) 6!
   (E) 10!

[Data Sufficiency Question]
7. Does the Set A contain only odd prime numbers?

   (1) A contains only odd numbers.
   (2) A contains only prime numbers.

[Data Sufficiency Question]
8. What is the probability that a person selected randomly from a group of people is a woman in pink attire?

   (1) Of the women in the group, 4% are wearing pink attire.
   (2) Of the people in the group, 40% are women.

9. x is a two-digit number. The digits of the number differ by 6, and the squares of the digits differ by 60. Which one of the following could x equal?

   (A) 17
   (B) 28
   (C) 39
   (D) 71
   (E) 93

[Data Sufficiency Question]
10. If p and q are both positive integers, then is p divisible by 9?

   (1) $p/10 + q/10$ is an integer.
   (2) $p/9 + q/10$ is an integer.

[Data Sufficiency Question]
11. A function is expressed as $f(x) = mx + c$. Does $f(p) - f(q)$ equal $p - q$?

   (1) $m = 1$
   (2) $c = 1$

12. A set has exactly five consecutive positive integers starting with 1. Which one of the following is the closest percentage decrease in the average of the numbers when the greatest one of the numbers is removed from the set?

   (A) 5
   (B) 8.5
   (C) 12.5
   (D) 15.2
   (E) 16.66

GMAT Math Tests

13. In the figure, what is the value of *a* ?

    (A) 30
    (B) 45
    (C) 60
    (D) 72
    (E) 90

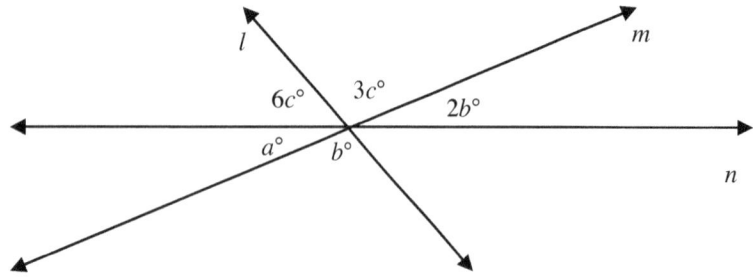

[Data Sufficiency Question]
14. In the figure, *ABCD* is a square, and *OB* is a radius of the circle. Is *BC* a tangent to the circle?

    (1) $PC = 2$
    (2) Area of the square is 16.

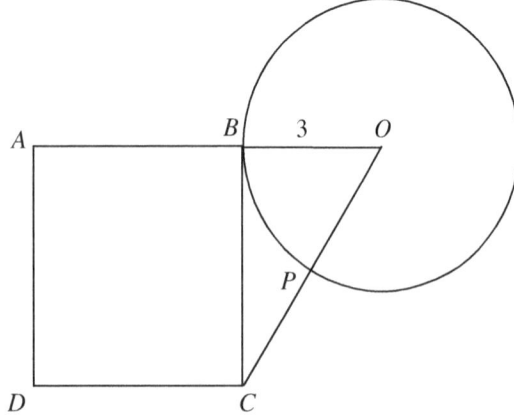

[Data Sufficiency Question]
15. Is the integer k a prime number?

   (1) $k + 1$ is prime.
   (2) $k + 2$ is not prime.

16. In quadrilateral $ABCD$, $\angle A$ measures 20 degrees more than the average of the other three angles of the quadrilateral. Then $\angle A =$

   (A) $70°$
   (B) $85°$
   (C) $95°$
   (D) $105°$
   (E) $110°$

17. The five numbers 1056, 1095, 1098, 1100, and 1126 are represented on a number line by the points A, B, C, D, and E, respectively, as shown in the figure. Which one of the following points represents the average of the five numbers?

   (A)   Point A
   (B)   Point B
   (C)   Point C
   (D)   Point D
   (E)   Point E

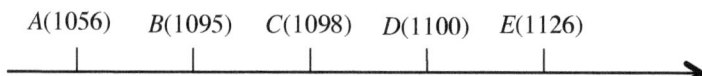

GMAT Math Tests

18. Set S is the set of all numbers from 1 through 100, inclusive. What is the probability that a number randomly selected from the set is divisible by 3?

   (A) 1/9
   (B) 33/100
   (C) 34/100
   (D) 1/3
   (E) 66/100

[Data Sufficiency Question]
19. What is the height of a rectangular tank?

   (1) The area of the base of the tank is 100 sq. ft.
   (2) It takes 20 seconds to fill up the tank with water poured at the rate of 25 cubic feet per second.

20. In the figure, lines l and m are parallel. Which one of the following, if true, makes lines p and q parallel?

   (A) $a = b$
   (B) $a = c$
   (C) $c = d$
   (D) $d = b$
   (E) $b = c$

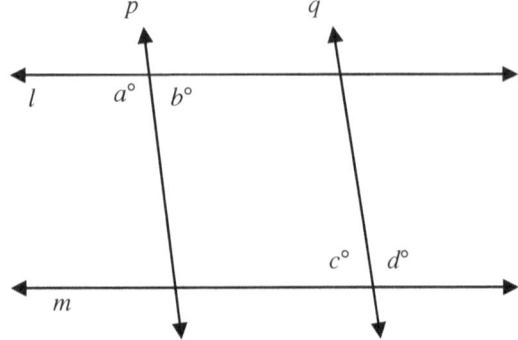

21. If $x = a$, $y = 2b$, $z = 3c$, and $x : y : z = 1 : 2 : 3$, then $\dfrac{x+y+z}{a+b+c} =$

(A) 1/3
(B) 1/2
(C) 2
(D) 3
(E) 6

22. $\dfrac{4\left(\sqrt{6}+\sqrt{2}\right)}{\sqrt{6}-\sqrt{2}} - \dfrac{2+\sqrt{3}}{2-\sqrt{3}} =$

(A) 1
(B) $\sqrt{6}-\sqrt{2}$
(C) $\sqrt{6}+\sqrt{2}$
(D) 8
(E) 12

USE THIS SPACE FOR SCRATCHWORK.

Questions 23–27 refer to the following graph.

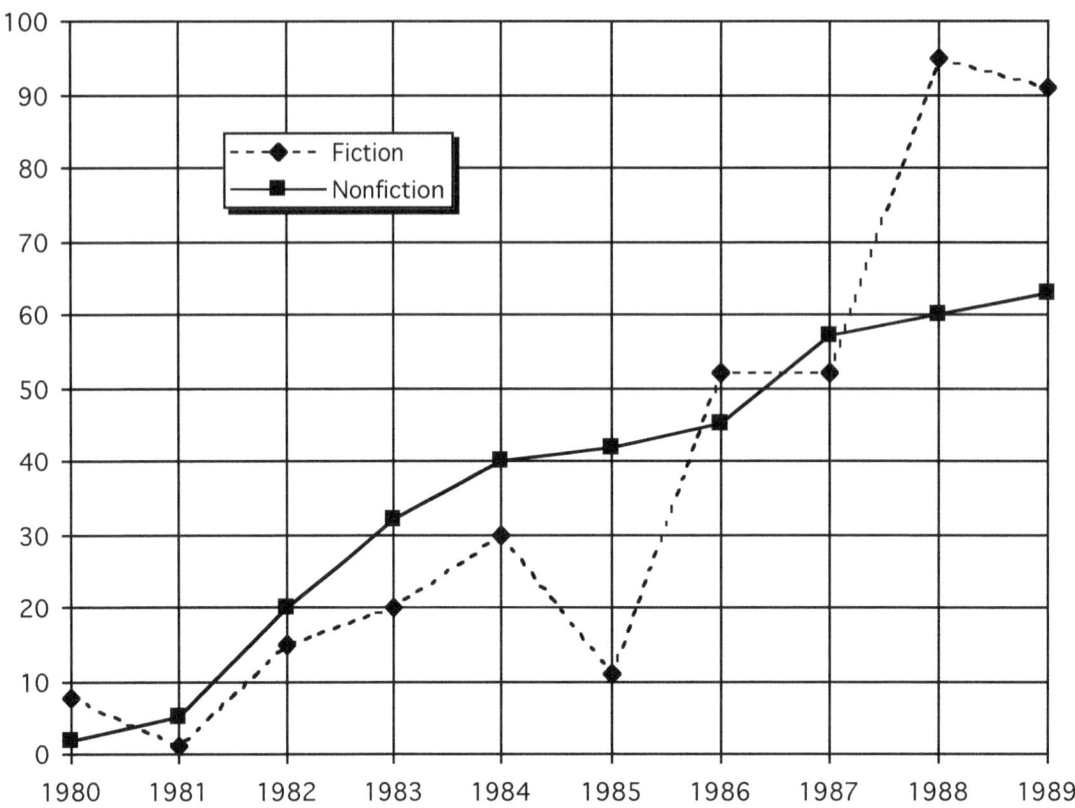

23. In how many years did the sales of nonfiction titles exceed the sales of fiction titles ?

(A) 2
(B) 3
(C) 4
(D) 5
(E) 6

24. Which of the following best approximates the amount by which the increase in sales of fiction titles from 1985 to 1986 exceeded the increase in sales of fiction titles from 1983 to 1984?

   (A) 31.5 thousand
   (B) 40 thousand
   (C) 49.3 thousand
   (D) 50.9 thousand
   (E) 68 thousand

25. Which of the following periods showed a continual increase in the sales of fiction titles?

   (A) 1980–1982
   (B) 1982–1984
   (C) 1984–1986
   (D) 1986–1988
   (E) 1987–1989

26. What was the approximate average number of sales of fiction titles from 1984 to 1988?

   (A) 15 thousand
   (B) 30 thousand
   (C) 40 thousand
   (D) 48 thousand
   (E) 60 thousand

27. By approximately what percent did the sale of nonfiction titles increase from 1984 to 1987?

    (A) 42%
    (B) 50%
    (C) 70%
    (D) 90%
    (E) 110%

[Data Sufficiency Question]

28. The operator $a*$ is defined on a number a as equal to $(-1)^m \cdot a$, where m is an integer. If a is not equal to zero, what is $(a*)* - a$?

    (1) $a* + a = 0$
    (2) $a* \cdot a + a^2 = 0$

Data Sufficiency Question]
29. In the figure, is the line AB perpendicular to the line CD?

   (1) $x + y = 180$
   (2)   AOC is an isosceles triangle

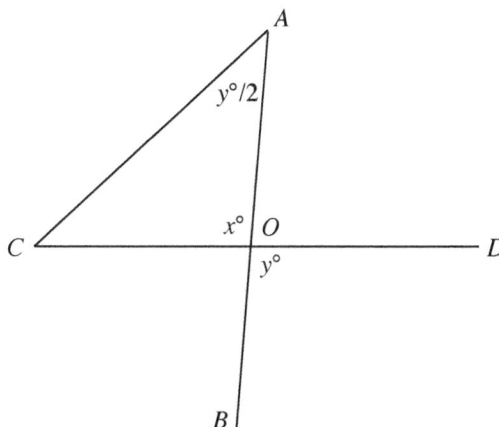

The dimensions in the figure may be different from what they appear to be.

[Data Sufficiency Question]
30. What is the remainder when m is divided by 3?

   (1)   The remainder when m is divided by 6 is 2.
   (2)   The remainder when m is divided by 12 is 2.

31. In what proportion must rice at $0.8 per pound be mixed with rice at $0.9 per pound so that the mixture costs $0.825 per pound?

    (A)   1 : 3
    (B)   1 : 2
    (C)   1 : 1
    (D)   2 : 1
    (E)   3 : 1

[Data Sufficiency Question]
32. Is p greater than 0.3 ?

    (1) $p \geq 3/10$
    (2) $3 - 2p < 2.4$

33. In a box of 5 eggs, 2 are rotten. What is the probability that two eggs chosen at random from the box are rotten?

    (A)   1/16
    (B)   1/10
    (C)   1/5
    (D)   2/5
    (E)   3/5

[Data Sufficiency Question]
34. A regular hexagon is inscribed in a circle. What is the area of the hexagon?

    (1)   The radius of the circle is 10.

    (2)   The perimeter of the hexagon is $40\sqrt{3}$.

35. If $x/a = 4$, $a/y = 6$, $a^2 = 9$, and $ab^2 = -8$, then $x + 2y =$

    (A)   −2
    (B)   −5
    (C)   −10
    (D)   −13
    (E)   −15

[Data Sufficiency Question]
36. If $2x + 3 = y + 1/y$, then $x + y =$

    (1) $x = -1/4$
    (2) $y = 2$

37. From the figure, which of the following must be true?

    (I) $x + y = 90$
    (II) x is 35 units greater than y
    (III) x is 35 units less than y

    (A) I only
    (B) II only
    (C) III only
    (D) I and II only
    (E) I and III only

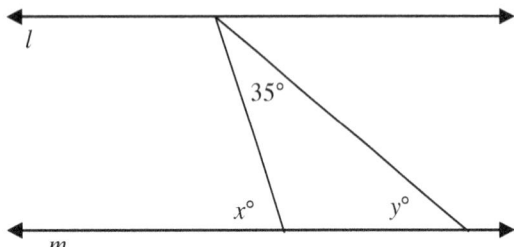

Test 10—Answers and Solutions

Answers and Solutions Test 10:

1. B	11. A	21. C	31. E
2. B	12. E	22. A	32. B
3. D	13. D	23. E	33. B
4. C	14. C	24. A	34. D
5. D	15. E	25. B	35. D
6. D	16. D	26. D	36. B
7. C	17. B	27. A	37. B
8. C	18. B	28. D	
9. B	19. C	29. A	
10. B	20. E	30. D	

---

1. The product of two integers is odd when both integers are themselves odd. Hence, the probability of the product being odd equals the probability of both numbers being odd. Since there is one odd number in every two numbers (there are 10 odd numbers in the 20 numbers 1 through 20, inclusive), the probability of a number being odd is 1/2. The probability of both numbers being odd (independent case) is

$$1/2 \times 1/2 = 1/4$$

The answer is (B).

---

2. Translating the sentence into an equation gives $a + 3a = b + 3b - 4$
Combining like terms gives $4a = 4b - 4$
Subtracting $4b$ from both sides gives $4a - 4b = -4$
Finally, dividing by 4 gives $a - b = -1$

Hence, the answer is (B).

---

3. The average of N numbers is their sum divided by N, that is,

$$average = \frac{sum}{N}$$

By the definition of an average, we get

$$\frac{x + 2x + 6}{3} = \frac{3x + 6}{3} = \frac{3(x + 2)}{3} = x + 2$$

Hence, the answer is (D).

---

4. Compound interest is the concept of adding accumulated interest to the principal so that interest is earned on the new principal from that moment onward. The act of declaring interest to be principal is called compounding (i.e., interest is compounded).

To calculate the interest earned or the balance at any point, apart from the interest earned, we also need the frequency of compounding of the interest. Hence, both statements are required to answer the question. The answer is (C).

5. Substitute the values for *a* and *b* shown in the answer-choices into the expression $(a - b)(a + b)$:

   Choice (A): $(7 - 13)(7 + 13) = -6 \times 20$

   Choice (B): $(5 - 15)(5 + 15) = -10 \times 20$

   Choice (C): $(3 - 10)(3 + 10) = -7 \times 13$

   Choice (D): $(-10 - 3)(-10 + 3) = -13 \times (-7) = 7 \times 13$

   Choice (E): $(-3 - (-10))(-3 + (-10)) = 7 \times (-13)$

Since only choice (D) equals the product 7×13, the answer is (D).

---

6. $3!(7 - 2)! = 3! \cdot 5!$

As defined, $3! = 3 \cdot 2 \cdot 1 = 6$ and $5! = 5 \cdot 4 \cdot 3 \cdot 2 \cdot 1$.

Hence, $3!(7 - 2)! = 3! \cdot 5! = 6(5 \cdot 4 \cdot 3 \cdot 2 \cdot 1) = 6 \cdot 5 \cdot 4 \cdot 3 \cdot 2 \cdot 1 = 6!$, as defined.

The answer is (D).

---

7. Statement (1) says that *A* contains only odd numbers, which does not mean it contains all the odd numbers.

Statement (2) says that *A* contains only prime numbers, which does not mean it contains all the prime numbers.

Thus, both statements are under-determined in the sense that they do not fully define (list the elements in) *A*.

The question is adequately defined in the sense that it asks us to check whether all the elements (one by one) are odd and prime. This requirement is clearly defined.

The difference is that the statements are about listing while the question is about checking requirements. That's why the question is adequately defined and the statements are under-defined.

Now, joining the statements, we get *A* is a set of odd prime numbers only. The answer is "Yes." The answer is (C).

Test 10—Answers and Solutions

8. In the question setup, the condition to the left of "is" is "a person selected randomly from a group of people."

So, the required ratio is

The number of women in pink/The number of people in the group =
(The number of women in pink/The number of women in the group) ×
(The number of women in the group/The number of people in the group)

The first fraction is 4% [from Statement (1)], and the second fraction is 40% [from Statement (2)]. So, the probability equals

$$4\% \times 40\% = 4/100 \times 40/100 = 160/10{,}000 = 16/1{,}000 = 2/125$$

Hence, both statements are required, and the answer is (C).

---

9. Since the digits differ by 6, let a and $a + 6$ be the digits. The difference of their squares, which is $(a + 6)^2 - a^2$, equals 60 (given). Hence, we have

$$(a + 6)^2 - a^2 = 60$$
$$a^2 + 12a + 36 - a^2 = 60$$
$$12a + 36 = 60$$
$$12a = 24$$
$$a = 2$$

The other digit is $a + 6 = 2 + 6 = 8$. Hence, 28 and 82 are the two possible answers. The answer is (B).

---

10. From Statement (1) alone, we have that $p/10 + q/10$ is an integer. Suppose $p = 20$ and $q = 10$. Then $p/10 + q/10 = 20/10 + 10/10 = 2 + 1 = 3$, an integer. Here, p is not divisible by 9.

Now, suppose $p = 90$ and $q = 10$. Then $p/10 + q/10 = 90/10 + 10/10 = 9 + 1 = 10$, an integer. Here, p is divisible by 9.

Hence, we have a double case, and Statement (1) alone is not sufficient.

If p is not divisible by 9 and q is not divisible by 10, then $p/9$ results in a non-terminating decimal and $q/10$ results in a terminating decimal and the sum of the two would not result in an integer. [Because (a terminating decimal) + (a non-terminating decimal) is always a non-terminating decimal, and a non-terminating decimal is not an integer.]

Since we are given that the expression is an integer, p must be divisible by 9. Hence, Statement (2) alone is sufficient.

For example, if $p = 1$ and $q = 10$, the expression equals $1/9 + 10/10 = 1.11...$, not an integer.

If $p = 9$ and $q = 5$, the expression equals $9/9 + 5/10 = 1.5$, not an integer.

If $p = 9$ and $q = 10$, the expression equals $9/9 + 10/10 = 2$, an integer.

The answer is (B).

11. From the rule, $f(p) = mp + c$ and $f(q) = mq + c$. Their difference is

$$f(p) - f(q) = (mp + c) - (mq + c)$$
$$= mp - mq$$
$$= m(p - q)$$
$$= 1(p - q) \quad \text{from Statement (1), } m = 1$$
$$= p - q$$

Hence, Statement (1) alone is sufficient.

The parameter m is independent of the parameter c. So, knowing c does not determine m. Regardless of the value of c, if m equals 1, the objective $f(p) - f(q) = p - q$ is achieved. Hence, Statement (2) is not needed. So, Statement (2) is not sufficient.

The answer is (A).

---

12. The average of the five consecutive positive integers 1, 2, 3, 4, and 5 is $(1 + 2 + 3 + 4 + 5)/5 = 15/5 = 3$. After dropping 5 (the greatest number), the new average becomes $(1 + 2 + 3 + 4)/4 = 10/4 = 2.5$. The percentage drop in the average is

$$\frac{\text{Old average} - \text{New average}}{\text{Old average}} \cdot 100 =$$

$$\frac{3 - 2.5}{3} \cdot 100 =$$

$$\frac{100}{6} =$$

$$16.66\%$$

The answer is (E).

---

13. Equating vertical angles in the figure yields $a = 2b$ and $b = 3c$. From the first equation, we have $b = a/2$. Plugging this into the second equation yields $a/2 = 3c$, from which we can derive $c = a/6$. Since the angle made by a line is 180°, we have for line l that $b + a + 6c = 180$. Replacing b with $a/2$ and c with $a/6$ in this equation yields $a/2 + a + 6(a/6) = a/2 + a + a = 180$. Summing the left-hand side yields $5a/2 = 180$, and multiplying both sides by 2/5 yields $a = 180(2/5) = 72$. The answer is (D).

---

14. Since OB is a radius, B is a point on the circle. Now, BC is a tangent to the circle only if $\angle CBO$ is right angled. In this case, $\triangle CBO$ is right triangle, and by The Pythagorean Theorem $OC^2 = OB^2 + BC^2$. Hence, the question can be reduced to "Is $OC^2 = OB^2 + BC^2$?"

We know that $OB = 3$ (given in figure). Now, we need the other two sides OC and BC to answer the question.

From Statement (1), we have $PC = 2$, and we know $OP = radius = 3$. Hence, $OC = OP + PC = 3 + 2 = 5$. But, we still do not have the value of BC. Hence, Statement (1) is *not* sufficient.

From Statement (2), we have the area of the square is 16. By the formula, the area of a square $= side^2$, we have $BC^2 = 16$; and by square rooting, we have $BC = 4$. But, from this Statement alone, we cannot determine the value of OC. Hence, Statement (2) alone is *not* sufficient.

From the statements together, we have $OC = 5$, $BC = 4$, and we already have $OB = 3$. Now, we have all the details to determine whether OC^2 equals $OB^2 + BC^2$. Hence, both statements are required, and the answer is (C).

Test 10—Answers and Solutions

15. The properties we know are

> k is an integer.
> k is an unknown property. Hence, $k + 1$ and $k + 2$ are unknown properties as well.

What do we do? Substitute for unknown properties.

Suppose $k = 2$ (chosen such that $k + 1 = 3$ is prime and $k + 2 = 4$ is not prime). Now, both statements are satisfied, and here k is prime.

Suppose $k = 4$ (chosen such that $k + 1 = 5$ is prime and $k + 2 = 6$ is not prime). Now, both statements are satisfied as well, and here k is not prime.

Hence, we have a double case and therefore the statements together are *not* sufficient. The answer is (E).

---

16. Setting the angle sum of the quadrilateral to 360° yields $\angle A + \angle B + \angle C + \angle D = 360$. Subtracting $\angle A$ from both sides yields $\angle B + \angle C + \angle D = 360 - \angle A$. Forming the average of the three angles $\angle B$, $\angle C$, and $\angle D$ yields $(\angle B + \angle C + \angle D)/3$ and this equals $(360 - \angle A)/3$, since we know that $\angle B + \angle C + \angle D = 360 - \angle A$. Now, we are given that $\angle A$ measures 20 degrees more than the average of the other three angles. Hence, $\angle A = (360 - \angle A)/3 + 20$. Solving the equation for $\angle A$ yields $\angle A = 105$. The answer is (D).

---

17. The average of the five numbers 56, 95, 98, 100, and 126 is

$$\frac{56 + 95 + 98 + 100 + 126}{5} = \frac{475}{5} = 95$$

Hence, the average of the five numbers 1056 (= 1000 + 56), 1095 (= 1000 + 95), 1098 (= 1000 + 98), 1100 (= 1000 + 100), and 1126 (= 1000 + 126) must be 1000 + 95 = 1095. The point that represents the number on the number line is point B. Hence, the answer is (B).

---

18. The count of the numbers 1 through 100, inclusive, is 100.

Now, let $3n$ represent a number divisible by 3, where n is an integer.

Since we have the numbers from 1 through 100, we have $1 \leq 3n \leq 100$. Dividing the inequality by 3 yields $1/3 \leq n \leq 100/3$. The possible values of n are the integer values between $1/3$ (≈ 0.33) and $100/3$ (≈ 33.33). The possible numbers are 1 through 33, inclusive. The count of these numbers is 33.

Hence, the probability of randomly selecting a number divisible by 3 is 33/100. The answer is (B).

19. The formula for the volume of a rectangular tank is (*area of base*) × *height*. Hence, we have

   volume = (*area of base*) × *height*
   or
   height = *volume*/(*area of base*)

This equation shows that we need the area of the base and the volume of the tank to calculate its height. The area of the base is given in Statement (1), but Statement (1) alone does not yield the volume of the tank. So, we just need the volume of the tank to calculate the height (to answer the question). Now, from Statement (2), we are given that it takes 20 seconds to fill the tank at the rate of 25 cubic feet per second. Hence, the volume of the tank = rate × time = 25 cubic feet × 20 seconds = 500 cubic feet. Using this, the height can be calculated and therefore the question can be answered. Since statements (1) and (2) together are sufficient to answer the question, the answer is (C).

---

20. Superimposing parallel line *m* on line *l* yields a figure like this:

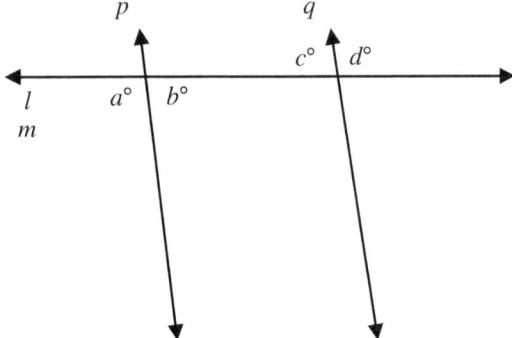

Now, when two lines (here *p* and *q*) cut by a transversal (here *l*) are parallel, we have

(I)   Corresponding angles are equal: No corresponding angles are listed in the figure.
(II) Alternate interior angles are equal: $b = c$. In choice (E).
(III) Alternate exterior angles are equal: $a = d$. Not listed in any answer-choice.
(IV) Interior angles are supplementary.
(V)   Exterior angles are supplementary.

The answer is (E).

---

21. We are given the equations $x = a$, $y = 2b$, $z = 3c$ and the proportion $x : y : z = 1 : 2 : 3$. Substituting the first three equations in the last equation (ratio equation) yields $a : 2b : 3c = 1 : 2 : 3$. Forming the resultant ratio yields $a/1 = 2b/2 = 3c/3$. Simplifying the equation yields $a = b = c$. Thus, we have that both *a* and *b* equal *c*. Hence, from the given equations, we have $x = a = c$, $y = 2b = 2c$, and $z = 3c$.

Now, $\dfrac{x+y+z}{a+b+c} =$

$\dfrac{c + 2c + 3c}{c + c + c} =$ because $x = a, y = 2c, z = 3c$, and $a = b = c$

$\dfrac{6c}{3c} =$

2

The answer is (C).

22. Let's rationalize the denominators of both fractions by multiplying top and bottom of each fraction by the conjugate of its denominator:

$$\frac{\sqrt{6}+\sqrt{2}}{\sqrt{6}-\sqrt{2}}$$

$$= \frac{\sqrt{6}+\sqrt{2}}{\sqrt{6}-\sqrt{2}} \cdot \frac{\sqrt{6}+\sqrt{2}}{\sqrt{6}+\sqrt{2}} \qquad \text{the conjugate is } \sqrt{6}+\sqrt{2}$$

$$= \frac{\left(\sqrt{6}+\sqrt{2}\right)^2}{\left(\sqrt{6}\right)^2 - \left(\sqrt{2}\right)^2} \qquad \text{by the formula } (a+b)(a-b) = a^2 - b^2$$

$$= \frac{\left(\sqrt{6}\right)^2 + \left(\sqrt{2}\right)^2 + 2\sqrt{6}\sqrt{2}}{6-2}$$

$$= \frac{6+2+4\sqrt{3}}{4}$$

$$= 2+\sqrt{3}$$

$$\frac{4\left(\sqrt{6}+\sqrt{2}\right)}{\sqrt{6}-\sqrt{2}} = 4\left(2+\sqrt{3}\right) = 8+4\sqrt{3}$$

$$\frac{2+\sqrt{3}}{2-\sqrt{3}}$$

$$= \frac{2+\sqrt{3}}{2-\sqrt{3}} \cdot \frac{2+\sqrt{3}}{2+\sqrt{3}} \qquad \text{the conjugate is } 2+\sqrt{3}$$

$$= \frac{4+3+4\sqrt{3}}{4-3}$$

$$= 7+4\sqrt{3}$$

Hence, $\frac{4\left(\sqrt{6}+\sqrt{2}\right)}{\sqrt{6}-\sqrt{2}} - \frac{2+\sqrt{3}}{2-\sqrt{3}} = \left(8+4\sqrt{3}\right) - \left(7+4\sqrt{3}\right) = 8+4\sqrt{3}-7-4\sqrt{3} = 1$. The answer is (A).

23. The graph shows that nonfiction sales exceeded fiction sales in '81, '82, '83, '84, '85, and '87. The answer is (E).

24. The graph shows that the increase in sales of fiction titles from 1985 to 1986 was approximately 40 thousand and the increase in sales of fiction titles from 1983 to 1984 was approximately 10 thousand. Hence, the difference is

$$40 - 10 = 30$$

Choice (A) is the only answer-choice close to 30 thousand.

25. According to the chart, sales of fiction increased from 15,000 to 20,000 to 30,000 between 1982 and 1984. The answer is (B).

26. The following chart summarizes the sales for the years 1984 to 1988:

Year	Sales
1984	30 thousand
1985	11 thousand
1986	52 thousand
1987	52 thousand
1988	95 thousand

Forming the average yields:

$$\frac{30 + 11 + 52 + 52 + 95}{5} = 48$$

The answer is (D).

Note, it is important to develop a feel for how the writers of the GMAT approximate when calculating. We used 52 thousand to calculate the sales of fiction in 1986, which is the actual number. But from the chart, it is difficult to tell whether the actual number is 51, 52, or 53 thousand. However, using any of the these numbers, the average would still be nearer to 40 than to any other answer-choice.

27. Recall that the percentage increase (decrease) is formed by dividing the absolute increase (decrease) by the original amount:

$$\frac{57 - 40}{40} = .425$$

The answer is (A).

28.
Statement (1): $a* + a = 0$.

Subtracting a from both sides of the equation $a* + a = 0$ yields

$$a* = -a$$

By definition $a* = (-1)^m \cdot a$. Hence,

$$(-1)^m \cdot a = -a$$

Dividing by a (which is not zero) yields

$$(-1)^m = -1$$

Plugging $(-1)^m = -1$ in the definition $a* = (-1)^m \cdot a$ yields $a* = (-1)^m \cdot a = -1 \cdot a = -a$.

Now, $(a*)* - a = (-a)* - a = -(-a) - a = a - a = 0$.

The statement is sufficient.

The answer is (D).

Statement (2): $a* \cdot a + a^2 = 0$.

Factoring a from the terms of the equation $a* \cdot a + a^2 = 0$ yields

$$a(a* + a) = 0$$

This happens when a is zero or $a* + a = 0$. Since a is given not equal to zero, $a* + a$ must equal 0. This is what Statement (1) directly says. Therefore, Statement (2) is sufficient just as Statement (1) is.

Test 10—Answers and Solutions

29. In the figure, x equals y (vertical angles are equal); and if AB is perpendicular to CD, then the angles x and y must each equal $90°$.

Now, from Statement (1) alone, we have

$$x + y = 180$$
$$x + x = 180 \quad \text{(since } x = y\text{)}$$
$$2x = 180$$
$$x = 180/2 = 90$$

Since we have the value of x, from Statement (1) alone the statement is sufficient. The answer to the question is "Yes. AB is perpendicular to CD."

From Statement (2) alone, we have that AOC is an isosceles triangle. Since x equals y (earlier result) and neither equals $0°$, $\angle A$ ($= x°$) cannot equal $\angle AOC$ (which actually equals $y/2$). Hence, A and O are not the equal angles of the triangle.

Now, suppose $\angle C = \angle AOC$ (hence, isosceles). Then $\angle C = \angle AOC = x°$, and summing the angles of the triangle to $180°$ yields

$$\angle AOC + \angle C + \angle A = 180$$
$$x + x + y/2 = 180 \quad \text{(by substituting known values)}$$
$$x + x + x/2 = 180 \quad \text{(since } y = x\text{)}$$

Solving the equation for x yields $x = 72$. Here, x is not $90°$, hence, AB is not perpendicular to CD.

Now, suppose $\angle C = \angle A$ (hence, the triangle is isosceles). Then $\angle C = \angle A = y/2$. Summing the angles of the triangle AOC to $180°$ yields

$$\angle AOC + \angle C + \angle A = 180$$
$$x + y/2 + y/2 = 180$$
$$x + y = 180$$
$$x + x = 180 \text{ (since } y = x\text{)}$$
$$2x = 180; x = 180/2 = 90$$

Here, x equals $90°$, hence, AB is perpendicular to CD.

Hence, we have a double case, and Statement (2) alone is not sufficient.

Hence, the answer is (A).

30.

Statement (1): The remainder when m is divided by 6 is 2.

Statement (2): The remainder when m is divided by 12 is 2.

Here, m can be represented as $6p + 2$, where p is an integer. Now, $m/3 = (6p + 2)/3 = 2p + 2/3$, 2 is the remainder

Here, m can be represented as $12q + 2$, where q is an integer. Now, $m/3 = (12q + 2)/3 = 4q + 2/3$, 2 is the remainder.

Hence, either statement is sufficient. The answer is (D).

31. Let 1 pound of the rice of the first type ($0.8 per pound) be mixed with p pounds of the rice of the second type ($0.9 per pound). Then the total cost of the $1 + p$ pounds of the rice is

($0.8 per pound × 1 pound) + ($0.9 per pound × p pounds) =

$0.8 + 0.9p$

Hence, the cost of the mixture per pound is

$$\frac{\text{Cost}}{\text{Weight}} = \frac{0.8 + 0.9p}{1 + p}$$

If this equals $0.825 per pound (given), then we have the equation

$$\frac{0.8 + 0.9p}{1 + p} = 0.825$$
$0.8 + 0.9p = 0.825(1 + p)$
$0.8 + 0.9p = 0.825 + 0.825p$
$0.9p - 0.825p = 0.825 - 0.8$
$900p - 825p = 825 - 800$
$75p = 25$
$p = 25/75 = 1/3$

Hence, the proportion of the two rice types is $1 : 1/3$, which also equals $3 : 1$. Hence, the answer is (E).

32.

Statement (1): $p \geq 3/10$

The statement says $p \geq 3/10$. Hence, p could equal $3/10$ (here p is not greater than 0.3) or p could be greater than $3/10$. This is a double case and therefore the statement is *not* sufficient.

Statement (2): $3 - 2p < 2.4$

Subtracting 3 from both sides of the inequality $3 - 2p < 2.4$ yields $-2p < -0.6$. Dividing both sides by -2 and flipping the direction of the inequality yields

$-2p/-2 > -0.6/-2$
$p > 0.3$

This statement is sufficient to say "Yes, p is greater than 0.3."

The answer is (B).

---

33. Since 2 of the 5 eggs are rotten, the chance of selecting a rotten egg the first time is 2/5. For the second selection, there is only one rotten egg, out of the 4 remaining eggs. Hence, there is a 1/4 chance of selecting a rotten egg again.

Hence, the probability selecting 2 rotten eggs in a row is $2/5 \times 1/4 = 1/10$. The answer is (B).

Test 10—Answers and Solutions

34. A unique regular hexagon can be drawn given the radius of the circle in which it is inscribed. The area can be later measured. Hence, Statement (1) alone is sufficient.

The perimeter of the hexagon is $40\sqrt{3}$. Hence, the sum of the 6 equal sides is $40\sqrt{3}$, and the side length of each is $\dfrac{40\sqrt{3}}{6}$. Given the side length of a regular hexagon, a unique figure can be drawn for the hexagon. The area of the figure can then be measured. Hence, Statement (2) alone is also sufficient.

Hence, the answer is (D).

35. Square rooting the given equation $a^2 = 9$ yields two solutions: $a = 3$ and $a = -3$. In the equation $ab^2 = -8$, b^2 is positive since the square of any nonzero number is positive. Since $ab^2 = -8$ is a negative number, a must be negative. Hence, keep only negative solutions for a. Thus, we get $a = -3$.

Substituting this value of a in the given equation $x/a = 4$ yields

$x/(-3) = 4$
$x = -12$

Substituting of $a = -3$ in the given equation $a/y = 6$ yields

$-3/y = 6$
$y = -3/6 = -1/2$

Hence, $x + 2y = -12 + 2(-1/2) = -13$. The answer is (D).

36.

Statement (1): $x = -1/4$

Substituting $x = -1/4$ in the equation $2x + 3 = y + 1/y$ yields

$$2\left(-\frac{1}{4}\right) + 3 = y + \frac{1}{y}$$

$$-\frac{1}{2} + 3 = y + \frac{1}{y}$$

$$2\frac{1}{2} = y + \frac{1}{y}$$

$$2 + \frac{1}{2} = y + \frac{1}{y}$$

By comparing the left and right sides of the equation, we can say that y could be 2 or 1/2.

Hence, $x + y$ could be $-\frac{1}{4} + 2 = 1\frac{3}{4}$.

Or $x + y$ could be $-\frac{1}{4} + \frac{1}{2} = \frac{1}{4}$.

Since we have two different solutions (which means no unique answer), the statement is *not* sufficient.

The answer is (B).

Statement (2): $y = 2$

Substituting $y = 2$ in the equation $2x + 3 = y + 1/y$ yields

$$2x + 3 = 2 + \frac{1}{2}$$

$$2x = -3 + 2\frac{1}{2}$$

$$2x = -\frac{1}{2}$$

$$x = -\frac{1}{4}$$

Hence, $x + y = -\frac{1}{4} + 2 = 1\frac{3}{4}$, and the statement is sufficient.

37. Angle x is an exterior angle of the triangle and therefore equals the sum of the remote interior angles, 35 and y. That is, $x = y + 35$. This equation says that x is 35 units greater than y. So, (II) is true and (III) is false. Now, if x is an obtuse angle ($x > 90$), then $x + y$ is greater than 90. Hence, $x + y$ need not equal 90. So, (I) is not necessarily true. The answer is (B).

Test 11

Questions: 37
Time: 75 minutes

1. If $b = a + c$ and $b = 3$, then $ab + bc =$

   (A) $\sqrt{3}$
   (B) 3
   (C) $3\sqrt{3}$
   (D) 9
   (E) 27

2. Two data sets S and R are defined as follows:

   Data set S: 28, 30, 25, 28, 27
   Data set R: 22, 19, 15, 17, 21, 25

   By how much is the median of data set S greater than the median of data set R?

   (A) 5
   (B) 6
   (C) 7
   (D) 8
   (E) 9

3. If $\sqrt{3 - 2x} = 1$, then what is the value of $(3 - 2x) + (3 - 2x)^2$?

   (A) 0
   (B) 1
   (C) 2
   (D) 3
   (E) 4

[Data Sufficiency Question]
4. Is $x = 9$?

   (1) $x^2 - 7x - 18 = 0$
   (2) $x^2 - 10x + 9 = 0$

5. $ABCD$ is a square and one of its sides AB is also a chord of the circle as shown in the figure. What is the area of the square?

   (A) 3
   (B) 9
   (C) 12
   (D) $12\sqrt{2}$
   (E) 18

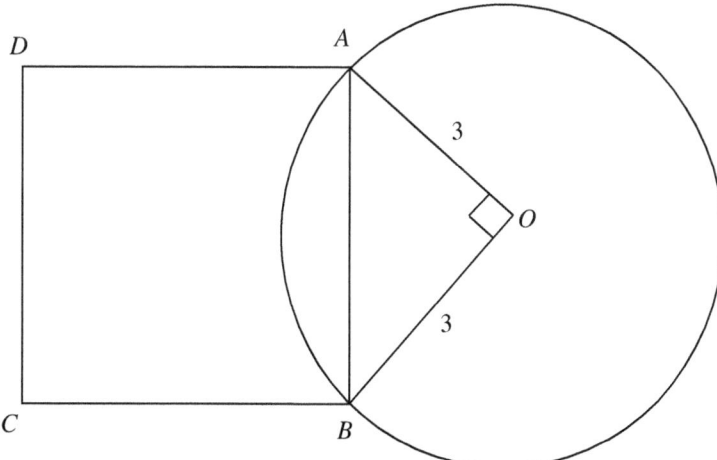

6. The annual exports of the company NeuStar increased by 25% last year. This year, it increased by 20%. If the increase in the exports was 1 million dollars last year, then what is the increase (in million dollars) this year?

   (A) 0.75
   (B) 0.8
   (C) 1
   (D) 1.2
   (E) 1.25

[Data Sufficiency Question]
7. In which quadrant does the point (p, q) lie?

   (1) $2p + 3q = 5$
   (2) $4p - q = 7$

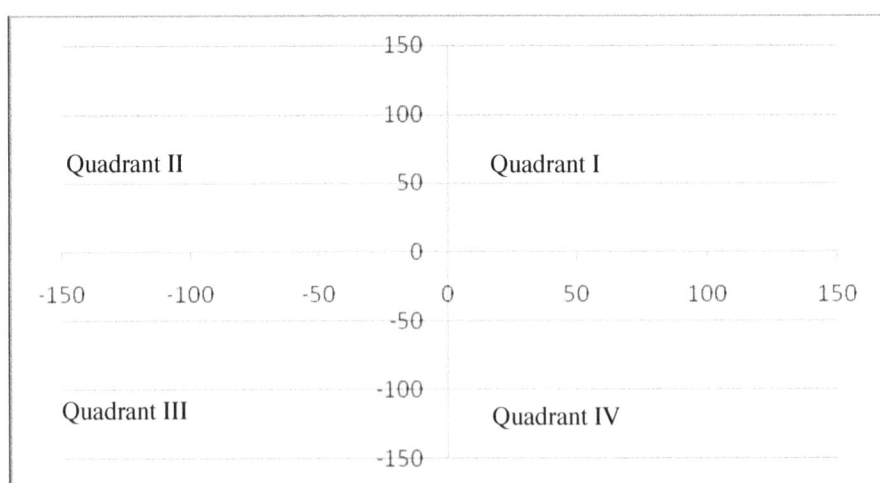

[Data Sufficiency Question]
8. Is $x = 9$?

    (1) $x^2 - 7x - 18 = 0$
    (2) $x^2 - 10x + 10 = 0$

9. In a market, a dozen eggs cost as much as a pound of rice, and a half-liter of kerosene costs as much as 8 eggs. If the cost of each pound of rice is $0.33, then how many cents does a liter of kerosene cost? [One dollar has 100 cents.]

    (A) 0.33
    (B) 0.44
    (C) 0.55
    (D) 44
    (E) 55

[Data Sufficiency Question]
10. Is r a multiple of s?

    (1) $r + 2s$ is a multiple of s.
    (2) $2r + s$ is a multiple of s.

[Data Sufficiency Question]
11. Is the integer *k* a prime number?

    (1) $k + 1$ is prime.
    (2) $k + 2$ is not prime.

12. In the figure, what is the average of the five angles shown inside the circle?

    (A) 36
    (B) 45
    (C) 60
    (D) 72
    (E) 90

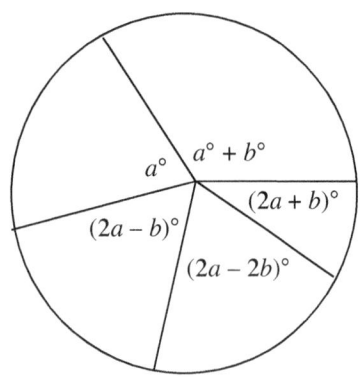

13. If x and y are two positive integers and x + y = 5, then what is the probability that x equals 1?

    (A) 1/2
    (B) 1/3
    (C) 1/4
    (D) 1/5
    (E) 1/6

[Data Sufficiency Question]
14. What is the sum of the two numbers x and y?

    (1) The ratio of the sum of the reciprocals of x and y to the product of the reciprocals of x and y is 1 : 3.
    (2) The product of x and y is 11/36 units greater than the sum of x and y.

[Data Sufficiency Question]
15. If $x^2 - 5x + 6 = 0$, then x =

    (1) $x \neq 1$
    (2) $x \neq 2$

16. Mr. Smith's average annual income over the years 1966 and 1967 is x dollars. His average annual income in over the years 1968, 1969, and 1970 is y dollars. What is his average annual income over the five continuous years 1966 through 1970?

(A) $2x/5 + 3y/5$
(B) $x/2 + y/2$
(C) $5(x + y)$
(D) $5x/2 + 5y/2$
(E) $3x/5 + 2y/5$

USE THIS SPACE FOR SCRATCHWORK.

17. Carlos & Co. generated revenue of $1,250 in 2006. This was 12.5% of its gross revenue. In 2007, the gross revenue grew by $2,500. What is the percentage increase in the revenue in 2007?

(A) 12.5%
(B) 20%
(C) 25%
(D) 50%
(E) 66.3%

USE THIS SPACE FOR SCRATCHWORK.

18. *AD* is the longest side of the right triangle *ABD* shown in the figure. What is the length of longest side of △*ABC* ?

   (A) 2
   (B) 3
   (C) $\sqrt{41}$
   (D) 9
   (E) 41

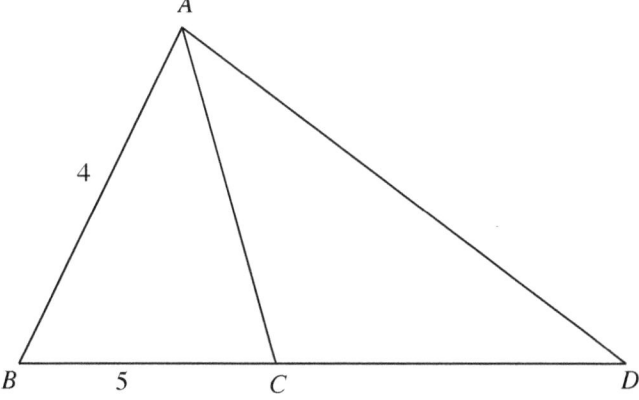

The figure is not drawn to scale

[Data Sufficiency Question]
19. If $xyz = tyz$, is $x = t$?

   (1) $x = 0$
   (2) $y \neq 0$

20. The sequence of numbers a, ar, ar^2, and ar^3 are in geometric progression. The sum of the first four terms in the series is 5 times the sum of first two terms and $r \neq -1$. How many times larger is the fourth term than the second term?

(A) 1
(B) 2
(C) 4
(D) 5
(E) 6

USE THIS SPACE FOR SCRATCHWORK.

21. On average, a sharpshooter hits the target once every 3 shots. What is the probability that he will hit the target in 4 shots?

(A) 1
(B) 1/81
(C) 1/3
(D) 65/81
(E) 71/81

USE THIS SPACE FOR SCRATCHWORK.

22. In the figure, triangles *ABC* and *ABD* are right triangles. What is the value of *x* ?

   (A) 20
   (B) 30
   (C) 50
   (D) 70
   (E) 90

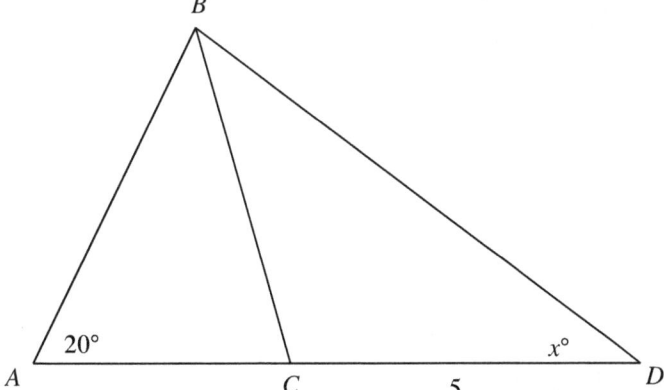

Questions 23–27 refer to the following graphs.

AUTOMOBILE ACCIDENTS IN COUNTRY X: 1990 TO 1994
(in ten thousands)

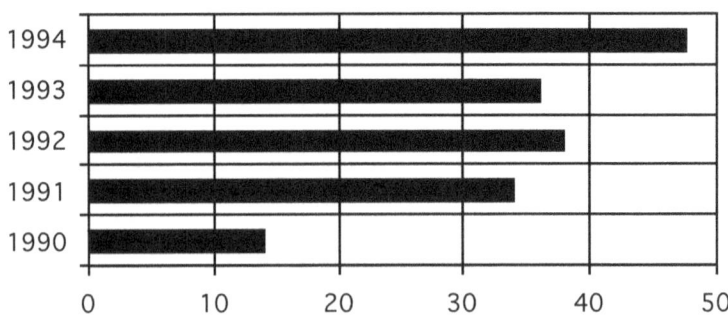

CARS IN COUNTRY X
(in millions)

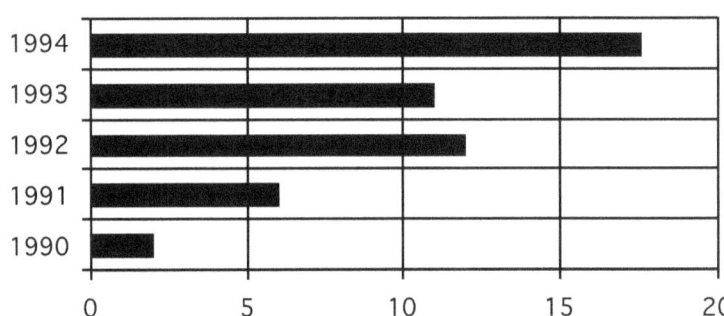

23. Approximately how many millions of cars were in Country X in 1994?

   (A) 1.0
   (B) 4.7
   (C) 9.0
   (D) 15.5
   (E) 17.5

24. The amount by which the number of cars in 1990 exceeded the number of accidents in 1991 was approximately

   (A) 0.3 million
   (B) 0.7 million
   (C) 1.0 million
   (D) 1.7 million
   (E) 2.5 million

25. The number of accidents in 1993 was approximately what percentage of the number of cars?

   (A) 1%
   (B) 1.5%
   (C) 3%
   (D) 5%
   (E) 10%

26. In which of the following years will the number of accidents exceed 500 thousand?

   (A) 1994
   (B) 1995
   (C) 1998
   (D) 2000
   (E) It cannot be determined from the information given.

27. If no car in 1993 was involved in more than four accidents, what is the minimum number of cars that could have been in accidents in 1993?

   (A) 50 thousand
   (B) 60 thousand
   (C) 70 thousand
   (D) 80 thousand
   (E) 90 thousand

[Data Sufficiency Question]
28. Are all the integers arranged in order in Sequence A consecutive integers?

   (1) The average of the sequence is not equal to the median of the sequence.
   (2) There is an odd number of integers in the set.

Data Sufficiency Question]
29. m is negative, and n is an integer. Is m^n positive?

   (1) m is odd.
   (2) n is odd.

[Data Sufficiency Question]

30. If r and s are two positive numbers, what is the value of the ratio r/s ?

    (1) r is 25% greater than s.
    (2) r is 25 units greater than s.

USE THIS SPACE FOR SCRATCHWORK.

31. The frequency distribution for x is as given below. What is the range of f ?

x	f
0	1
1	5
2	4
3	4

(A) 0
(B) 1
(C) 3
(D) 4
(E) 5

USE THIS SPACE FOR SCRATCHWORK.

[Data Sufficiency Question]

32. In the figure, A and B are the centers of the two circles. The circles intersect each other at C and D. What is the value of the common area of the two circles?

    (1) The radius of the circle with center A is 5.
    (2) ∠CAD = 120°.

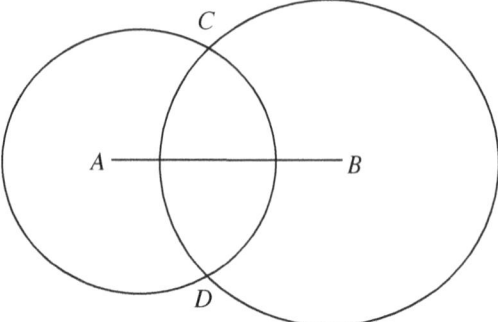

33. In an acoustics class, 120 students are male and 100 students are female. 25% of the male students and 20% of the female students are engineering students. 20% of the male engineering students and 25% of the female engineering students passed the final exam. What percentage of engineering students passed the exam?

    (A) 5%
    (B) 10%
    (C) 16%
    (D) 22%
    (E) 25%

[Data Sufficiency Question]

34. Which one is greater on Richard's farm: the total number of pigs and horses, or the number of chickens?

    (1) The ratio of the number of chickens to the number of pigs to the number of horses on his farm is 33 : 17 : 21.
    (2) The total number of chickens, pigs, and horses on his farm is 142.

35.
$$g(x) = (2x - 3)^{1/4} + 1$$

In the function above, for what values of x is $g(x)$ a real number?

(A) $x \geq 0$
(B) $x \geq 1/2$
(C) $x \geq 3/2$
(D) $x \geq 2$
(E) $x \geq 3$

[Data Sufficiency Question]

36. Train X leaves Los Angeles at 10:00 AM and travels East at a constant speed of x miles per hour. If another Train Y leaves Los Angeles at 11:30 AM and travels East along the same tracks at speed y, then at what time will Train Y catch Train X?

    (1) $y = 4x/3$
    (2) $x = 60$ miles per hour

37. In the figure, ABC is a right triangle. What is the value of y ?

    (A) 20
    (B) 30
    (C) 50
    (D) 70
    (E) 90

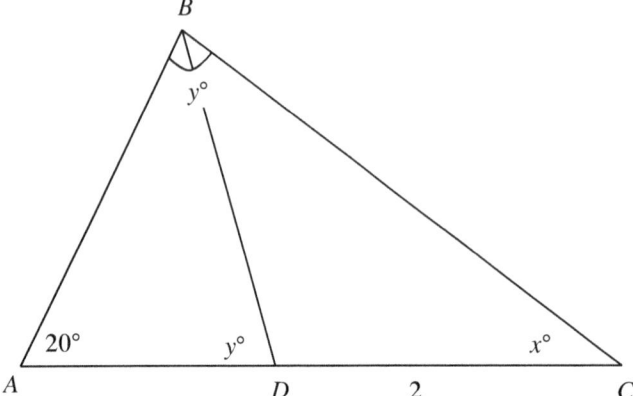

Test 11—Answers and Solutions

Answers and Solutions Test 11:

1.	D	11.	E	21.	D	31.	D
2.	B	12.	D	22.	D	32.	E
3.	C	13.	C	23.	E	33.	D
4.	C	14.	A	24.	D	34.	A
5.	E	15.	B	25.	C	35.	C
6.	C	16.	A	26.	E	36.	A
7.	C	17.	C	27.	E	37.	E
8.	B	18.	C	28.	A		
9.	D	19.	E	29.	B		
10.	A	20.	C	30.	A		

---

1. Factoring the common factor b from the expression $ab + bc$ yields

$$b(a + c) =$$
$$b \cdot b = \quad \text{(since } a + c = b\text{)}$$
$$b^2 = 3^2 = 9$$

The answer is (D).

---

2. The definition of *median* is "When a set of numbers is arranged in order of size, the *median* is the middle number. If a set contains an even number of elements, then the median is the average of the two middle elements."

Data set S (arranged in increasing order of size) is

$$25, 27, 28, 28, 30$$

The median of the set is the third number 28.

Data set R (arranged in increasing order of size) is

$$15, 17, 19, 21, 22, 25$$

The median is the average of the two middle numbers (the 3rd and 4th numbers):

$$(19 + 21)/2 = 40/2 = 20$$

The difference of 28 and 20 is 8. The answer is (B).

---

3. We have $\sqrt{3 - 2x} = 1$. Squaring both sides of the equation yields $(3 - 2x) = 1$. Squaring both sides of the equation again yields $(3 - 2x)^2 = 1$. Hence,

$$(3 - 2x) + (3 - 2x)^2 = 1 + 1 = 2$$

The answer is (C).

4. Substitute $x = 9$ to check whether either statement supports x being 9.

Statement (1): $x^2 - 7x - 18 = 9^2 - 7(9) - 18 = 81 - 63 - 18 = 0$.

Hence, Statement (1) says "yes x could be 9, but not sure x equals only 9." That is, it doesn't confirm that 9 is the only solution. The concern is that the equation $x^2 - 7x - 18 = 0$ is of degree 2 and therefore can have two different solutions (including 9) since the expression is not a perfect square trinomial. (If it were a perfect square trinomial, we would have a single solution.) We do not need to evaluate the other solution since we are sure there exists another solution other than 9. Since x could be 9 or the other solution, we have a double case. The statement is *not* sufficient.

Similarly, Statement (2) $x^2 - 10x + 9 = 9^2 - 10(9) + 9 = 81 - 90 + 9 = -9 + 9 = 0$ satisfies x being 9, but says one solution other than 9 exists as well. Hence, again, we have a double case, and therefore the statement is *not* sufficient.

Now, the statements together $x^2 - 7x - 18 = 0$ and $x^2 - 10x + 9 = 0$ indicate that each of them has exactly 2 solutions and exactly one of them is common (regardless, that is 9). Hence, with the statements together, we have a single solution, which can be compared with 9 (the solution equals 9) and answered. The answer is (C), the statements together are sufficient.

5. Side AB is the hypotenuse of the $\triangle AOB$. Hence, by The Pythagorean Theorem, we have $AB^2 = AO^2 + BO^2 = 3^2 + 3^2 = 18$. Hence, the area of the square $ABCD$ equals $side^2 = AB^2 = 18$. The answer is (E).

6. Let x be the annual exports of the company before last year. It is given that the exports increased by 25% last year. The increase equals $\frac{25}{100} \cdot x = \frac{1}{4} x$. We are given that the increase equaled 1 million dollars. Hence, $\frac{1}{4} x = 1$ million dollars. Now, the net exports equals $x + x/4 = 5x/4$. This year, the exports increased by 20%. Hence, $\frac{20}{100} \cdot (5x/4) = \frac{1}{4} x$. Since we know $\frac{1}{4} x = 1$, the increase in exports this year equals 1 million dollars. The answer is (C).

7.

Statement (1): $2p + 3q = 5$

$p = 1$ and $q = 1$ is a solution of Statement (1) since $2(1) + 3(1) = 5$, and the point $(p, q) = (1, 1)$ lies in Quadrant I (from the figure both x and y coordinates are positive in Quadrant I only).

Now, $p = -1$ and $q = 7/3$ is also a solution since $2(-1) + 3(7/3) = 5$, and the point $(p, q) = (-1, 7/3)$ lies in Quadrant II (from the figure, the x-coordinate is negative and the y-coordinate is positive in Quadrant II only).

This is a double case, so the statement is *not* sufficient.

Statement (2): $4p - q = 7$

$p = 1$ and $q = -3$ is a solution of Statement (2) since $4(1) - (-3) = 7$, and the point $(p, q) = (1, -3)$ lies in Quadrant IV (from the figure, the x-coordinate is positive and the y-coordinate negative in Quadrant IV only).

Now, $p = -1$ and $q = -11$ is a solution of Statement (2) since $4(-1) - (-11) = 7$, and the point $(p, q) = (-1, -11)$ lies in Quadrant III (from the figure, both x- and y-coordinates are negative only in Quadrant III).

This is a double case, so the statement is *not* sufficient.

With the two different linear equations, we have a single point, which lies in only one quadrant. Hence, the statements together are sufficient, and the answer is (C).

8. Statement (1) supports x being 9. But since it is a quadratic equation and not a perfect square trinomial, it will have one more solution as well. Hence, the statement is *not* sufficient.

Statement (2) does not support $x^2 - 10x + 10 = 0$ being 9. Hence, Statement (2) says $x = 9$ is false. The statement is sufficient.

The answer is (B).

---

9. One pound of rice costs 0.33 dollars. A dozen eggs cost as much as one pound of rice, and a dozen has 12 items. Hence, 12 eggs cost 0.33 dollars.

Now, since half a liter of kerosene costs as much as 8 eggs, one liter must cost 2 times the cost of 8 eggs, which equals the cost of 16 eggs.

Now, suppose 16 eggs cost x dollars. We know that 12 eggs cost 0.33 dollars. So, forming the proportion yields

$$\frac{0.33 \text{ dollars}}{12 \text{ eggs}} = \frac{x \text{ dollars}}{16 \text{ eggs}}$$

$$x = 16 \times \frac{0.33}{12} = 4 \times \frac{0.33}{3} = 4 \times 0.11$$

$$= 0.44 \text{ dollars} = 0.44 \ (100 \text{ cents}) \qquad \text{since one dollar has 100 cents}$$

$$= 44 \text{ cents}$$

The answer is (D).

---

10. Any number (integer or decimal or non-terminating number) can be a multiple of the another if the ratio of the former to later is an integer other than 0. For example, 4.5 is a multiple of 1.5 by 3 (= 4.5/1.5 which happens to be an integer) times.

Statement (1): $r + 2s$ is a multiple of s.

This means $(r + 2s) \div s$ is an integer. Let's express this as

$(r + 2s) \div s$ = integer
$r/s + 2s/s$ = integer
$r/s + 2$ = integer
r/s = integer − 2 = another integer.

So, r is a multiple of s. The statement is sufficient.

Statement (2): $2r + s$ is a multiple of s.

This means $(2r + s) \div s$ is an integer. Let's express this as

$(2r + s) \div s$ = integer
$2r/s + s/s$ = integer
$2r/s + 1$ = integer
$2r/s$ = integer − 1 = another integer
r/s = another integer/2

An integer divided by 2 may or may not be an integer. For example, 2/2 = 1 is an integer, but 3/2 = 1.5 is not an integer. So, the statement is *not* sufficient.

The answer is (A).

11. Suppose $k = 2$. Then $k + 1 = 3$ is prime and $k + 2 = 4$ is not prime (both statements satisfied). Here, k is prime.

Suppose $k = 4$. Then $k + 1 = 5$ is prime and $k + 2 = 6$ is not prime (both statements satisfied). Here, k is not prime.

Since we have a double case, the statements together are *not* sufficient. The answer is (E).

---

12. The average of the five angles is

$$\frac{\text{Sum of the five angles}}{5} = \frac{360}{5} = 72$$

The answer is (D).

---

13. The possible positive integer solutions x and y of the equation $x + y = 5$ are $\{x, y\} = \{1, 4\}, \{2, 3\}, \{3, 2\},$ and $\{4, 1\}$. Each solution is equally probable. Exactly one of the 4 possible solutions has x equal to 1. Hence, the probability that x equals 1 is one in four ways, which equals 1/4. The answer is (C).

---

14. From Statement (1) alone, we have that the ratio of the sum of the reciprocals of x and y to the product of the reciprocals of x and y is $1 : 3$. Writing this as an equation yields

$$\frac{\frac{1}{x} + \frac{1}{y}}{\frac{1}{x} \cdot \frac{1}{y}} = \frac{1}{3}$$

$$\frac{\frac{x+y}{xy}}{\frac{1}{xy}} = \frac{1}{3}$$

$$\frac{x+y}{xy} \cdot \frac{xy}{1} = \frac{1}{3}$$

$$x + y = \frac{1}{3} \qquad \text{by canceling } xy \text{ from the numerator and denominator}$$

Hence, Statement (1) alone is sufficient.

From Statement (2) alone, we have that the product of x and y is $11/36$ units greater than the sum of x and y. Writing this as an equation yields

$$xy - (x + y) = 11/36$$
$$x + y = xy - 11/36 \qquad \text{by solving for } x + y$$

Since we do not know the value of xy, we cannot determine the value of $x + y$. Hence, Statement (2) alone is not sufficient.

The answer is (A).

Test 11—Answers and Solutions

15. $x^2 - 5x + 6 = 0$
    $x^2 - 2x - 3x + 6 = 0$
    $x(x - 2) - 3(x - 2) = 0$ by factoring
    $(x - 2)(x - 3) = 0$
    $x - 2 = 0$ or $x - 3 = 0$
    $x = 2$ or 3

We have two solutions. The statement that constrains the number of solutions to just one will be the sufficient statement.

Statement (1) says $x \neq 1$, but we already know this since x equals only 2 or 3. The statement could not constrain number of solutions to one. Therefore, the statement is *not* sufficient.

Statement (2) says $x \neq 2$, which eliminates the solution $x = 2$. We now have only one possible solution, $x = 3$. The statement is sufficient.

The answer is (B).

---

16. Since Mr. Smith's average annual income over the two years 1966 and 1967 is x dollars, his total income in the two years is $2 \cdot x = 2x$.

Since Mr. Smith's average annual income in each of the next three years 1968 through 1970 is y dollars, his total income in the three years is $3 \cdot y = 3y$.

Hence, the total income in the five continuous years is $2x + 3y$.

Hence, the average income in the five years is

(the net income) ÷ 5 =

$(2x + 3y)/5 =$

$2x/5 + 3y/5$

The answer is (A).

---

17. We are given that Carlos & Co. generated revenue of $1,250 in 2006 and that this was 12.5% of the gross revenue. Hence, if 1250 is 12.5% of the revenue, then 100% (gross revenue) is

$(100/12.5)(1250) = 10,000$

Hence, the total revenue by end of 2007 is $10,000. In 2006, revenue grew by $2500. This is a growth of

$(2500/10000) \times 100 = 25\%$

The answer is (C).

GMAT Math Tests

18. In a right triangle, the angle opposite the longest side is the right angle. Since AD is the longest side of the right triangle ABD, $\angle B$ must be a right angle and $\triangle ABC$ must be a right triangle. Applying The Pythagorean Theorem to the right triangle ABC yields

$$AC^2 = AB^2 + BC^2$$
$$AC = \sqrt{AB^2 + BC^2}$$
$$AC = \sqrt{4^2 + 5^2}$$
$$AC = \sqrt{16 + 25}$$
$$AC = \sqrt{41}$$

The answer is (C).

---

19. Subtracting tyz from both sides of the equation yields $xyz - tyz = 0$, or $yz(x - t) = 0$. The expression $yz(x - t)$ equals 0 when A) $z = 0$ or B) $y = 0$ or C) $x = t$.

There are three possibilities. Not all may be true. Again, the three possibilities are:

A) $z = 0$ or B) $y = 0$ or C) $x = t$.

Statement (1): $x = 0$

The statement does not eliminate any possibility. The possibility $x = t$ may or may not be simultaneously true along with $x = 0$. We have a double case and therefore the statement is *not* sufficient.

Statement (2): $y \neq 0$

The statement eliminates the second possibility but we still have two possibilities open: A) and C). The possibilities may not be simultaneously true or they might. We have a double case and therefore the statement is *not* sufficient.

With the statements together, we could eliminate the possibility B) and affirm the possibility A) $z = 0$. But the possibility C) may be false or simultaneously true along with A) in case $t = 0$. The statements together are *not* sufficient. The answer is (E).

---

20. In the given progression, the sum of first two terms is $a + ar$, and the sum of first four terms is $a + ar + ar^2 + ar^3$. Since "the sum of the first four terms in the series is 5 times the sum of the first two terms," we have

$$a + ar + ar^2 + ar^3 = 5(a + ar)$$
$$\frac{a + ar + ar^2 + ar^3}{a + ar} = 5 \qquad \text{by dividing both sides by } a + ar \ (\neq 0 \text{ because } r \neq -1)$$
$$\frac{(a + ar) + r^2(a + ar)}{a + ar} = 5$$
$$\frac{(a + ar)(1 + r^2)}{a + ar} = 5 \qquad \text{by factoring out the common term } a + ar$$
$$1 + r^2 = 5 \qquad \text{by canceling } a + ar \text{ from both numerator and denominator}$$
$$r^2 = 5 - 1 = 4.$$

Now, the fourth term is $ar^3/ar = r^2 = 4$ times the second term. Hence, the answer is (C).

21. The sharpshooter hits the target once in 3 shots. Hence, the probability of hitting the target is 1/3. The probability of not hitting the target is 1 – 1/3 = 2/3.

Now, (the probability of not hitting the target even once in 4 shots) + (the probability of hitting at least once in 4 shots) equals 1, because these are the only possible cases.

Hence, the probability of hitting the target at least once in 4 shots is

1 – (the probability of not hitting even once in 4 shots)

The probability of not hitting in the 4 chances is $\frac{2}{3} \cdot \frac{2}{3} \cdot \frac{2}{3} \cdot \frac{2}{3} = \frac{16}{81}$. Now, 1 – 16/81 = 65/81. The answer is (D).

22. In triangle ABC, ∠A is 20°. Hence, the right angle in △ABC is either ∠ABC or ∠BCA. If ∠ABC is the right angle, then ∠ABD, of which ∠ABC is a part, would be greater than the right angle (90°) and ABD would be an obtuse angle, not a right triangle. So, ∠ABC is not 90° and therefore ∠BCA must be a right angle. Since AD is a line, ∠ACB + ∠BCD = 180°. Solving for ∠BCD yields ∠BCD = 180 – 90 = 90. Hence, △BCD is also a right triangle, with right angle at C. Since there can be only one right angle in a triangle, ∠D is not a right angle. But, we are given that △ABD is right angled, and from the figure ∠A equals 20°, which is not a right angle. Hence, the remaining angle ∠ABD is right angled. Now, since the sum of the angles in a triangle is 180°, in △ABC, we have 20 + 90 + x = 180. Solving for x yields x = 70. The answer is (D).

23. In the bottom chart, the bar for 1994 ends half way between 15 and 20. Thus, there were about 17.5 million cars in 1994. The answer is (E).

24. From the bottom chart, there were 2 million cars in 1990; and from the top chart, there were 340 thousand accidents in 1991. Forming the difference yields

2,000,000 – 340,000 = 1,660,000

Rounding 1.66 million off yields 1.7 million. The answer is (D).

25. From the charts, the number of accidents in 1993 was 360,000 and the number of cars was 11,000,000. Forming the percentage yields

$$\frac{360,000}{11,000,000} \approx 3\%$$

The answer is (C).

26. From the graphs, there is no way to predict what will happen in the future. The number of accidents could continually decrease after 1994. The answer is (E).

27. The number of cars involved in accidents will be minimized when each car has exactly 4 accidents. Now, from the top chart, there were 360,000 accidents in 1993. Dividing 360,000 by 4 yields

$$\frac{360,000}{4} = 90,000$$

The answer is (E).

---

28. If all the integers in Sequence A are consecutive, then the average of the sequence must equal the median of the sequence.

For example, the average of the sequence 1, 2, 3 is 2, which is also the median.

And the average of the sequence 1, 2, 4 is 2.33, which does not equal the median (2).

Statement (1): The average of the sequence is not equal to the median of the sequence.	Statement (2): There is an odd number of integers in the set.
Statement (1) says that the median of sequence A is not the average of the sequence, and therefore sequence A is not a set of consecutive integers. So, Statement (1) is sufficient.	Not all sequences containing an odd number of elements are consecutive or vice versa. So, the statement does not help in any way.
	For example, both series mentioned above 1, 2, 3 and 1, 2, 4 have an odd number of integers. But one consists of only consecutive integers and the other does not. This is a double case and therefore Statement (2) alone does not answer the question.

The answer is (A).

---

29. Note that even numbers and odd numbers are as likely to be negative as positive.

Statement (1): m is odd.	Statement (2): n is odd.
Statement (1) is irrelevant because m^n could be negative or positive whether m is odd or even. m^n is negative only if m is negative, and m^n is positive only if m is positive or n is even or 0. So, we have the double case, and the statement alone is not sufficient.	A negative number raised to an odd power (positive or negative) is always negative. So, the statement says that m^n is negative (not positive). For example, $(-3)^3 = -27$ is negative, and $(-3)^{-3} = 1/(-3)^3 = 1/(-27)$ is negative. So, the statement alone is sufficient.

The answer is (B).

---

30. From Statement (1) alone, we have that r is 25% greater than s. Hence, $r = (1 + 25/100)s$. Hence, $r/s = 1 + 25/100 = 1.25$. Hence, Statement (1) alone is sufficient.

From Statement (2) alone, we have that r is 25 units greater than s. Hence, we have the equation $r = s + 25$. Dividing the equation by s yields $r/s = s/s + 25/s = 1 + 25/s$. Since s is unknown, $1 + 25/s$ cannot be calculated. Hence, Statement (2) alone is not sufficient.

The answer is (A).

31. The *range* of f is the greatest value of f minus the smallest value of f: $5 - 1 = 4$. The answer is (D).

32. Draw a circle of radius 5. So, Statement (1) would be satisfied. Now, from its center, say A, locate two points C and D which subtend an angle 120° with the center ($\angle CAD = 120°$). Now, any circle passing through the points C and D (any one in the figure shown) satisfies the two statements along with the main circle. Each one has a different common area with the main circle. So, the two statements together do not yield a unique value for the common area and the answer is (E), the two statements together is not sufficient.

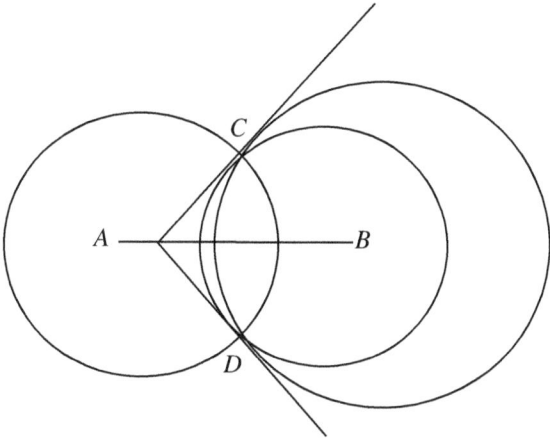

33. There are 100 female students in the class, and 20% of them are Engineering students. Now, 20% of 100 equals $20/100 \times 100 = 20$. Hence, the number of female engineering students in the class is 20.

Now, 25% of the female engineering students passed the final exam: 25% of 20 = $25/100 \times 20 = 5$. Hence, the number of female engineering students who passed is 5.

There are 120 male students in the class. And 25% of them are engineering students. Now, 25% of 120 equals $25/100 \times 120 = 1/4 \times 120 = 30$. Hence, the number of male engineering students is 30.

Now, 20% of the male engineering students passed the final exam: 20% of 30 = $20/100 \times 30 = 6$. Hence, the number of male engineering students who passed is 6.

Hence, the total number of Engineering students who passed is

(Female Engineering students who passed) + (Male Engineering students who passed) =

$5 + 6 =$

11

The total number of Engineering students in the class is

(Number of female engineering students) + (Number of male engineering students) =
$30 + 20 =$
50

Hence, the percentage of engineering students who passed is

$$\frac{\text{Total number of engineering students who passed}}{\text{Total number of engineering students}} \times 100 =$$

$11/50 \times 100 =$

22%

The answer is (D).

34. Let the number of chickens, pigs and horses on Richard's farm be $c, p,$ and h. From Statement (1), we have that the ratio of the three is $c : p : h = 33 : 17 : 21$. So, let c equal $33k$, p equal $17k$, and h equal $21k$, where k is some positive integer (such that $c : p : h = 33 : 17 : 21$). Then the total number of pigs and horses is $17k + 21k = 38k$; and since this is greater than $33k$, the number of chickens, the answer to the question is "The total number of pigs and horses is greater than the number of chickens." Hence, Statement (1) alone is sufficient to answer the question.

Next, Statement (2) alone gives the total number of the three species available, which is of no use. Hence, Statement (2) alone is not sufficient.

Hence, the answer is (A).

---

35. Let's change the fractional notation to radical notation: $g(x) = \sqrt[4]{2x-3} + 1$. Since we have an even root, the expression under the radical must be greater than or equal to zero. Hence, $2x - 3 \geq 0$. Adding 3 to both sides of this inequality yields $2x \geq 3$. Dividing both sides by 2 yields $x \geq 3/2$. The answer is (C).

---

36. Train X started at 10:00AM. Let the time it has been traveling be t. Since Train Y started at 11:30AM, it has been traveling an hour and a half less. So, represent its time as $t - 1\ 1/2 = t - 3/2$.

Train X travels at speed x miles per hour, and Train Y travels at speed y miles per hour. By the formula *Distance = Speed · Time*, the respective distances they travel before meeting equals xt and $y(t - 3/2)$. Since the trains started from same point and traveled in the same direction, they will have traveled the same distance when they meet. Hence, we have

$$xt = y\left(t - \frac{3}{2}\right)$$

$$\frac{xt}{y} = t - \frac{3}{2} \qquad \text{by dividing both sides by } y$$

$$\frac{xt}{y} - t = -\frac{3}{2}$$

$$t\left(\frac{x}{y} - 1\right) = -\frac{3}{2} \qquad \text{by factoring out the common factor } t$$

$$t = -\frac{\frac{3}{2}}{\frac{x}{y} - 1} \qquad \ldots (1)$$

From Statement (1), we have $x/y = 3/4$. Substituting this in equation (1) yields

$$t = -\frac{\frac{3}{2}}{\frac{3}{4} - 1}$$

$$= -\frac{\frac{3}{2}}{-\frac{1}{4}}$$

$$= \frac{3}{2} \cdot \frac{4}{1}$$

$$= 6 \text{ hours}$$

Test 11—Answers and Solutions

Hence, Train *Y* will catch Train *X* at 4PM (10AM plus 6 hours is 4PM), so Statement (1) alone is sufficient.

From Statement (2), we have $x = 60$. Substituting this in the equation (1) yields

$$t = -\frac{\frac{3}{2}}{\frac{60}{y} - 1}$$

Since we do not know the value of *y*, Statement (2) alone is not sufficient.

Hence, the answer is (A): Statement (1) alone is sufficient and Statement (2) alone is not.

---

37. In the given right triangle, $\triangle ABC$, $\angle A$ is 20°. Hence, $\angle A$ is not the right angle in the triangle. Hence, either of the other two angles, $\angle C$ or $\angle B$, must be right angled.

Now, $\angle BDA$ (= $\angle ABC$ = $y°$, from the figure) is an exterior angle to $\triangle BCD$ and therefore equals the sum of the remote interior angles $\angle C$ and $\angle DBC$. Clearly, the sum is larger than $\angle C$ and therefore if $\angle C$ is a right angle, $\angle BDA$ (= $\angle ABC$) must be larger than a right angle, so $\angle BDA$, hence, $\angle ABC$ must be obtuse. But a triangle cannot accommodate a right angle and an obtuse angle simultaneously because the angle sum of the triangle would be greater than 180°. So, $\angle C$ is not a right angle and therefore the other angle, $\angle B$, is a right angle. Hence, $y° = \angle B = 90°$. The answer is (E).

Test 12

GMAT Math Tests

Questions: 37
Time: 75 minutes

1. If $a^3 + a^2 - a - 1 = 0$, then which one of the following could be the value of a?

    (A) 0
    (B) 1
    (C) 2
    (D) 3
    (E) 4

2. Which one of the following is true regarding the triangle shown in figure?

    (A) $x > y > z$
    (B) $x < y < z$
    (C) $x = y = z$
    (D) $2x = 3y/2 = z$
    (E) $x/2 = 2y/3 = z$

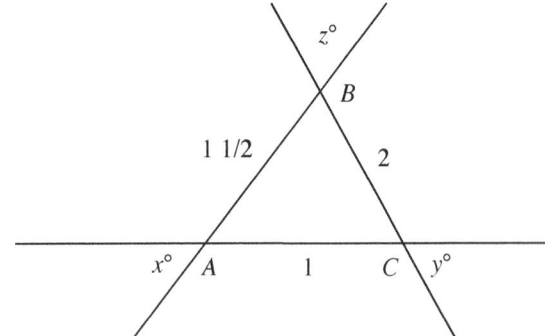

314

3. A function @ is defined on positive integers as @(a) = @(a − 1) + 1. If the value of @(1) is 1, then @(3) equals which one of the following?

   (A) 0
   (B) 1
   (C) 2
   (D) 3
   (E) 4

[Data Sufficiency Question]
4. If m and n are positive integers, then is $m + 2n$ an even integer?

   (1) $m = 3n + 1$
   (2) Exactly one of the two numbers m and n is even.

5. If $42.42 = k(14 + 7/50)$, then what is the value of k?

   (A) 1
   (B) 2
   (C) 3
   (D) 4
   (E) 5

6. In the figure, ABCD is a rectangle, and the area of △ACE is 10. What is the area of the rectangle?

   (A) 18
   (B) 22.5
   (C) 36
   (D) 44
   (E) 45

[Data Sufficiency Question]
7. What is the value of $x + y$?

   (1) $a = 3x$ and $b = 4y$
   (2) $d = x + y/2$

[Data Sufficiency Question]
8. The sides AC and BC of △ABC are parallel, respectively, to the lines l and m outside the triangle. What is the value of x?

   (1) $\angle B = 40°$
   (2) $y = 100°$

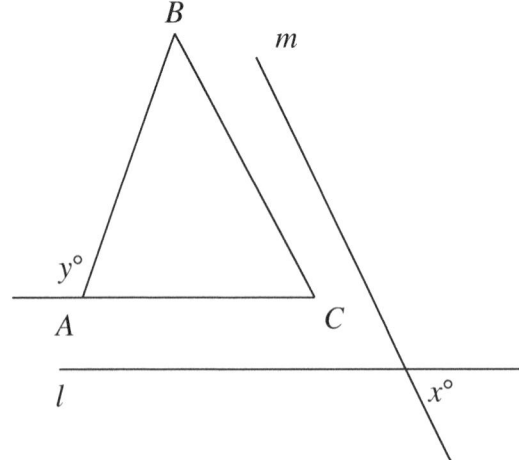

9. The following values represent the number of cars owned by the 20 families on Pearl Street.

   1, 1, 2, 3, 2, 5, 4, 3, 2, 4, 5, 2, 6, 2, 1, 2, 4, 2, 1, 1

   What is the probability that a family randomly selected from Pearl Street has at least 3 cars?

   (A) 1/6
   (B) 2/5
   (C) 9/20
   (D) 13/20
   (E) 4/5

[Data Sufficiency Question]
10. What is x ?

    (1) $x = y + 3$
    (2) $(x + y - 2)(x + 2y) = 0$

[Data Sufficiency Question]
11. A class consists of boys and girls only. On a final exam in History, the average score of the girls is 72 and the average score of the boys is 70. Is the average score of the class 71?

    (1) Smith is one of the classmates and Smith has the same number of boy classmates as girl classmates.
    (2) The number of students in the class is 101.

12. Evans sold apples at 125% of what it cost him. What is the percentage of profit made by selling 100 apples?

(A) 0%
(B) 20%
(C) 25%
(D) 33.3%
(E) 50%

USE THIS SPACE FOR SCRATCHWORK.

13. If x, y, and z are positive integers such that $x < y < z$ and $x + y + z = 6$, then what is the value of z ?

(A) 1
(B) 2
(C) 3
(D) 4
(E) 5

USE THIS SPACE FOR SCRATCHWORK.

[Data Sufficiency Question]

14. Is $\frac{(a-b)+(c-b)}{d} > 0$?

(1) $a + \text{c} < 2b$
(2) $d < 0$

USE THIS SPACE FOR SCRATCHWORK.

[Data Sufficiency Question]
15. Is $a + b = 0$?
    (1) $a/b > 1$
    (2) $ab > 1$

16. If $p - 10$ is divisible by 6, then which one of the following must also be divisible by 6?

    (A) p
    (B) $p - 4$
    (C) $p + 4$
    (D) $p - 6$
    (E) $p + 6$

17. Which of the following must be true?

    (I)   The area of triangle P.
    (II) The area of triangle Q.
    (III) The area of triangle R.

    (A) I = II = III
    (B) I < II < III
    (C) I > II > III
    (D) III < I < II
    (E) III > I > II

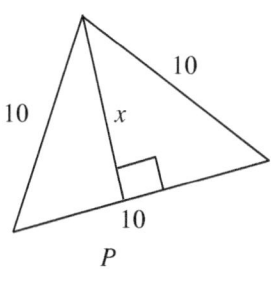

P

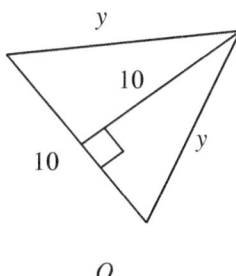

Q

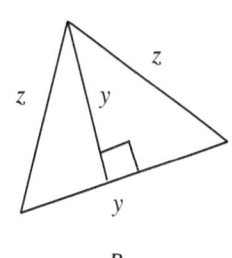

R

18. If $p = 216^{-1/3} + 243^{-2/5} + 256^{-1/4}$, then which one of the following is an integer?

   (A) $p/19$
   (B) $p/36$
   (C) p
   (D) $19/p$
   (E) $36/p$

[Data Sufficiency Question]
19. Is the integer k a prime number?
   (1) $k + 1$ is prime.
   (2) $k + 2$ is a multiple of 6.

20. A spirit and water solution is sold in a market. The cost per liter of the solution is directly proportional to the part (fraction) of spirit (by volume) the solution has. A solution of 1 liter of spirit and 1 liter of water costs 50 cents. How many cents does a solution of 1 liter of spirit and 2 liters of water cost?

   (A) 13
   (B) 33
   (C) 50
   (D) 51
   (E) 52

21. In the figure, ABCD is a parallelogram. Which one of the following is true?

    (A) $x < y$
    (B) $x > q$
    (C) $x > p$
    (D) $y > p$
    (E) $y > q$

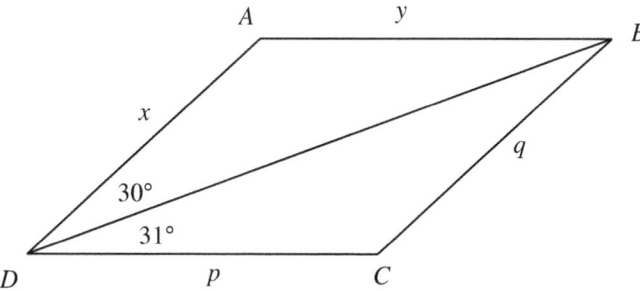

22. a, b, c, d, and e are five consecutive numbers in increasing order of size. Deleting one of the five numbers from the set decreased the sum of the remaining numbers in the set by 20%. Which one of the following numbers was deleted?

    (A) a
    (B) b
    (C) c
    (D) d
    (E) e

Questions 23–27 refer to the following graphs.

DISTRIBUTION OF IMPORTS AND EXPORTS FOR COUNTRY X IN 2014.

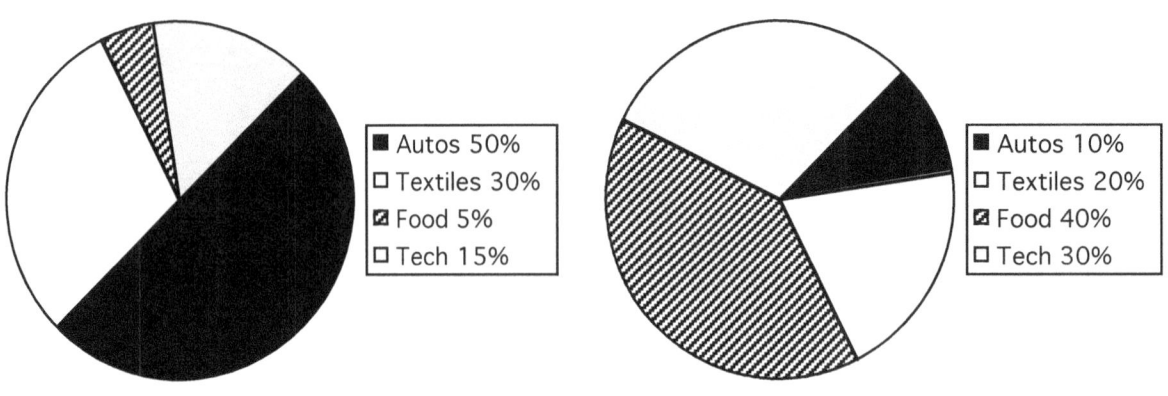

23. How many autos did Country X export in 2014?

    (A) 10 million
    (B) 15 million
    (C) 16 million
    (D) 20 million
    (E) 30 million

24. In how many categories did the total number of items (import and export) exceed 75 million?

    (A) 1
    (B) 2
    (C) 3
    (D) 4
    (E) none

25. The ratio of the number of technology items imported in 2014 to the number of textile items exported in 2014 is

    (A) 1/3
    (B) 3/5
    (C) 1
    (D) 6/5
    (E) 3/2

26. If in 2015 the number of autos exported was 16 million, then the percent increase from 2014 in the number of autos exported is

    (A) 40%
    (B) 47%
    (C) 50%
    (D) 60%
    (E) 65%

27. In 2014, if twice as many autos imported to Country X broke down as autos exported from Country X and 20 percent of the exported autos broke down, what percent of the imported autos broke down?

    (A) 1%
    (B) 1.5%
    (C) 2%
    (D) 4%
    (E) 5.5%

[Data Sufficiency Question]
28. Is *p* an odd prime integer?

    (1)   *p* is odd
    (2)   *p* is prime

[Data Sufficiency Question]
29. Are *x* and *y* integers?

    (1) $x + y$ is an odd.
    (2) $x - y$ is an even.

[Data Sufficiency Question]
30. If Ms. Ana and Mr. Mathew are children of Mrs. Smith, how many brothers and sisters are there in Mrs. Smith's family?

    (1)   Ms. Ana has the same number of brothers and sisters.
    (2)   Mr. Mathew has twice as many sisters as brothers.

31. The number m yields a remainder p when divided by 14 and a remainder q when divided by 7. If $p = q + 7$, then which one of the following could be the value of m ?

(A) 45
(B) 53
(C) 72
(D) 85
(E) 100

USE THIS SPACE FOR SCRATCHWORK.

[Data Sufficiency Question]
32. Does Set A contain only odd prime numbers?

(1) *A* contains odd numbers.
(2) *A* contains prime numbers.

USE THIS SPACE FOR SCRATCHWORK.

33. If a, b, and c are not equal to 0 or 1 and if $a^x = b$, $b^y = c$, and $c^z = a$, then $xyz =$

(A) 0
(B) 1
(C) 2
(D) a
(E) abc

USE THIS SPACE FOR SCRATCHWORK.

GMAT Math Tests

[Data Sufficiency Question]
34. What is the sum of numbers in the series?

    (1) All the numbers in the series are 3-digit numbers.
    (2) All the numbers in the series leave a remainder of 2 when divided by 3.

35. What is the maximum value of m such that 7^m divides into 14! evenly?

    (A) 1
    (B) 2
    (C) 3
    (D) 4
    (E) 5

[Data Sufficiency Question]
36. The graph shows two lines, one on the left of the y-axis and one on the right, that represent the curve $f(x)$. What is the value of $f(4) \cdot f(-4)$?

    (1) $a = 3$
    (2) $b = 5$

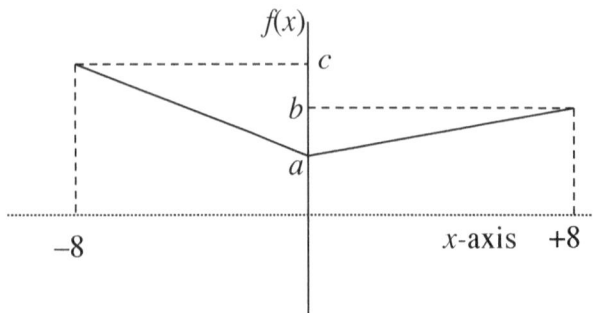

326

37. In the figure, *ABCD* is a parallelogram, what is the value of *b* ?

    (A) 46
    (B) 48
    (C) 72
    (D) 84
    (E) 96

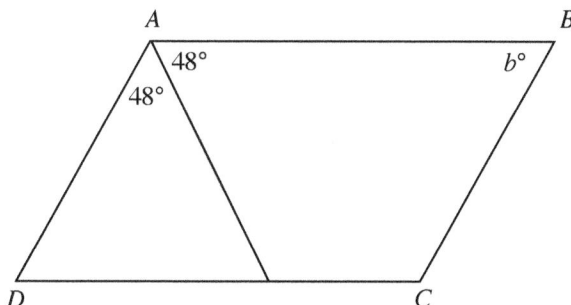

Answers and Solutions Test 12:

1.	B	11.	D	21.	C	31.	B
2.	A	12.	C	22.	C	32.	E
3.	D	13.	C	23.	A	33.	B
4.	E	14.	C	24.	B	34.	E
5.	C	15.	D	25.	E	35.	B
6.	C	16.	B	26.	D	36.	E
7.	E	17.	B	27.	D	37.	D
8.	C	18.	D	28.	C		
9.	B	19.	B	29.	C		
10.	E	20.	C	30.	C		

1. Let's test which answer-choice satisfies the equation $a^3 + a^2 - a - 1 = 0$.

Choice (A): $a = 0$. $a^3 + a^2 - a - 1 = 0^3 + 0^2 - 0 - 1 = -1 \neq 0$. Reject.
Choice (B): $a = 1$. $a^3 + a^2 - a - 1 = 1^3 + 1^2 - 1 - 1 = 0$. Correct.
Choice (C): $a = 2$. $a^3 + a^2 - a - 1 = 2^3 + 2^2 - 2 - 1 = 9 \neq 0$. Reject.
Choice (D): $a = 3$. $a^3 + a^2 - a - 1 = 3^3 + 3^2 - 3 - 1 = 32 \neq 0$. Reject.
Choice (E): $a = 4$. $a^3 + a^2 - a - 1 = 4^3 + 4^2 - 4 - 1 = 75 \neq 0$. Reject.

The answer is (B).

Method II (This problem can also be solved by factoring.)

$$a^3 + a^2 - a - 1 = 0$$
$$a^2(a + 1) - (a + 1) = 0$$
$$(a + 1)(a^2 - 1) = 0$$
$$(a + 1)(a + 1)(a - 1) = 0$$
$$a + 1 = 0 \text{ or } a - 1 = 0$$

Hence, $a = 1$ or -1. The answer is (B).

---

2. From the figure, we have the following inequality between the sides of the triangle:

$$BC (= 2) > AB (= 1\ 1/2) > AC (= 1)$$

In a triangle, the longer the side, the bigger the angle opposite it. Hence, we have the following inequality between the angles of the triangle: $\angle A > \angle C > \angle B$. Replacing the angles in the inequality with their respective vertical angles in the figure yields $x > y > z$. The answer is (A).

---

3. The function @ is defined on positive integers by the rule $@(a) = @(a - 1) + 1$.

Using the rule for $a = 2$ yields $@(2) = @(2 - 1) + 1 = @(1) + 1 = 1 + 1 = 2$. [Since $@(1) = 1$, given.]
Using the rule for $a = 3$ yields $@(3) = @(3 - 1) + 1 = @(2) + 1 = 2 + 1 = 3$. [Since $@(2) = 2$, derived.]

Hence, $@(3) = 3$, and the answer is (D).

Test 12—Answers and Solutions

4. From Statement (1) alone, we have $m = 3n + 1$.

Hence, $m + 2n = (3n + 1) + 2n = 5n + 1$

If n is even, then $5n$ is even and $5n + 1$ is odd.

If n is odd, then $5n$ is odd and $5n + 1$ is even.

Thus, we have a double case, and Statement (1) alone is not sufficient. Also, in either case, only one of the two numbers m and n is even. Hence, Statement (2) is a derivation of Statement (1). Hence, we can use the same two cases in Statement (1) to determine that Statement (2) alone is not sufficient. The answer is (E).

5. The given equation is

$$42.42 = k(14 + 7/50)$$

$$42.42 = k(14 + 14/100)$$

$$42.42 = k(14 + 0.14)$$

$$42.42 = k(14.14)$$

$$42.42/14.14 = k$$

$$3 = k$$

The answer is (C).

6. The formula for the area of a triangle is $1/2 \times base \times height$. Hence, the area of $\triangle ACE$ (which is given to equal 10) is $1/2 \times CE \times AB$. Hence, we have

$1/2 \times CE \times AB = 10$
$1/2 \times 5 \times AB = 10$ (from the figure, $CE = 5$)
$AB = 4$

Now, the formula for the area of a rectangle is $length \times width$. Hence, the area of the rectangle $ABCD = BC \times AB$

$= (BE + EC) \times (AB)$ from the figure, $BC = BE + EC$
$= (4 + 5) \times 4$ from the figure, $BE = 4$ and $EC = 5$
$= 9 \times 4$
$= 36$

The answer is (C).

7.

Statement (1): $a = 3x$ and $b = 4y$

Solving $a = 3x$ for x yields $x = a/3$. And solving $b = 4y$ for y yields $y = b/4$. Hence,

$$x + y = a/3 + b/4$$

Since we do not know a and b, which are new and have been constraining x and y, the statements are irrelevant and the statement is not sufficient.

Statement (2): $d = x + y/2$

Since d is a new variable used in Statement (1) constraining x and y, the statement is new and irrelevant information.

Since each statement has irrelevant information, the statements together cannot solve. The answer is (E).

8. Since the pair of lines AC and BC are parallel to the pair of lines l and m, respectively, corresponding angles between the pairs are equal. So, $\angle C$ equals $x°$, and the question transforms to "What is $\angle C$?" with the parallel lines l and m now out of the picture. We do not need them anymore. So, this is now a triangle problem.

From the figure, it is clear that

$$y° = \angle B + \angle C$$
(An exterior angle equals the sum of the remote interior angles)

Now, $\angle C$ equals $y° - \angle B$. This says that both $y°$ and $\angle B$ are needed unless either derives the other. Now, angles $y°$ and $\angle B$ are independent of each other and neither derives the other. Therefore, both statements are needed and sufficient. The answer is (C).

$$\angle C = y° - \angle B = 100° \text{ [from Statement (2)]} - 40° \text{ [from Statement (1)]} = 60°$$

9. From the distribution given, the 4th, 6th, 7th, 8th, 10th, 11th, 13th, and 17th families, a total of 8, have at least 3 cars. Hence, the probability of selecting a family having at least 3 cars out of the available 20 families is 8/20, which reduces to 2/5. The answer is (B).

Test 12—Answers and Solutions

10.

Statement (1): $x = y + 3$

Here, x depends on y (x varies with y). For example, if $y = 2$, x equals 5; and if $y = 3$, x equals 6.

Since we do not know y, we cannot determine x. The statement is not sufficient.

Statement (2): $(x + y - 2)(x + 2y) = 0$

We have the equation $(x + y - 2)(x + 2y) = 0$.

The equation equals zero when either $x + y - 2 = 0$ or $x + 2y = 0$. Either way, x depends on y, and therefore the statement is *not* sufficient.

From the statements together, we have two different possible systems:

$x = y + 3$
$x + y - 2 = 0$

Adding the two equations yields

$x + x + y - 2 = y + 3$
$2x = 5$
$x = 5/2$

$x = y + 3$
$x + 2y = 0$

Subtracting 3 from both sides of the first equation yields

$y = x - 3$

Substituting this into the second equation yields

$x + 2(x - 3) = 0$
$3x - 6 = 0$
$3x = 6$
$x = 6/3 = 2$

Since the statements together still yield two solutions (not a unique solution), the statements together are not sufficient. The answer is (E).

---

11. The average score of the class will be exactly in the middle between 70 and 72 (at 71) only if the weight of the number of boys equals the weight of the number of girls. The weight of the boys equals the weight of the girls only if the number of boys equals the number of girls.

So, the question can be transformed to "In the class, is the number of girls *equal to* the number of boys?"

Statement (1): Smith is one of the classmates and Smith has the same number of boy classmates as girl classmates.

Statement (1) says Smith has as many boy classmates as girl classmates. If Smith is a girl, the class will have one girl more; and if Smith is a boy, the class will have one boy more. So, whether Smith is a girl or a boy is irrelevant. The average is *not* in the middle. The statement answers the question as "No."

Statement (2): The number of students in the class is 101.

Suppose we have an equal number of boys and girls, and suppose the number is n. Then the class size is $n + n = 2n$, which must be even. But we are given that the class size is 101, which is odd. Hence, our assumption that we have an equal number of boys and girls is false. Hence, there is an unequal weight of boys and girls, and the average is *not* in the middle. The statement is sufficient to answer the question as "No."

The answer is (D).

12. Let the cost of each apple to Evans be x. Then the cost of 100 apples is $100x$. Since he sold the apples at 125% of the cost [each apple sold at 125% of x, which equals $(125/100)x = 5x/4$], the profit he made is

Selling price − Cost =

$5x/4 - x =$

$x/4$

The profit on 100 apples is $100(x/4) = 25x$. Hence, percentage of profit equals (Profit/Cost)100 = $(25x/100x)100 = 25\%$. The answer is (C).

---

13. From the given inequality $x < y < z$, it is clear that the positive integers $x, y,$ and z are different and are in the increasing order of size.

Assume $x > 1$. Then $y > 2$ and $z > 3$. Adding the inequalities yields $x + y + z > 6$. This contradicts the given equation $x + y + z = 6$. Hence, the assumption $x > 1$ is false. Since x is a positive integer, x must be 1.

Next, assume $y > 2$. Then $z > 3$ and $x + y + z = 1 + y + z > 1 + 2 + 3 = 6$, so $x + y + z > 6$. This contradicts the given equation $x + y + z = 6$. Hence, the assumption $y > 2$ is incorrect. Since we know y is a positive integer and greater than $x (= 1)$, y must be 2.

Now, the substituting known values in equation $x + y + z = 6$ yields $1 + 2 + z = 6$, or $z = 3$. The answer is (C).

Method II (without substitution):
We have the inequality $x < y < z$ and the equation $x + y + z = 6$. Since x is a positive integer, $x \geq 1$. From the inequality $x < y < z$, we have two inequalities: $y > x$ and $z > y$. Applying the first inequality ($y > x$) to the inequality $x \geq 1$ yields $y \geq 2$ (since y is also a positive integer, given); and applying the second inequality ($z > y$) to the second inequality $y \geq 2$ yields $z \geq 3$ (since z is also a positive integer, given). Summing the inequalities $x \geq 1, y \geq 2,$ and $z \geq 3$ yields $x + y + z \geq 6$. But we have $x + y + z = 6$, exactly. This happens only when $x = 1, y = 2,$ and $z = 3$ (not when $x > 1, y > 2,$ and $z > 3$). Hence, $z = 3$, and the answer is (C).

---

14. The question is about the fraction $\dfrac{(a-b)+(c-b)}{d}$. The numerator of the fraction is $(a - b) + (c - b)$ and the denominator is d.

From Statement (1), we do not have any information about d. So, if $(a - b) + (c - b)$ is negative and d is positive, the fraction is negative; and if $(a - b) + (c - b)$ is negative and d is negative, the fraction is positive. Hence, Statement (1) alone is *not* sufficient.

From Statement (2), we do not have any information about the numerator $(a - b) + (c - b)$. So, if the numerator is negative and the denominator d is negative, the fraction is positive; and if the numerator is positive and the denominator d is negative, the fraction is negative. Hence, we have a double case and Statement (2) alone is *not* sufficient.

Now, the numerator is $(a - b) + (c - b) = a + c - 2b$ and according to Statement (1) alone, we have the expression is negative (< 0). Now, from statement (2) alone, we have the denominator d is negative. So, the fraction Numerator/Denominator = a Negative Number ÷ a Negative Number = a Positive Number. So, the answer is "Yes. $\dfrac{(a-b)+(c-b)}{d} > 0$". Hence, the answer is (C), the statements together are sufficient.

Test 12—Answers and Solutions

15. Subtracting b from both sides, we get $a + b$ equals 0 only when $a = -b$.

Statement (1): $a/b > 1$

Dividing both sides of the equation $a = -b$ by b yields $a/b = -1$. However, Statement (1) says $a/b > 1$ and therefore prevents the possibility of a/b equaling -1. So, the statement is sufficient.

Statement (2): $ab > 1$

Multiplying both sides of the equation $a = -b$ by b yields $ab = -b^2$, which is zero or negative. However, Statement (2) says $ab > 1$ and therefore prevents the possibility of a equaling $-b$. So, the statement is sufficient.

The answer is (D).

Method II:
Subtracting b from both sides yields $a + b$ equals 0 only when $a = -b$. This means, $a + b$ equals 0 only when a and b are both equal numerically but are on opposite sides of 0 on the number line (are at equal distance to either side of 0 on the number line). Both statements individually prevent a and b from being zero. So, each statement is sufficient. The answer is (D).

16. Since $p - 10$ is divisible by 6, let's represent it as $6n$, where n is an integer. Then we have $p - 10 = 6n$. Adding 10 to both sides of the equation yields

$$p = 6n + 10$$

Let's plug this result into each answer-choice to find out which one is a multiple of 6 and therefore divisible by 6.

Choice (A): $p = 6n + 10 = 6n + 6 + 4 = 6(n + 1) + 4$. Hence, p is not a multiple of 6. Reject.

Choice (B): $p - 4 = (6n + 10) - 4 = 6n + 6 = 6(n + 1)$. Hence, p is a multiple of 6 and therefore divisible by 6. Correct.

Choice (C): $p + 4 = (6n + 10) + 4 = 6n + 14 = 6n + 12 + 2 = 6(n + 2) + 2$. Hence, p is not a multiple of 6. Reject.

Choice (D): $p - 6 = (6n + 10) - 6 = 6n + 4$. Hence, p is not a multiple of 6. Reject.

Choice (E): $p + 6 = (6n + 10) + 6 = 6n + 16 = 6n + 12 + 4 = 6(n + 2) + 4$. Hence, p is not a multiple of 6. Reject.

The answer is (B).

17. In the figure, triangle *P* is equilateral, with each side measuring 10 units. So, as in any equilateral triangle, the altitude (*x* here) is shorter than any of the other sides of the triangle. Hence, *x* is less than 10. Now,

$$\begin{aligned} I &= \text{Area of Triangle } P \\ &= 1/2 \times base \times height \\ &= 1/2 \times 10 \times x \\ &= 5x \text{ and this is less than 50, since } x \text{ is less than 10} \end{aligned}$$

Triangle *Q* has both base and altitude measuring 10 units, and the area of the triangle is

$$1/2 \times base \times height = 1/2 \times 10 \times 10 = 50$$

So, II = 50. We have one more detail to pick up: *y*, being the hypotenuse in the right triangle in figure *Q*, is greater than any other side of the triangle. Hence, *y* is greater than 10, the measure of one leg of the right triangle.

Triangle *R* has both the base and the altitude measuring *y* units. Hence,

$$\begin{aligned} II &= \text{area of the triangle } R \\ &= 1/2 \times base \times height \\ &= 1/2 \times y \times y \\ &= (1/2)y^2, \text{ and this is greater than } 1/2 \times 10^2 \text{ (since } y > 10\text{), which equals 50} \end{aligned}$$

Summarizing, the three results I < 50, II = 50, and III > 50 into a single inequality yields I < II < III. The answer is (B).

---

18. Simplifying the given equation yields

$$\begin{aligned} p &= 216^{-1/3} + 243^{-2/5} + 256^{-1/4} \\ &= (6^3)^{-1/3} + (3^5)^{-2/5} + (4^4)^{-1/4} \\ &= 6^{3(-1/3)} + 3^{5(-2/5)} + 4^{4(-1/4)} \\ &= 6^{-1} + 3^{-2} + 4^{-1} \\ &= \frac{1}{6} + \frac{1}{9} + \frac{1}{4} \\ &= \frac{6+4+9}{36} \\ &= \frac{19}{36} \end{aligned}$$

because $216 = 6^3$, $243 = 3^5$, and $256 = 4^4$

Now,

Choice (A): $p/19 = (19/36)/19 = 1/36$, not an integer. Reject.
Choice (B): $p/36 = (19/36)/36 = 19/36^2$, not an integer. Reject.
Choice (C): $p = 19/36$, not an integer. Reject.
Choice (D): $19/p = 19/(19/36) = 19 \cdot 36/19 = 36$, an integer. Correct.
Choice (E): $36/p = 36/(19/36) = 36^2/19$, not an integer. Reject.

The answer is (D).

Test 12—Answers and Solutions

19.

Statement (1): $k + 1$ is prime.

Suppose $k = 2$. Then $k + 1 = 3$ is prime (the statement is satisfied). Here, k is prime.

Suppose $k = 4$. Then $k + 1 = 5$ is prime (the statement is satisfied). Here, k is *not* prime.

Hence, the statement being satisfied is not an indication of whether k is prime or not. The statement is *not* sufficient.

Statement (2): $k + 2$ is a multiple of 6.

Here, $k + 2$ must be an even number (multiples of even numbers are even).

Hence, $k =$ even number $- 2 =$ even. No even number other than 2 is prime since even numbers are multiples of 2. If k were 2, $k + 2 = 4$ would not be a multiple of 6. Hence, the statement is sufficient.

The answer is (B).

20. Since the cost of *each* liter of the spirit water solution is directly proportionally to the part (fraction) of spirit the solution has, the cost per liter can be expressed as kf, where f is the fraction (part of) of pure spirit the solution has.

Now, each liter of the m liters of the solution containing n liters of the spirit ($f = n/m$) should cost $kf = k(n/m)$. The m liters cost $m \cdot k(n/m) = kn$. Hence, the solution is only priced for the content of the spirit the solution has (n here). Hence, the cost of the two samples given in the problem must be the same since both have exactly 1 liter of spirit. Hence, the answer is (C), 50 cents.

21. Since $ABCD$ is a parallelogram, opposite sides are equal. So, $x = q$ and $y = p$. Now, line BD is a transversal cutting opposite sides AB and DC in the parallelogram. So, the alternate interior angles $\angle ABD$ and $\angle BDC$ both equal 31°. Hence, in $\triangle ABD$, $\angle B$ (which equals 31°) is greater than $\angle D$ (which equals 30°, from the figure). Since the sides opposite greater angles in a triangle are greater, we have $x > y$. But, $y = p$ (we know). Hence, $x > p$, and the answer is (C).

22. Since $a, b, c, d,$ and e are consecutive numbers in the increasing order, we have

$$b = a + 1, c = a + 2, d = a + 3 \text{ and } e = a + 4$$

The sum of the five numbers is $a + (a + 1) + (a + 2) + (a + 3) + (a + 4) = 5a + 10$.

Now, we are given that the sum decreased by 20% when one number was deleted. Hence, the new sum should be

$$(5a + 10)(1 - 20/100) = (5a + 10)(1 - 1/5) = (5a + 10)(4/5) = 4a + 8$$

Now, since New Sum = Old Sum – Dropped Number, we have $(5a + 10) = (4a + 8) +$ Dropped Number. Hence, the number dropped is $(5a + 10) - (4a + 8) = a + 2$. Since $c = a + 2$, the answer is (C).

23. The graph shows that 100 million items were exported in 2014 and 10% were autos. Hence, 10 million autos were exported. The answer is (A).

24. The following chart summarizes the items imported and exported:

	Imports	Exports	Total
Autos	100	10	110
Textiles	60	20	80
Food	10	40	50
Tech	30	30	60

The chart shows that only autos and textiles exceeded 75 million total items. The answer is (B).

---

25. In 2014, there were 200 million items imported of which 15% were technology items. Thus, the number of technology items imported was

$$(15\%)(200 \text{ million}) = (.15)(200 \text{ million}) = 30 \text{ million}$$

In 2014, there were 100 million items exported of which 20% were textile items. Thus, the number of textile items exported was

$$(20\%)(100 \text{ million}) = (.20)(100 \text{ million}) = 20 \text{ million}$$

Forming the ratio of the above numbers yields

$$\frac{number\ of\ technology\ items\ imported}{number\ of\ textile\ items\ exported} = \frac{30}{20} = \frac{3}{2}$$

The answer is (E).

---

26. Remember, to calculate the percentage increase, find the absolute increase and divide it by the original number. Now, in 2014, the number of autos exported was 10 million (100x10%), and in 2015 it was 16 million. The absolute increase is thus:

$$16 - 10 = 6$$

Hence the percent increase in the number of autos exported is

$$\frac{absolute\ increase}{original\ number} = \frac{6}{10} = 60\%$$

The answer is (D).

---

27. If 20% of the exports broke down, then 2 million autos broke down (20%x10). Since "twice as many autos imported to Country X broke down as autos exported from Country X," 4 million imported autos broke down. Further, Country X imported 100 million autos (50%x200). Forming the percentage yields

$$\frac{4}{100} = 0.04 = 4\%$$

The answer is (D).

Test 12—Answers and Solutions

28. Let's draw a Venn diagram to represent the odd numbers and the prime numbers (see figure below). Statement (1), p is odd, is represented by the region to the left in the Venn diagram. Statement (2), p is prime, is represented by the region to the right in the Venn diagram. Not all odd numbers are prime, and not all prime numbers are odd. Hence, the two regions have some exclusive space. There is at least one odd prime number. Hence, the common region of the two statements is not blank. But the common region expects a number to be both odd and prime. Hence, the statements together are sufficient because the common region equals neither of the two sets.

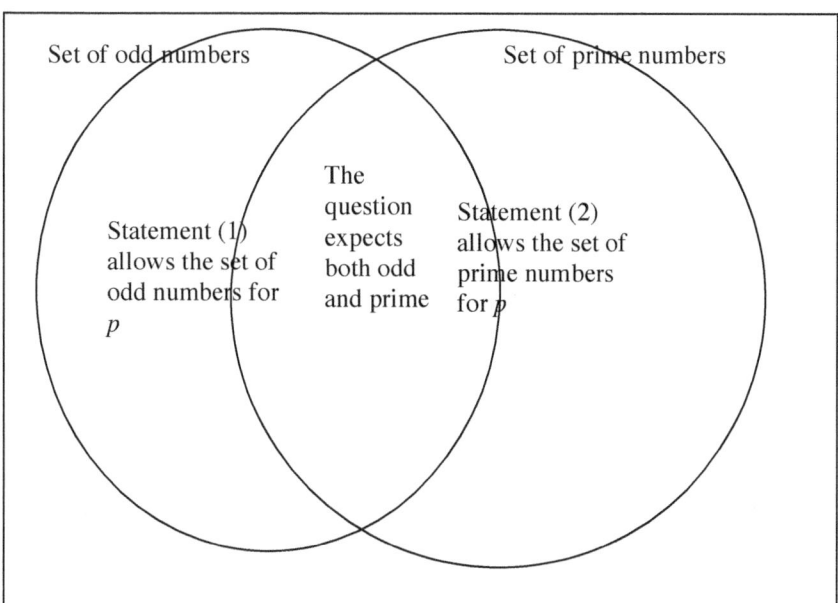

The answer is (C).

29. Suppose $x - y = e$, an even integer; and suppose $x + y = o$, an odd integer. Summing the two equations yields

$$(x + y) + (x - y) = o + e$$
$$2x = o + e$$
$$x = \frac{o + e}{2} = \frac{odd}{2}$$

Since $\frac{odd}{2}$ is never an integer, x is not an integer.

Subtracting the equation $x - y = e$ from the equation $x + y = o$ yields

$$(x + y) - (x - y) = o - e$$
$$2y = o - e$$
$$y = \frac{o - e}{2} = \frac{odd}{2}$$

Since $\frac{odd}{2}$ is never an integer, y is not an integer.

The statements together answer the question, and the answer is (C).

30. From Statement (1) alone, we have that Ms. Anna has the same number of brothers as sisters. If m is the number of male children Mrs. Smith has (so Anna has this many brothers), then she must have m sisters also. Hence, including Ms. Anna, Mrs. Smith must have $m + 1$ female children. Now, the number of children Mrs. Smith has equals $m + (m + 1) = 2m + 1$. But, we still do not know the value of m. Hence, Statement (1) alone is not sufficient.

From Statement (2) alone, we have that Mr. Mathew has twice as many sisters as brothers. Hence, if Mathew has, say, $m - 1$ brothers, then he must have $2(m - 1)$ sisters. Hence, the total number of children of Mrs. Smith equals

$m - 1$ brothers of Mathew + 1 (Mathew himself) + $2(m - 1)$ sisters = $m + 2(m - 1) = 3m - 2$

Since we do not know the value m, Statement (2) alone is not sufficient.

Equating the number of children from both statements yields $2m + 1 = 3m - 2$. Solving this equation for m yields $m = 3$. Hence, the number of children of Mrs. Smith is $2m + 1 = 2 \cdot 3 + 1 = 7$. Hence, the statements together answer the question.

The answer is (C).

---

31. Select the choice that satisfies the equation $p = q + 7$.

Choice (A): If $m = 45$, then $m/14 = 45/14 = 3 + 3/14$. So, the remainder is $p = 3$. Also, $m/7 = 45/7 = 6 + 3/7$. So, the remainder is $q = 3$. Here, $p \ne q + 7$. So, reject the choice.

Choice (B): If $m = 53$, then $m/14 = 53/14 = 3 + 11/14$. So, the remainder is $p = 11$. Also, $m/7 = 53/7 = 7 + 4/7$. So, the remainder is $q = 4$. Here, $p = q + 7$. So, select the choice.

Choice (C): If $m = 72$, then $m/14 = 72/14 = 5 + 2/14$. So, the remainder is $p = 2$. Now, $m/7 = 72/7 = 10 + 2/7$. So, the remainder is $q = 2$. Here, $p \ne q + 7$. So, reject the choice.

Choice (D): If $m = 85$, then $m/14 = 85/14 = 6 + 1/14$. So, the remainder is $p = 1$. Now, $m/7 = 85/7 = 12 + 1/7$. So, the remainder is $q = 1$. Here, $p \ne q + 7$. So, reject the choice.

Choice (E): If $m = 100.$, then $m/14 = 100/14 = 7 + 2/14$. So, the remainder is $p = 2$. Now, $m/7 = 100/7 = 14 + 2/7$. So, the remainder is $q = 2$. Here, $p \ne q + 7$. So, reject the choice.

Hence, the answer is (B).

---

32. Statement (1) allows odd numbers, and Statement (2) allows prime numbers. So, the statements together allow odd and prime numbers in Set A. This, of course, means there *could* be other numbers (not just odd or prime or both). If there are other numbers in Set A, the answer is "No"; and if there are not, the answer is "Yes." Hence, the answer to the question is "Can't say" and therefore the answer is (E).

33. We are given three equations $a^x = b$, $b^y = c$, and $c^z = a$. From the first equation, we have $b = a^x$. Substituting this in the second equation gives

$$(a^x)^y = c$$

We can replace a in this equation with c^z (according to the third equation $c^z = a$):

$$\left(\left(c^z\right)^x\right)^y = c$$

$c^{xyz} = c^1$ By multiplying the exponents and writing c as c^1
$xyz = 1$ By equating the exponents of c on both sides

The answer is (B).

---

34. Let the given series be represented by A.

Combining the two statements yields

"All the numbers in the series are 3-digit numbers that leave a remainder of 2 when divided by 3."

(Note: We need to be careful not to change the language while combining the statements.)

The list of all such numbers is

$$\{101, 104, 107, \ldots, 998\}$$

From the language of the problem, we are still not sure whether Set A contains all of these numbers $\{101, 104, 107, \ldots, 998\}$. So, the sum cannot be calculated, nor the average. The answer is (E).

If the statements adequately define the series, adding an extra condition will not violate or slice the already calculated Set A.

For example, adding Statement (3) "The numbers in the series are all even," which is a possibly valid statement, further reduces the Set A to

$$\{\cancel{101}, 104, \cancel{107}, \ldots, \cancel{995}, 998\} = \{104, 110, \ldots, 992, 998\}$$

So, if Statement (2) were "The series is the set of all numbers and only the numbers that are 3-digited and leave a remainder of 2 when divided by 3," then no other kind of statement such as Statement (3) can slice the Set A further. If Statement (3) is slicing or adding new elements to the already fully defined set, the statement is invalid.

---

35. The term 14! equals the product of the numbers 1, 2, 3, 4, 5, 6, 7, 8, 9, 10, 11, 12, 13, and 14. Only two of these numbers are divisible by 7. The numbers are 7 and 14. Hence, 14! can be expressed as the product of

$$k \cdot 7 \cdot 14, \text{ where } k \text{ is not divisible by } 7$$

Now, since there are two 7s in 14!, the numbers 7 and 7^2 divide 14! evenly. 7^3 and further powers of 7 leave a remainder when divided into 14!. Hence, the maximum value of m is 2. The answer is (B).

36. Draw the *xy*-axes. On the *x*-axis, plot two points one on either side of the *y*-axis that are 8 units from the *y*-axis.

Now, using Statements (1) and (2), we can plot the points $A(0, a)$ and $B(8, b)$. Thus, the positive side of the curve can be constructed and thereby the value of $f(4)$ can be evaluated.

But since we still do not know what c is, we cannot construct the negative side of the curve. So, $f(-4)$ can vary; it is not fixed. Hence, $f(4) \cdot f(-4)$ cannot be calculated. Data is not sufficient.

The answer is (E).

---

37. From the figure, $\angle A = 48 + 48 = 96$. Since the sum of any two adjacent angles of a parallelogram equals 180°, we have

$$\angle A + b = 180$$

or

$$96 + b = 180$$

Solving for b yields $b = 180 - 96 = 84$. The answer is (D).

Test 13

GMAT Math Tests

Questions: 37
Time: 75 minutes

1. If the ratio of *y* to *x* is equal to 3 and the sum of *y* and *x* is 80, what is the value of *y*?

    (A) −10
    (B) −2
    (C) 5
    (D) 20
    (E) 60

2. The number 3072 is divisible by both 6 and 8. Which one of the following is the first integer larger than 3072 that is also divisible by both 6 and 8?

    (A) 3078
    (B) 3084
    (C) 3086
    (D) 3090
    (E) 3096

3. A *perfect square* is a number that becomes an integer when square rooting it. *A*, *B*, and *C* are three positive integers. The ratio of the three numbers is 1 : 2 : 3, respectively. Which one of the following expressions must be a perfect square?

    (A) $A + B + C$
    (B) $A^2 + B^2 + C^2$
    (C) $A^3 + B^3 + C^3$
    (D) $3A^2 + B^2 + C^2$
    (E) $3A^2 + 4B^2 + 4C^2$

342

[Data Sufficiency Question]
4. Is 2*p* − 3*q* not equal to 0?

   (1) 4*p* is not equal to 6*q*.
   (2) *p* is not equal to *q*.

5. The following frequency distribution shows the number of cars owned by the 20 families on Pearl Street.

x	The number of families having *x* number of cars
1	2
2	2
3	*a*
4	4
5	5
6	2

   What is the probability that a family randomly selected from the street has at least 4 cars?

   (A) 1/10
   (B) 1/5
   (C) 3/10
   (D) 9/20
   (E) 11/20

6. In the figure, the area of rectangle EFGH is 3 units greater than the area of rectangle ABCD. What is the value of ab if $a + b = 8$?

   (A) 9
   (B) 12
   (C) 15
   (D) 18
   (E) 21

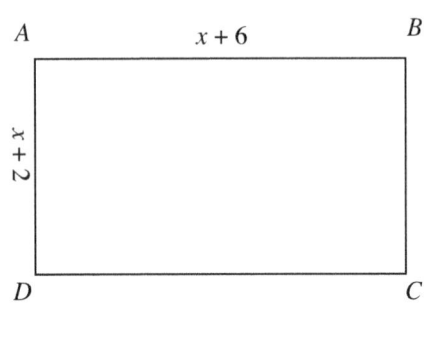
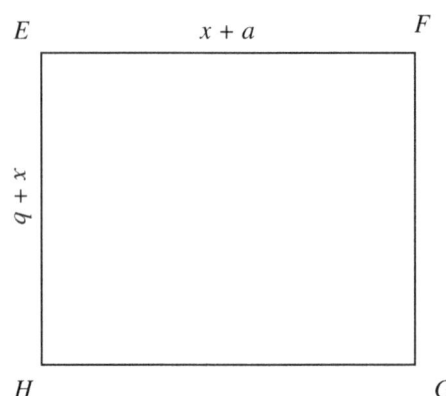

[Data Sufficiency Question]
7. Is x divisible by 14?

   (1) $x/4$ is a positive integer.
   (2) $x/6$ is a positive integer.

[Data Sufficiency Question]
8. If $x^2 - y^2 = 15$, is $x + y > x - y$?

   (1) $x - y = 5$
   (2) $x + y = 3$

9. In the figure shown, the line l represents the function f. What is the value of $f(10)$?

   (A) 2
   (B) 5
   (C) 8
   (D) 10
   (E) 12

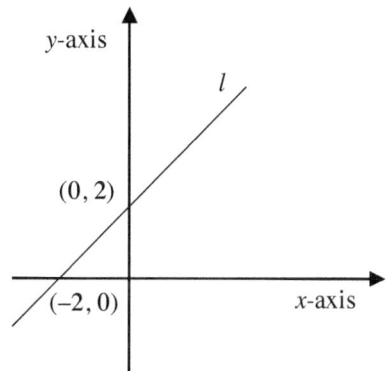

[Data Sufficiency Question]
10. Is $2y = 20 - p$?

    (1) $x = y + p$
    (2) $x + y = 10$

[Data Sufficiency Question]

11. Is $x = 1$, $y = 2$, and $z = 3$?

 (1) $5x + 2z = 3x + 4y = y + 3z$
 (2) $5x + 2z = 3x + 4y$ and $3x + 4y = y + 3z$

USE THIS SPACE FOR SCRATCHWORK.

12. Which one of the following equals the maximum difference between the squares of two single-digit numbers that differ by 4?

 (A) 13
 (B) 25
 (C) 45
 (D) 56
 (E) 63

USE THIS SPACE FOR SCRATCHWORK.

13. In the figure, AB and CD are the diameters of the circle. What is the value of x?

    (A) 16°
    (B) 18°
    (C) 26°
    (D) 32°
    (E) 58°

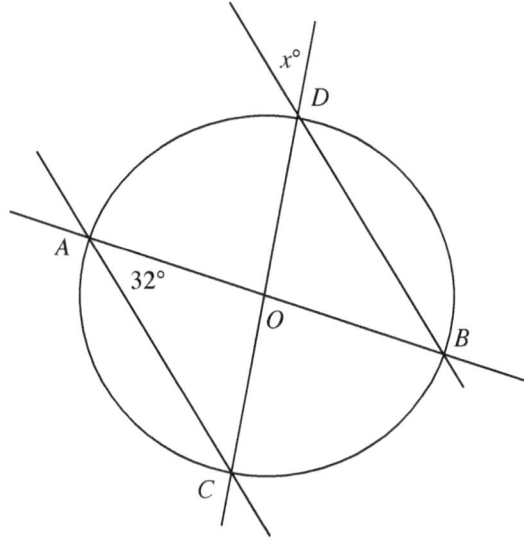

[Data Sufficiency Question]
14. Is $b > a$?

    (1) $a^4 + b^4 + c^4 = 0$
    (2) $a^3 + b^3 + c^3 = 0$

GMAT Math Tests

[Data Sufficiency Question]
15. $3x + 4y = C$
    $Kx + 12y = 36$

    What are the values of x and y ?

    (1) $C = 12$
    (2) $K = 9$

16. What is the probability that the sum of two different numbers randomly picked (without replacement) from the set $S = \{1, 2, 3, 4\}$ is 5?

    (A) 1/5
    (B) 3/16
    (C) 1/4
    (D) 1/3
    (E) 1/2

17. If p and q are positive, $p^2 + q^2 = 16$, and $p^2 - q^2 = 8$, then $q =$

    (A) 2
    (B) 4
    (C) 8
    (D) $2\sqrt{2}$
    (E) $2\sqrt{6}$

348

18. △ABC and △DEF are right triangles. Each side of triangle ABC is twice the length of the corresponding side of triangle DEF. $\dfrac{\text{The area of } \triangle DEF}{\text{The area of } \triangle ABC} =$

    (A) 4
    (B) 2
    (C) 1
    (D) 1/2
    (E) 1/4

[Data Sufficiency Question]
19. Is $x = 3$?

    (1) $\dfrac{(x-3)(x-4)}{(x-3)} = 0$
    (2) $(x-4)(x+4) = 0$

20. The percentage of integers from 1 through 100 whose squares end with the digit 1 is $x\%$, and the percentage of integers from 1 through 200 whose squares end with the digit 1 is $y\%$. Which one of the following is true?

    (A) $x = y$
    (B) $x = 2y$
    (C) $x = 4y$
    (D) $y = 2x$
    (E) $y = 4x$

21. In the figure, which one of the following angles is the greatest?

   (A)   ∠A
   (B)   ∠B
   (C)   ∠C
   (D)   ∠D
   (E)   ∠CDB

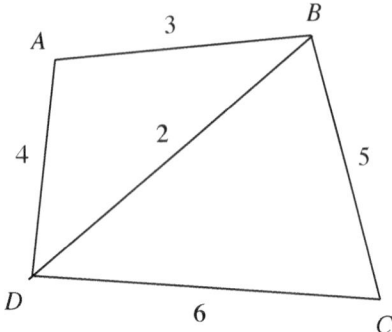

The figure is not drawn to scale.

22. The ratio of the number of red balls, to yellow balls, to green balls in a urn is 2 : 3 : 4. What is the probability that a ball chosen at random from the urn is a red ball?

   (A)   2/9
   (B)   3/9
   (C)   4/9
   (D)   5/9
   (E)   7/9

23. How much funding did the Education & Health Services get through state and central funding in the year?

    (1) The thick shaded region in Chart A represents 3,54,300 dollars.
    (2) The thick shaded region in Chart B represents 2,32,482 dollars.

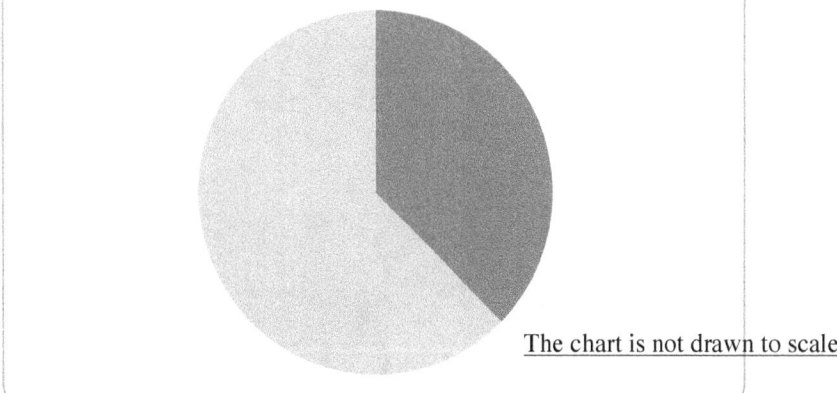

Chart A:

Distribution of usage of state tax for Education & Health Services for every 1 million dollars.

The chart is not drawn to scale

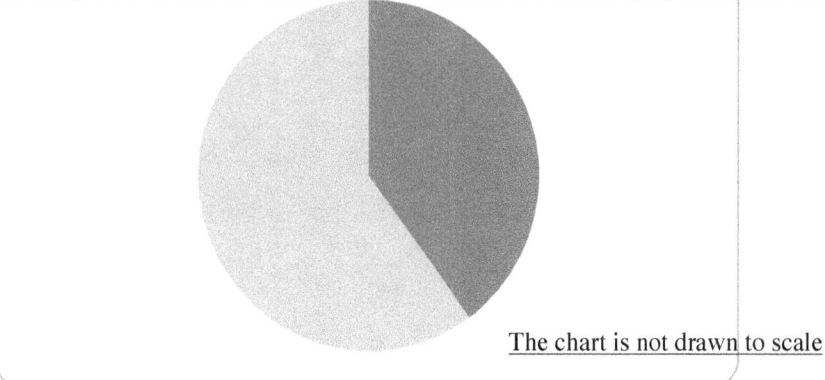

Chart B:

Distribution of usage of central tax for Education & Health Services for every 1 million dollars.

The chart is not drawn to scale

GMAT Math Tests

24. The graph shows the exports by the state of Ohio in 2006 and 2007. By how many times in dollars did the American corn export increase over Wheat export from 2006 to 2007?

   (1) The exports of Rice and American Corn together in the two years are $2 million and $3 million, respectively.

   (2) The exports of Wheat and Rice together in the two years are $4 million and $7 million, respectively.

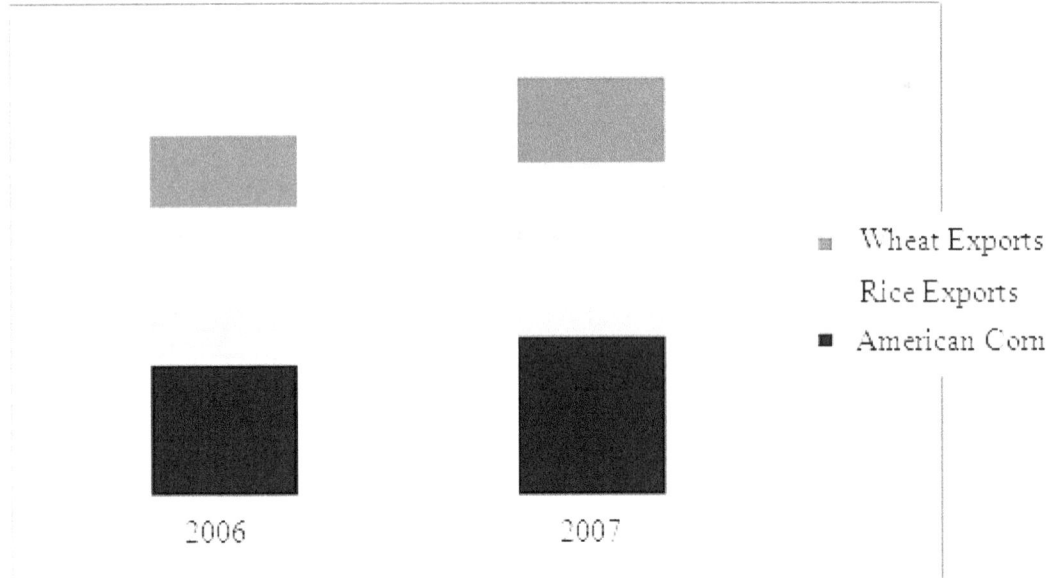

Graph not plotted to scale

25. An expense reduction consulting company needs to analyze tips to cut cost in a company. To help in doing this, they need the fraction of R & D expenditure that's funded through the non-chain market. The charts above show the distribution of the profits to different categories of expenses of Robert's shoe making company. What's the fraction as calculated by the consulting company, assuming the calculations it did are correct?

   (1) Dossier has the true information: R & D in the chain account chart represents 4,22,051 dollars.
   (2) Dossier has the true information: R & D in the non-chain account chart represents 3,33,235 dollars.

Chain Account usage: Distribution of usage of every 1 million dollars profit from chain market this fiscal year to Research & Development by Robert's shoe making company.

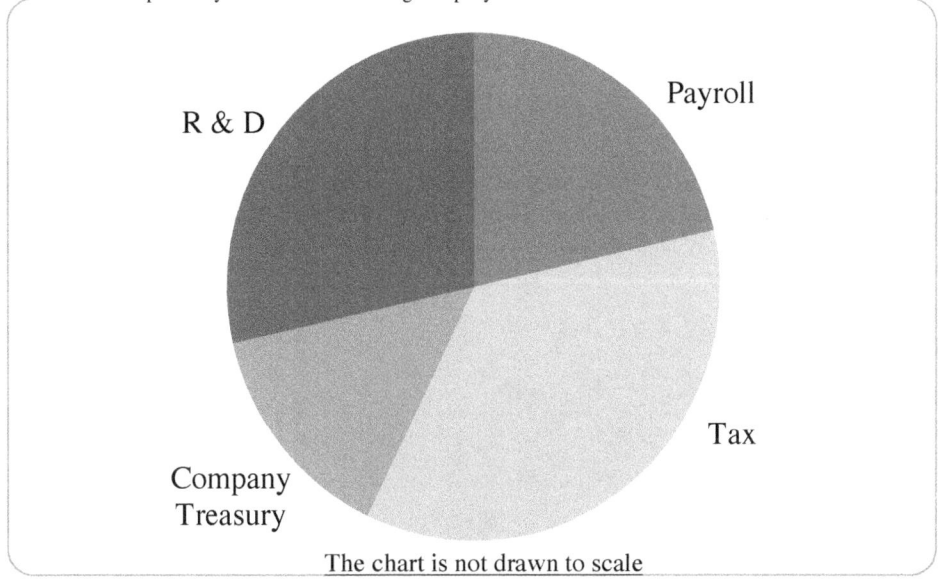

The chart is not drawn to scale

Non-Chain Account usage: Distribution of usage of every 1 million dollars profit from non-chain market this fiscal year to Research & Development by Robert's shoe making company.

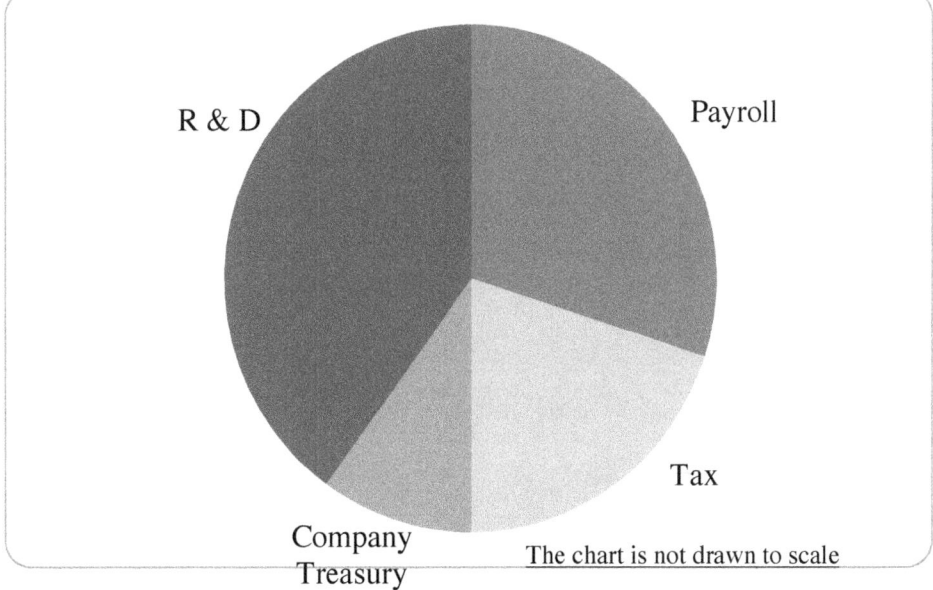

The chart is not drawn to scale

26. If $2 < x < 5$ and $3 < y < 5$, which of the following best describes $x - y$?

    (A) $-3 < x - y < 2$
    (B) $-3 < x - y < 5$
    (C) $0 < x - y < 2$
    (D) $3 < x - y < 5$
    (E) $2 < x - y < 5$

27. In 2007, the arithmetic mean of the annual incomes of Jack and Jill was $3800. The arithmetic mean of the annual incomes of Jill and Jess was $4800, and the arithmetic mean of the annual incomes of Jess and Jack was $5800. What is the arithmetic mean of the incomes of the three?

    (A) $4000
    (B) $4200
    (C) $4400
    (D) $4800
    (E) $5000

[Data Sufficiency Question]

28. Waugh jogged to a restaurant at x miles per hour, and jogged back home along the same route at y miles per hour. He took 30 minutes for the whole trip. What is the average speed at which he jogged for the whole trip?

    (1) The restaurant is 2 miles from home.
    (2) $x = 12$ and $y = 6$.

Data Sufficiency Question]
29. What is the average temperature from Monday through Saturday of a week?

   (1)   The average temperature from Monday through Wednesday of the week is 36°C.
   (2)   The minimum and maximum temperatures between Thursday and Saturday of the week are 25°C and 38°C, respectively.

[Data Sufficiency Question]
30. Does Set A contain at least one odd prime number?

   (1)   A contains odd numbers.
   (2)   A contains prime numbers.

31. In the figure, ∠P =

   (A)   15°
   (B)   30°
   (C)   35°
   (D)   40°
   (E)   50°

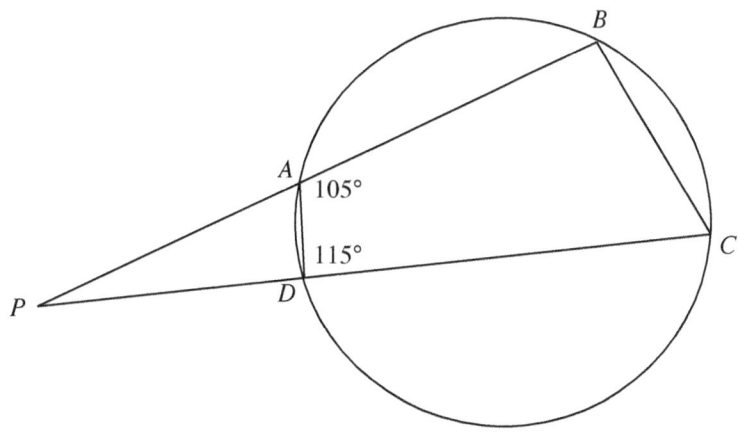

[Data Sufficiency Question]
32. How many families in the town of Windsor have exactly one car?

    (1)   250 families have at least one car.
    (2)   60 families have at least two cars.

33. There are 87 balls in a jar. Each ball is painted with at least one of two colors, red or green. It is observed that 2/7 of the balls that have red color also have green color, while 3/7 of the balls that have green color also have red color. What fraction of the balls in the jar have both red and green colors?

    (A)   6/14
    (B)   2/7
    (C)   6/35
    (D)   6/29
    (E)   6/42

[Data Sufficiency Question]
34. What is Set A?

    (1)   Set A contains only even numbers.
    (2)   Set A contains all the even numbers.

35. The diagonal length of a square is 14.1 sq. units. What is the area of the square, rounded to the nearest integer? ($\sqrt{2}$ is approximately 1.41.)

    (A) 96
    (B) 97
    (C) 98
    (D) 99
    (E) 100

[Data Sufficiency Question]

36. What is the average speed of the car during its entire trip?

    (1) The car traveled at 75 mph for the first half (by time) of the trip and at 40 mph for the second half of the trip.
    (2) The car would have taken 5 hrs. to complete the trip if it traveled at 75 mph for the entire trip.

37. A meeting is attended by 750 professionals. 450 of the attendees are females. Half the female attendees are less than thirty years old, and one-fourth of the male attendees are less than thirty years old. If one of the attendees of the meeting is selected at random to receive a prize, what is the probability that the person selected is less than thirty years old?

    (A) 1/8
    (B) 1/2
    (C) 3/8
    (D) 2/5
    (E) 3/4

Answers and Solutions Test 13:

1.	E	11.	E	21.	A	31.	D
2.	E	12.	D	22.	A	32.	C
3.	D	13.	D	23.	E	33.	D
4.	A	14.	A	24.	C	34.	C
5.	E	15.	E	25.	E	35.	D
6.	C	16.	D	26.	A	36.	A
7.	E	17.	A	27.	D	37.	D
8.	D	18.	E	28.	D		
9.	E	19.	A	29.	E		
10.	C	20.	A	30.	E		

1. Translating *"the ratio of y to x is equal to 3"* into an equation yields

$$\frac{y}{x} = 3$$

Translating *"the sum of y and x is 80"* into an equation yields

$$y + x = 80$$

Solving the first equation for y gives $y = 3x$. Substituting this into the second equation yields

$$3x + x = 80$$
$$4x = 80$$
$$x = 20$$

Hence, $y = 3x = 3 \cdot 20 = 60$. The answer is (E).

2. Any number divisible by both 6 and 8 must be a multiple of the least common multiple of the two numbers, which is 24. Hence, any such number can be represented as $24n$. If 3072 is one such number and is represented as $24n$, then the next such number should be $24(n + 1) = 24n + 24 = 3072 + 24 = 3096$. The answer is (E).

3. Forming the given ratio yields

$$A/1 = B/2 = C/3 = k, \text{ for some integer}$$
$$A = k, B = 2k, \text{ and } C = 3k$$

Choice (A): $A + B + C = k + 2k + 3k = 6k$. This is a perfect square only when k is a product of 6 and a perfect square number. For example, when k is $6 \cdot 9^2$, $6k = 6^2 \cdot 9^2$, a perfect square. In all other cases (suppose $k = 2$, then $6k = 12$), it is not a perfect square. Hence, reject.

Choice (B): $A^2 + B^2 + C^2 = k^2 + (2k)^2 + (3k)^2 = k^2 + 4k^2 + 9k^2 = 14k^2$. This is surely not a perfect square. For example, suppose k equals 2. Then $14k^2 = 56$, which is not a perfect square. Hence, reject.

Choice (C): $A^3 + B^3 + C^3 = k^3 + (2k)^3 + (3k)^3 = k^3 + 8k^3 + 27k^3 = 36k^3$. This is a perfect square only when k^3 is perfect square. For example, suppose $k = 2$. Then $36k^3 = 288$, which is not a perfect square. Hence, reject.

Choice (D): $3A^2 + B^2 + C^2 = 3k^2 + (2k)^2 + (3k)^2 = 3k^2 + 4k^2 + 9k^2 = 16k^2 = 4^2k^2 = (4k)^2$. The square root of $(4k)^2$ is $4k$ and is an integer for any integer value of k. Hence, this expression must always result in a perfect square. Choose (D).

Choice (E): $3A^2 + 4B^2 + 4C^2 = 3k^2 + 4(2k)^2 + 4(3k)^2 = 3k^2 + 16k^2 + 36k^2 = 55k^2$. This is surely not a perfect square. Hence, reject.

The answer is (D).

Test 13—Answers and Solutions

4. From Statement (1) alone, we have that $4p \neq 6q$. Dividing both sides by 2 yields $2p \neq 3q$. Subtracting $3q$ from both sides yields $2p - 3q \neq 0$. Hence, Statement (1) alone is sufficient to answer the question.

From Statement (2) alone, we have $p \neq q$. Multiplying both sides by 2 yields $2p \neq 2q$. Subtracting $3q$ from both sides yields $2p - 3q \neq -q$. Now, if q equals 0, then $2p - 3q$ does not equal 0. But if q does not equal 0, then $2p - 3q$ may equal 0 [For example, when $p = 3$ and $q = 2$, then $2p - 3q = 2(3) - 3(2) = 0$]. Hence, we have a double case, and Statement (2) alone is not sufficient.

Since Statement (1) alone is sufficient, the answer is (A).

5. From the distribution given, there are

   4 families having exactly 4 cars
   5 families having exactly 5 cars
   2 families having exactly 6 cars

Hence, there are $4 + 5 + 2 = 11$ families with at least 4 cars. Hence, the probability of picking one such family from the 20 families is 11/20. The answer is (E).

6. The formula for the area of a rectangle is *length × width*. Hence, the area of rectangle *ABCD* is

$$(x + 6)(x + 2) = x^2 + 8x + 12$$

and the area of the rectangle *EFGH* is

$$(x + a)(x + b) = x^2 + (a + b)x + ab = x^2 + 8x + ab \text{ (given that } a + b = 8\text{)}$$

Now, we are given that the area of the rectangle *EFGH* is 3 units greater than the area of the rectangle *ABCD*. Hence, we have

$x^2 + 8x + ab = (x^2 + 8x + 12) + 3$
$ab = 12 + 3$ (by canceling x^2 and $8x$ from both sides)
$ab = 15$

The answer is (C).

7. Statement (1): $x/4$ is a positive integer when x is a multiple of 4. Now, not every multiple of 4 is divisible by 14. For example, 28 is a multiple of 4 and divisible by 14, but 32 is a multiple of 4 and not divisible by 14. Hence, Statement (1) alone is not sufficient.

Statement (2): $x/6$ is a positive integer when x is a multiple of 6. Now, not every multiple of 6 is divisible by 14. For example, 42 is a multiple of 6 and divisible by 14, but 48 is a multiple of 6 and not divisible by 14. Hence, Statement (2) alone is not sufficient.

With statements (1) and (2) together, we have that x is a multiple of both 4 and 6. Hence, x must be a multiple of the least common multiple of 4 and 6, which is 12. Hence, x is a multiple of 12. Now, not every multiple of 12 is divisible by 14. For example, 84 is a multiple of 12 and divisible by 14, but 24 is a multiple of 12 and not divisible by 14. Hence, even statements (1) and (2) together do not answer the question. The answer is (E).

8. We are given the expression $x^2 - y^2 = 15$. Applying the Difference of Squares formula $(a + b)(a - b) = a^2 - b^2$ to the left-hand side yields $(x + y)(x - y) = 15$.

From Statement (1) alone, we have $x - y = 5$. Plugging this in the equation $(x + y)(x - y) = 15$ yields $(x + y)(5) = 15$. Dividing both sides by 5 yields $x + y = 3$. Hence, $x + y < x - y$ because $3 < 5$. Hence, Statement (1) alone is sufficient. The answer is "No. $x + y > x - y$ is false."

From Statement (2) alone, we have $x + y = 3$. Plugging this in the equation $(x + y)(x - y) = 15$ yields $3(x - y) = 15$. Dividing both sides by 3 yields $x - y = 5$. Hence, $x + y < x - y$ because $3 < 5$ Hence, Statement (2) alone is sufficient. The answer is "No. $x + y$ is not greater than $x - y$."

The answer is (D).

9. We know that the slope of a line through any two points (x_1, y_1) and (x_2, y_2) is given by $\dfrac{y_2 - y_1}{x_2 - x_1}$.

Since $(-2, 0)$ and $(0, 2)$ are two points on the line $f(x)$, the slope of the line is $\dfrac{2-0}{0-(-2)} = \dfrac{2}{2} = 1$.

If $(10, f(10))$ is a point on the line, then using the point $(0, 2)$ the slope of the line is

$$\dfrac{f(10) - 2}{10 - 0} = 1$$
$$f(10) - 2 = 10$$
$$f(10) = 12$$

The answer is (E).

10. Adding p to both sides of the question "$2y = 20 - p$?" yields "Is $2y + p = 20$?" Let the expression to be checked "$2y + p$" be t. Then $p = t - 2y$.

Statement (1): $x = y + p$

We have $x = y + p$. Putting $t - 2y$ for p yields

$$x = y + t - 2y = t - y$$
$$t = x + y$$

Since $x + y$ is unknown, the statement alone is *not* sufficient.

Statement (2): $x + y = 10$

We have $x + y = 10$. Since there is no p in the statement, the statement does not constrain the value of t (which is a function of p as $2y + p$) from being a particular value. Hence, the statement is not sufficient alone.

With the statements together, we have $t = x + y$ [from Statement (1)] = 10 [from Statement (2)]. Hence, the statements together answer the question. The answer is (C).

Test 13—Answers and Solutions

11. Suppose $x = 1$, $y = 2$, and $z = 3$, which satisfy both statements. Next, suppose $x = 2$, $y = 4$, and $z = 6$, which also satisfy both statements. Both statements reveal the same and therefore together are not sufficient. The answer is (E).

---

12. Suppose a and b are the single-digit numbers. Then by the Difference of Squares formula

$$a^2 - b^2 = (a - b)(a + b) = 4(a + b) \text{ [Given that difference between the digits is 4]}$$

This is maximum when $(a + b)$ is maximum.

If a and b are single digit numbers, then $a + b$ would be a maximum when a is equal to 9 and $b = 9 - 4 = 5$ (given the numbers differ by 4). Hence, the maximum value of $a^2 - b^2$ is $9^2 - 5^2 = 56$. The answer is (D).

---

13. OA and OC are radii of the circle and therefore equal. Hence, the angles opposite the two sides in $\triangle AOC$ are equal: $\angle C = \angle A = 32°$ (from the figure). Now, summing the angles of the triangle to 180° yields $\angle A + \angle C + \angle AOC = 180$ or $32 + 32 + \angle AOC = 180$. Solving the equation for $\angle AOC$, we have $\angle AOC = 180 - (32 + 32) = 180 - 64 = 114$.

Since $\angle BOD$ and $\angle AOC$ vertical angles, they are equal. Hence, we have $\angle BOD = \angle AOC = 114$.

Now, OD and OB are radii of the circle and therefore equal. Hence, the angles opposite the two sides in $\triangle BOD$ are equal: $\angle B = \angle D$. Now, summing the angles of the triangle to 180° yields $\angle B + \angle D + \angle BOD = 180$ or $\angle D + \angle D + \angle BOD = 180$ or $2\angle D + 114 = 180$. Solving the equation yields $\angle D = 32$. Since $\angle D$ and angle $x°$ are vertical angles, x also equals 32.

The answer is (D).

14.

Statement (1): $a^4 + b^4 + c^4 = 0$

Unless $a = b = c = 0$, $a^4 + b^4 + c^4$ cannot equal 0. Hence, $a = b = c = 0$ must be true.

For example, if $a = -1$, $b = 0$, and $c = 1$. Then $a^4 = 1$ (becomes positive), $b^4 = 0$, and $c^4 = 1$ and the three sum to 2.

Hence, $b > a$ is false. The statement is sufficient.

Statement (2): $a^3 + b^3 + c^3 = 0$

Suppose $a = -1$, $b = 0$, and $c = 1$. Then $a^3 + b^3 + c^3 = (-1)^3 + 0^3 + 1^3 = -1 + 0 + 1 = 0$. Here, $b > a$ is true.

Suppose $a = 1$, $b = 0$, and $c = -1$. Then $a^3 + b^3 + c^3 = 1^3 + 0^3 + (-1)^3 = 1 + 0 + -1 = 0$. Here, $b > a$ is false.

We have a double case and therefore the statement is *not* sufficient.

The answer is (A).

15. To determine the system completely, we need both parameters C and K. Clearly, we need the statements together (neither statement alone is sufficient).

Substituting the values given in both statements into the system yields

$$3x + 4y = 12$$
$$9x + 12y = 36$$

Dividing the bottom equation by 3 yields the top equation. Hence, we effectively have a single equation and therefore any point (hence, there is more than one solution) on the line must be a solution. We do not have fixed solution for x and y. Hence, the statements together are not sufficient. The answer is (E).

---

16. The first selection can be done in 4 ways (by selecting any one of the numbers 1, 2, 3, and 4 of the set S). Hence, there are 3 elements remaining in the set. The second number can be selected in 3 ways (by selecting any one of the remaining 3 numbers in the set S). Hence, the total number of ways the selection can be made is $4 \times 3 = 12$.

The selections that result in the sum 5 are 1 and 4, 4 and 1, 2 and 3, 3 and 2, a total of 4 selections. So, 4 of the 12 possible selections have a sum of 5. Hence, the probability is the fraction $4/12 = 1/3$. The answer is (D).

---

17. Subtract the second equation from the first:

$$\begin{array}{r} p^2 + q^2 = 16 \\ (-)\ p^2 - q^2 = 8 \\ \hline 2q^2 = 8 \end{array}$$

Dividing both sides of the equation by 2 gives $q^2 = 4$

Finally, taking the square root of both sides gives $q = \pm 2$

Hence, the answer is (A).

---

18. We are given that each side of triangle ABC is twice the length of the corresponding side of triangle DEF. Hence, each leg of triangle ABC must be twice the length of the corresponding leg in triangle DEF. The formula for the area of a right triangle is $1/2 \cdot$ *product of the measures of the two legs*. Hence,

$$\frac{\text{The area of } \Delta DEF}{\text{The area of } \Delta ABC} =$$

$$\frac{\frac{1}{2}(\text{leg 1 of } \Delta DEF)(\text{leg 2 of } \Delta DEF)}{\frac{1}{2}(\text{leg 1 of } \Delta ABC)(\text{leg 2 of } \Delta ABC)} =$$

$$\frac{\frac{1}{2}(\text{leg 1 of } \Delta DEF)(\text{leg 2 of } \Delta DEF)}{\frac{1}{2}(2 \cdot \text{leg 1 of } \Delta DEF)(2 \cdot \text{leg 2 of } \Delta DEF)} =$$

$$\frac{\frac{1}{2}}{\frac{1}{2} \cdot 2 \cdot 2} =$$

$$\frac{1}{2 \cdot 2} =$$

$$\frac{1}{4}$$

The answer is (E).

Test 13—Answers and Solutions

19.

Statement (1): $\dfrac{(x-3)(x-4)}{(x-3)} = 0$

A fraction can equal 0 only when the numerator is 0 and the denominator is not zero. So, the numerator of equation above says x equals 3 or 4 while the denominator says x is not 3. The only solution left is $x = 4$. We can answer the question as "No. $x \neq 3$."

The answer is (A).

Statement (2): $(x-4)(x+4) = 0$

The expression $(x-4)(x+4)$ equals 0 when x equals 4 or x equals -4.

This is double case and therefore the statement is *not* sufficient.

---

20. The square of an integer ends with the digit 1 only if the integer itself either ends with the digit 1 or with the digit 9. For example, $11^2 = 121$ and $19^2 = 361$. Now, there are ten integers ending with 1 from 1 through 100. The numbers are 1, 11, 21, ..., 91. Also, there are ten integers ending with 9 from 1 through 100. They are 9, 19, 29, ..., 99. Hence, the total number of integers from 1 through 100 whose squares end with the digit 1 is 20. The number 20 is $20/100 \times 100 = 20\%$ of 100. Hence, $x = 20$.

Similarly, there are twenty integers (1, 11, 21... 191) ending with 1, and twenty integers (9, 19, 29, ..., 199) ending with 9. Hence, there are $20 + 20 = 40$ integers ending with 1 or 9. Now, 40 is $40/200 \times 100 = 20\%$ of the total 200 integers from 1 through 200. So, y also equals 20. Since $x = y$, the answer is (A).

---

21. In $\triangle ABD$, $AD = 4$, $AB = 3$, and $BD = 2$ (from the figure). Forming the inequality relation for the side lengths yields $AD > AB > BD$. Since in a triangle, the angle opposite the longer side is greater, we have a similar inequality for the angles opposite the corresponding sides: $\angle ABD > \angle BDA > \angle A$.

Similarly, in $\triangle BCD$, $DC = 6$, $BC = 5$, and $BD = 2$. Forming the inequality for the side lengths yields $DC > BC > BD$. Also the angles opposite the corresponding sides follow the relation $\angle DBC > \angle CDB > \angle C$.

Now, summing the two known inequalities $\angle ABD > \angle BDA > \angle A$ and $\angle DBC > \angle CDB > \angle C$ yields $\angle ABD + \angle DBC > \angle BDA + \angle CDB > \angle A + \angle C$; $\angle B > \angle D > \angle A + \angle C$. From this inequality, clearly $\angle B$ is the greatest angle. Hence, the answer is (B).

---

22. Let the number of red balls in the urn be $2k$, the number of yellow balls $3k$, and the number of green balls $4k$, where k is a common factor of the three. Now, the total number of balls in the urn is $2k + 3k + 4k = 9k$. Hence, the fraction of red balls from all the balls is $2k/9k = 2/9$. This also equals the probability that a ball chosen at random from the urn is a red ball. The answer is (A).

---

23. From the distribution in the two charts and the two statements, we have that the 3,54,300 dollars of every 1 million dollars of state tax is the funding from the part of the state tax that Education & Health services get. But we do not know how many millions of dollars is the state tax. Similarly, 2,32,482 dollars of every 1 million dollars of central tax is the funding from the part of the central tax to Educational & Health services. But we do not know how many millions of dollars is the central tax. Hence, we cannot determine the net contribution to the services. The answer is (E).

The net contribution would be $3,54,300/10,00,000 \times$ State tax $+ 2,32,482/10,00,000 \times$ Central tax.

24. Suppose Rice exports is r, the American Corn exports is a, and the Wheat exports is w, all in million dollars.

Then in 2006, $r + a = 2$ [from Statement (1)]; and in 2007, $w + r = 4$ [from Statement (2)].

And in 2007, $r + a = 4$ [from statement (1)]; and in 2007, $w + r = 7$ [from Statement (2)].

Subtracting the equation for 2006 $r + a = 2$ from the equation $w + r = 4$ yields $(w + r = 4) - (r + a = 2)$, or $w + r - (r + a) = 4 - 2$, or $w - a = 2$.

Subtracting the equation for 2007 $r + a = 4$ from the equation $w + r = 7$ yields $(w + r = 7) - (r + a = 4)$, or $w + r - (r + a) = 7 - 4$, or $w + r - r - a = 7 - 4$, or $w - a = 3$.

The answer is the ratio $w - a$ in 2007 to $w - a$ in 2006, which equals 3 : 2. The two statements are required to answer the question. The answer is (C).

---

25. If you thought we are not given the profit routes other than the chain and the non-chain profit routes, you are mistaken. If a chain is a particular profit route, a non-chain represents all other profit routes. So, you actually have all the needed profit routes to analyze.

From the distribution in the two charts and the two statements, we have the following two points:

The 4,22,051 dollars of every 1 million dollars of profit from chain account is funded to R & D.

Let's formulate it as 4,22,051/1 million × Profit from chain in dollars.

The 3,33,235 dollars of every 1 million dollars of profit from non-chain account is funded to R & D.

Let's formulate it as 3,33,235/1 million × Profit from non-chain in dollars.

The total of the two funds is the fund received by R & D. Hence, the part of it that is funded by non-chain equals

[3,33,235/1 million × Profit from non-chain]/[3,33,235/1 million × Profit from non-chain + 4,22,051/1 million × Profit from chain]

To calculate this we need at least the ratio of the profit of the chain to the profit of the non-chain. Since we do not have that, the statements together are *not* sufficient. The answer is (E).

---

26. Multiplying both sides of $3 < y < 5$ by -1 yields $-3 > -y > -5$. Now, we usually write the smaller number on the left side of the inequality. So $-3 > -y > -5$ becomes $-5 < -y < -3$. Add this inequality to the like inequality $2 < x < 5$:

$$2 < x < 5$$
$$(+) \quad -5 < -y < -3$$
$$\overline{-3 < x - y < 2}$$

The answer is (A).

Test 13—Answers and Solutions

---

27. Let a, b, and c be the annual incomes of Jack, Jill, and Jess, respectively. Now, we are given that

The arithmetic mean of the annual incomes of Jack and Jill was $3800. Hence, $(a + b)/2 = 3800$. Multiplying by 2 yields $a + b = 2 \times 3800 = 7600$.

The arithmetic mean of the annual incomes of Jill and Jess was $4800. Hence, $(b + c)/2 = 4800$. Multiplying by 2 yields $b + c = 2 \times 4800 = 9600$.

The arithmetic mean of the annual incomes of Jess and Jack was $5800. Hence, $(c + a)/2 = 5800$. Multiplying by 2 yields $c + a = 2 \times 5800 = 11{,}600$.

Summing these three equations yields

$$(a + b) + (b + c) + (c + a) = 7600 + 9600 + 11{,}600$$

$$2a + 2b + 2c = 28{,}800$$

$$a + b + c = 14{,}400$$

The average of the incomes of the three equals the sum of the incomes divided by 3:

$$(a + b + c)/3 =$$

$$14{,}400/3 =$$

$$4800$$

The answer is (D).

---

28. Remember that *Average Speed = Net Distance ÷ Time Taken*. We are given that the time taken for the full trip is 30 minutes. Hence, we need only the distance traveled.

From Statement (1) alone, we have that the restaurant is 2 miles from home. Since Waugh jogs back along the same route, the net distance he traveled is 2 miles + 2 miles = 4 miles. Hence, his average speed is 4 miles ÷ 30 minutes, which can be calculated. Hence, Statement (1) alone is sufficient.

From Statement (2) alone, we have that $x = 12$ and $y = 6$. Let d be the distance to the restaurant. Then the time taken to jog to the restaurant, by the formula *Time = Distance ÷ Speed*, equals $d \div x = d/12$; and to return home from restaurant, the time taken equals $d \div y = d \div 6$. Hence, the total time taken equals $d/12 + d/6$, which is given to be 30 minutes (1/2 hour). Hence, d can be calculated from this formula, and therefore the average speed can be calculated using

$$Distance \div Time = \frac{2d}{\frac{1}{2} \text{ hours}} = 4d$$

Hence, Statement (2) alone is also sufficient.

The answer is (D).

29. From Statement (1), we have information about the average temperature only for the period Monday through Wednesday. Since there is no relevant information for the rest of the week, Statement (1) alone is not sufficient.

Statement (2) has information about the minimum and the maximum temperatures for the period Thursday through Saturday. It does not help us evaluate the average temperature for the period.

With the two statements together, we do not have information about average temperatures for the complete week. Hence, the statements together are not sufficient to answer the question.

The answer is (E).

---

30. Statement (1) allows odd numbers but could contain other numbers that are not odd.

Statement (2) allows prime numbers but could contain other numbers that are not prime.

Statements (1) and (2) contain odd numbers and prime numbers. This does not necessarily mean that Set A contains at least a one odd prime number. 2 is a prime that is not odd. The set may contain only odd number and only prime number. For example, in the set $A = \{2, 9, 15\}$, both statements are satisfied and still not necessarily a single odd prime number is there. But if $A = \{3, 9, 15\}$, then both statements are satisfied and we have at least one odd-prime number, 3. Thus, we have a double case, and the answer is (E).

---

31. Since the angle in a line is 180°, we have $\angle PAD + \angle DAB = 180$, or $\angle PAD + 105 = 180$ (from the figure, $\angle DAB = 105°$). Solving for $\angle PAD$ yields $\angle PAD = 75$.

Since the angle in a line is 180°, we have $\angle ADP + \angle ADC = 180$, or $\angle ADP + 115 = 180$ (from the figure, $\angle ADC = 115°$). Solving for $\angle ADP$ yields $\angle ADP = 65$.

Now, summing the angles of the triangle PAD to 180° yields

$$\angle P + \angle PAD + \angle ADP = 180$$

$$\angle P + 75 + 65 = 180$$

$$\angle P = 40$$

The answer is (D).

Test 13—Answers and Solutions

32. Let A be the set of families having exactly one car. Then the question is how many families are there in set A.

Next, let B be the set of families having exactly two cars, and let C be the set of families having more than two cars.

Then the set of families having at least one car is the collection of the three sets A, B, and C. Since Statement (1) gives only the total number of families in the three sets, the statement is not sufficient.

Next, the set of families having at least two cars is the collection of the two sets B and C. Since Statement (2) does not have any information about set A, Statement (2) alone is not sufficient.

Now, from the statements together we have that

The number of families in all the three sets A, B, and C together = 250 [from Statement (1)]

and

The number of families in the two sets B and C together = 60 [from Statement (2)]

Since set A is the difference between a set containing the three families of A, B, and C and a set of families of B and C only, The number of families in set A =

(The number of families in sets A, B, and C together) – (the number of families in sets B and C) =

250 – 60 =

190

Hence, both statements are required to answer the question, and the answer is (C).

---

33. Let T be the total number of balls, R the number of balls having red color, G the number having green color, and B the number having both colors.

So, the number of balls having only red is $R - B$, the number having only green is $G - B$, and the number having both is B. Now, the total number of balls is

$$T = (R - B) + (G - B) + B = R + G - B$$

We are given that 2/7 of the balls having red color have green also. This implies that $B = 2R/7$. Also, we are given that 3/7 of the green balls have red color. This implies that $B = 3G/7$. Solving for R and G in these two equations yields $R = 7B/2$ and $G = 7B/3$. Substituting this into the equation $T = R + G - B$ yields $T = 7B/2 + 7B/3 - B$. Solving for B yields $B = 6T/29$. Hence, 6/29 of all the balls in the jar have both colors. The answer is (D). Note that we did not use the information: "There are 87 balls." Sometimes, not all information in a problem is needed.

34. Clearly, the question is asking for the listing of the series or the definition of the series that can be used to list the series.

Statement (1): Set A contains only even numbers.

Here, Set A could be

$\{2, 4\}$, or $\{6, 10\}$, or $\{4, 8, 18\}$, etc.

We do not have a unique solution and therefore the statement is *not* sufficient.

Statement (2): Set A contains all the even numbers.

Here, Set A must have the elements

..., –4, –2, 0, 2, 4, 6, ...

But the statement does not prevent Set A from containing elements that are not even. It just says that it contains all the even numbers. Thus, we could also have non-even integers and literally the series is not adequately defined. The statement is *not* sufficient.

Considering both statements, we derive that A contains all the even numbers and only even numbers. Thus, the statements together are sufficient.

The answer is (C).

---

35. If a is the length of a side of the square, then a diagonal divides the square into two congruent (equal) right triangles. Applying The Pythagorean Theorem to either triangle yields

$$diagonal^2 = side^2 + side^2 = a^2 + a^2 = 2a^2$$

Taking the square root of both sides of this equation yields $diagonal = a\sqrt{2}$. We are given that the diagonal length is 14.1. Hence, $a\sqrt{2} = 14.1$ or $a = \dfrac{14.1}{\sqrt{2}}$. Now, the area, a^2, equals

$$\left(\frac{14.1}{\sqrt{2}}\right)^2 = \frac{14.1^2}{\left(\sqrt{2}\right)^2} = \frac{14.1^2}{2} = \frac{198.81}{2} = 99.4$$

The number 99.4 is nearest to 99. Hence, the answer is (D).

Note: If you had approximated $\dfrac{14.1}{\sqrt{2}}$ with 10, you would have mistakenly gotten 100 and would have answered (E). Approximation is the culprit. Prefer doing it in the last.

Test 13—Answers and Solutions

36. Let *t* be the entire time of the trip.

Then from Statement (1) alone, we have that the car traveled at 75 mph for $t/2$ hours and at 40 mph for the remaining $t/2$ hours. Remember that *Distance = Speed × Time*. Hence, the net distance traveled during the two periods equals $75 \times t/2 + 40 \times t/2$. Now, remember that

$$Average\ Speed =$$

$$Net\ Distance\ /\ Time\ Taken =$$

$$\frac{75 \times t/2 + 40 \times t/2}{t} =$$

$$75 \times 1/2 + 40 \times 1/2$$

Hence, Statement (1) alone is sufficient.

Now, from Statement (2) alone, we have that if the car had constantly traveled at 75 mph, it would have needed 5 hrs. to complete the trip. But, we do not know how much time it has actually taken to complete the trip. Hence, we cannot find the average speed. So, Statement (2) alone is not sufficient.

The answer is (A).

---

37. The number of attendees at the meeting is 750 of which 450 are female. Hence, the number of male attendees is 750 – 450 = 300. Half of the female attendees are less than 30 years old. One half of 450 is 450/2 = 225. Also, one-fourth of the male attendees are less than 30 years old. One-fourth of 300 is 300/4 = 75.

Now, the total number of (male and female) attendees who are less than 30 years old is 225 + 75 = 300.

So, out of the total 750 attendees 300 attendees are less than 30 years old. Hence, the probability of randomly selecting an attendee less than 30 years old (equals the fraction of all the attendees who are less than 30 years old) is 300/750 = 2/5. The answer is (D).

Part Two
Summary of Math Properties

Arithmetic

1. A *prime number* is an integer that is divisible only by itself and 1.
2. An even number is divisible by 2, and can be written as $2x$.
3. An odd number is not divisible by 2, and can be written as $2x + 1$.
4. Division by zero is undefined.
5. Perfect squares: 1, 4, 9, 16, 25, 36, 49, 64, 81 . . .
6. Perfect cubes: 1, 8, 27, 64, 125 . . .
7. If the last digit of an integer is 0, 2, 4, 6, or 8, then it is divisible by 2.
8. An integer is divisible by 3 if the sum of its digits is divisible by 3.
9. If the last digit of an integer is 0 or 5, then it is divisible by 5.
10. Miscellaneous Properties of Positive and Negative Numbers:

    A. The product (quotient) of positive numbers is positive.
    B. The product (quotient) of a positive number and a negative number is negative.
    C. The product (quotient) of an even number of negative numbers is positive.
    D. The product (quotient) of an odd number of negative numbers is negative.
    E. The sum of negative numbers is negative.
    F. A number raised to an even exponent is greater than or equal to zero.

    $$even \times even = even$$
    $$odd \times odd = odd$$
    $$even \times odd = even$$

    $$even + even = even$$
    $$odd + odd = even$$
    $$even + odd = odd$$

11. Consecutive integers are written as $x, x + 1, x + 2, \ldots$
12. Consecutive even or odd integers are written as $x, x + 2, x + 4, \ldots$
13. The integer zero is neither positive nor negative, but it is even: $0 = 2 \cdot 0$.
14. Commutative property: $x + y = y + x$. Example: $5 + 4 = 4 + 5$.
15. Associative property: $(x + y) + z = x + (y + z)$. Example: $(1 + 2) + 3 = 1 + (2 + 3)$.
16. Order of operations: Parentheses, Exponents, Multiplication, Division, Addition, Subtraction.
17. $-\dfrac{x}{y} = \dfrac{-x}{y} = \dfrac{x}{-y}$. Example: $-\dfrac{2}{3} = \dfrac{-2}{3} = \dfrac{2}{-3}$
18.
    $33\dfrac{1}{3}\% = \dfrac{1}{3}$ $20\% = \dfrac{1}{5}$

    $66\dfrac{2}{3}\% = \dfrac{2}{3}$ $40\% = \dfrac{2}{5}$

    $25\% = \dfrac{1}{4}$ $60\% = \dfrac{3}{5}$

    $50\% = \dfrac{1}{2}$ $80\% = \dfrac{4}{5}$

19.
$\dfrac{1}{100} = .01 \qquad \dfrac{1}{10} = .1 \qquad \dfrac{2}{5} = .4$

$\dfrac{1}{50} = .02 \qquad \dfrac{1}{5} = .2 \qquad \dfrac{1}{2} = .5$

$\dfrac{1}{25} = .04 \qquad \dfrac{1}{4} = .25 \qquad \dfrac{2}{3} = .666\ldots$

$\dfrac{1}{20} = .05 \qquad \dfrac{1}{3} = .333\ldots \qquad \dfrac{3}{4} = .75$

20. Common measurements:
    1 foot = 12 inches
    1 yard = 3 feet
    1 quart = 2 pints
    1 gallon = 4 quarts
    1 pound = 16 ounces

21. Important approximations: $\sqrt{2} \approx 1.4 \qquad \sqrt{3} \approx 1.7 \qquad \pi \approx 3.14$

22. *"The remainder is r when p is divided by q"* means $p = qz + r$; the integer z is called the quotient. For instance, *"The remainder is 1 when 7 is divided by 3"* means $7 = 3 \cdot 2 + 1$.

23. $Probability = \dfrac{number\ of\ outcomes}{total\ number\ of\ possible\ outcomes}$

Algebra

24. Multiplying or dividing both sides of an inequality by a negative number reverses the inequality. That is, if $x > y$ and $c < 0$, then $cx < cy$.

25. Transitive Property: If $x < y$ and $y < z$, then $x < z$.

26. Like Inequalities Can Be Added: If $x < y$ and $w < z$, then $x + w < y + z$.

27. Rules for exponents:

$$x^a \cdot x^b = x^{a+b} \qquad \text{Caution, } x^a + x^b \neq x^{a+b}$$

$$\left(x^a\right)^b = x^{ab}$$

$$(xy)^a = x^a \cdot y^a$$

$$\left(\dfrac{x}{y}\right)^a = \dfrac{x^a}{y^a}$$

$$\dfrac{x^a}{x^b} = x^{a-b}, \text{ if } a > b. \qquad \dfrac{x^a}{x^b} = \dfrac{1}{x^{b-a}}, \text{ if } b > a.$$

$$x^0 = 1$$

28. There are only two rules for roots that you need to know for the test:

$$\sqrt[n]{xy} = \sqrt[n]{x}\sqrt[n]{y} \qquad \text{For example, } \sqrt{3x} = \sqrt{3}\sqrt{x}.$$

$$\sqrt[n]{\dfrac{x}{y}} = \dfrac{\sqrt[n]{x}}{\sqrt[n]{y}} \qquad \text{For example, } \sqrt[3]{\dfrac{x}{8}} = \dfrac{\sqrt[3]{x}}{\sqrt[3]{8}} = \dfrac{\sqrt[3]{x}}{2}.$$

$$\text{Caution: } \sqrt[n]{x+y} \neq \sqrt[n]{x} + \sqrt[n]{y}.$$

Summary of Math Properties

29. Factoring formulas:
$$x(y + z) = xy + xz$$
$$x^2 - y^2 = (x + y)(x - y)$$
$$(x - y)^2 = x^2 - 2xy + y^2$$
$$(x + y)^2 = x^2 + 2xy + y^2$$
$$-(x - y) = y - x$$

30. Adding, multiplying, and dividing fractions:

$\dfrac{x}{y} + \dfrac{z}{y} = \dfrac{x+z}{y}$ and $\dfrac{x}{y} - \dfrac{z}{y} = \dfrac{x-z}{y}$ Example: $\dfrac{2}{4} + \dfrac{3}{4} = \dfrac{2+3}{4} = \dfrac{5}{4}$.

$\dfrac{w}{x} \cdot \dfrac{y}{z} = \dfrac{wy}{xz}$ Example: $\dfrac{1}{2} \cdot \dfrac{3}{4} = \dfrac{1 \cdot 3}{2 \cdot 4} = \dfrac{3}{8}$.

$\dfrac{w}{x} \div \dfrac{y}{z} = \dfrac{w}{x} \cdot \dfrac{z}{y}$ Example: $\dfrac{1}{2} \div \dfrac{3}{4} = \dfrac{1}{2} \cdot \dfrac{4}{3} = \dfrac{4}{6} = \dfrac{2}{3}$.

31. $x\% = \dfrac{x}{100}$

32. Quadratic Formula: $x = \dfrac{-b \pm \sqrt{b^2 - 4ac}}{2a}$ are the solutions of the equation $ax^2 + bx + c = 0$.

Geometry

33. There are four major types of angle measures:

    An **acute angle** has measure less than 90°:

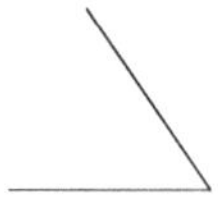

    A **right angle** has measure 90°:   90°

    An **obtuse angle** has measure greater than 90°:

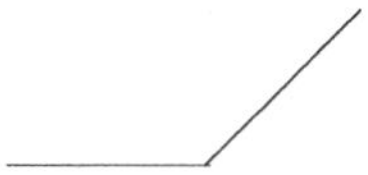

    A **straight angle** has measure 180°: 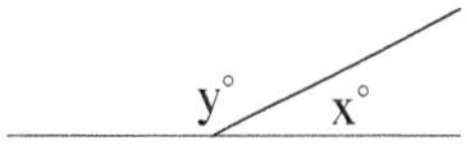   y° x°   x + y = 180°

34. Two angles are supplementary if their angle sum is 180°:   45° 135°
    45 + 135 = 180

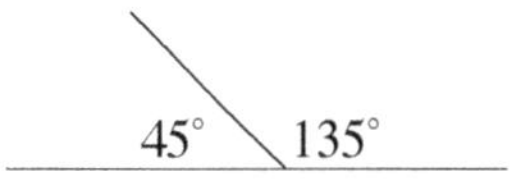

35. Two angles are complementary if their angle sum is 90°:   30° 60°
    30 + 60 = 90

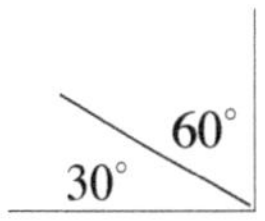

36. Perpendicular lines meet at right angles: 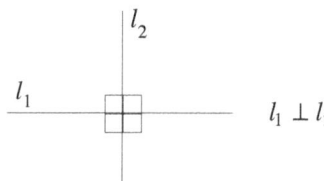 $l_1 \perp l_2$

37. When two straight lines meet at a point, they form four angles. The angles opposite each other are called vertical angles, and they are congruent (equal). In the figure, $a = b$, and $c = d$. 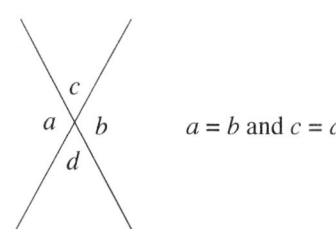 $a = b$ and $c = d$

38. When parallel lines are cut by a transversal, three important angle relationships exist:

    Alternate interior angles are equal. Corresponding angles are equal. Interior angles on the same side of the transversal are supplementary.

    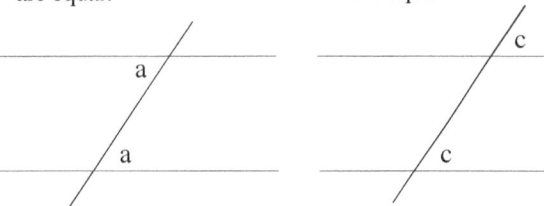 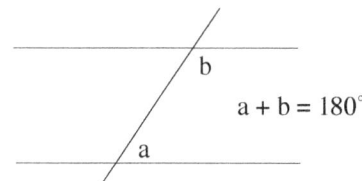
    $a + b = 180°$

39. The shortest distance from a point not on a line to the line is along a perpendicular line.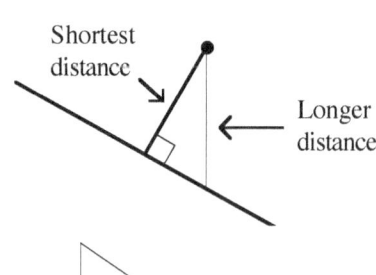

40. A triangle containing a right angle is called a *right triangle*. The right angle is denoted by a small square: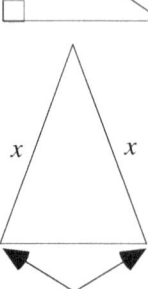

41. A triangle with two equal sides is called isosceles. The angles opposite the equal sides are called the base angles:

42. In an equilateral triangle, all three sides are equal and each angle is 60°: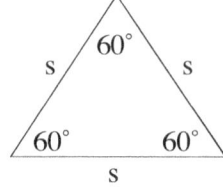

43. The altitude to the base of an isosceles or equilateral triangle bisects the base and bisects the vertex angle:

Isosceles: 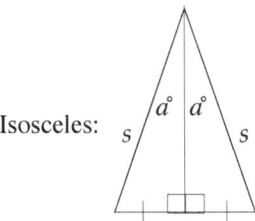   Equilateral: 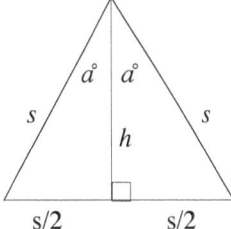 $h = \dfrac{s\sqrt{3}}{2}$

44. The angle sum of a triangle is 180°:

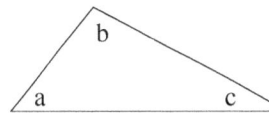 $a + b + c = 180°$

45. The area of a triangle is $\dfrac{1}{2}bh$, where b is the base and h is the height.

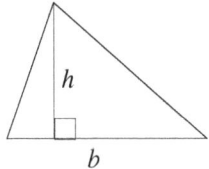 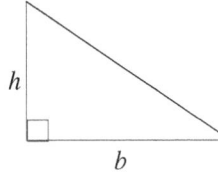 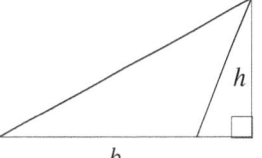 $A = \dfrac{1}{2}bh$

46. In a triangle, the longer side is opposite the larger angle, and vice versa:

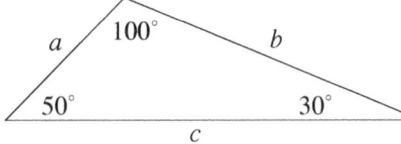   50° is larger than 30°, so side b is longer than side a.

47. Pythagorean Theorem (right triangles only): The square of the hypotenuse is equal to the sum of the squares of the legs.

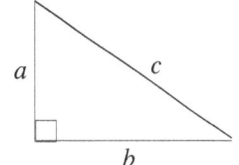 $c^2 = a^2 + b^2$

48. A Pythagorean triple: the numbers 3, 4, and 5 can always represent the sides of a right triangle and they appear very often: $5^2 = 3^2 + 4^2$.

49. Two triangles are similar (same shape and usually different size) if their corresponding angles are equal. If two triangles are similar, their corresponding sides are proportional:

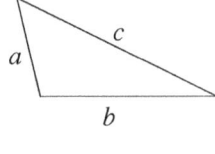 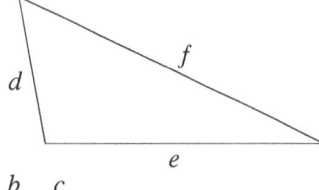

$$\dfrac{a}{d} = \dfrac{b}{e} = \dfrac{c}{f}$$

50. If two angles of a triangle are congruent to two angles of another triangle, the triangles are similar.
    In the figure, the large and small triangles are similar because both contain a right angle and they share $\angle A$.

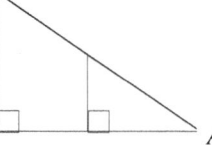

51. Two triangles are congruent (identical) if they have the same size and shape.

375

52. In a triangle, an exterior angle is equal to the sum of its remote interior angles and is therefore greater than either of them:

$e = a + b$ and $e > a$ and $e > b$

53. In a triangle, the sum of the lengths of any two sides is greater than the length of the remaining side:

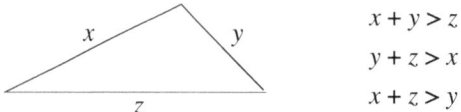

$x + y > z$
$y + z > x$
$x + z > y$

54. In a 30°–60°–90° triangle, the sides have the following relationships:

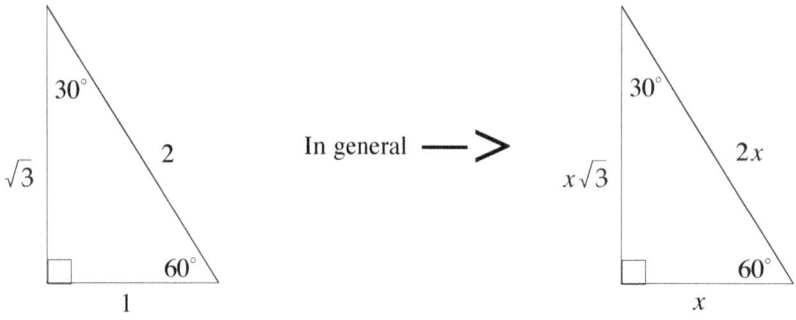

55. In a 45°–45°–90° triangle, the sides have the following relationships:

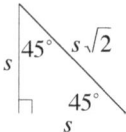

56. Opposite sides of a parallelogram are both parallel and congruent:

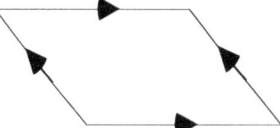

57. The diagonals of a parallelogram bisect each other:

58. A parallelogram with four right angles is a *rectangle*. If w is the width and l is the length of a rectangle, then its area is $A = lw$ and its perimeter is $P = 2w + 2l$:

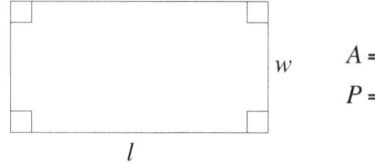

$A = l \cdot w$
$P = 2w + 2l$

59. If the opposite sides of a rectangle are equal, it is a square and its area is $A = s^2$ and its perimeter is $P = 4s$, where s is the length of a side:

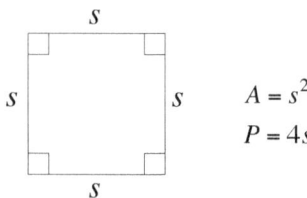

$A = s^2$
$P = 4s$

Summary of Math Properties

60. The diagonals of a square bisect each other and are perpendicular to each other:

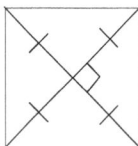

61. A quadrilateral with only one pair of parallel sides is a *trapezoid*. The parallel sides are called *bases*, and the non-parallel sides are called *legs*:

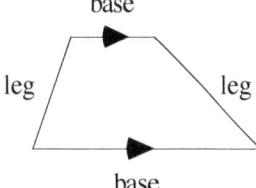

62. The area of a trapezoid is the average of the bases times the height:

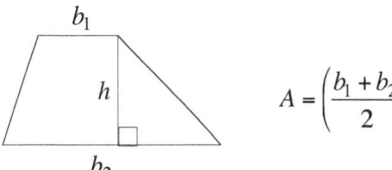

$$A = \left(\frac{b_1 + b_2}{2}\right)h$$

63. The volume of a rectangular solid (a box) is the product of the length, width, and height. The surface area is the sum of the area of the six faces:

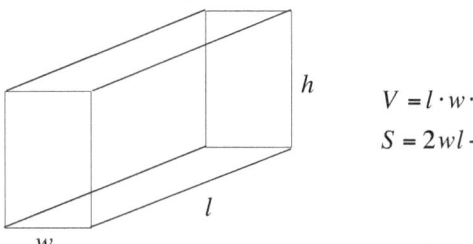

$$V = l \cdot w \cdot h$$
$$S = 2wl + 2hl + 2wh$$

64. If the length, width, and height of a rectangular solid (a box) are the same, it is a cube. Its volume is the cube of one of its sides, and its surface area is the sum of the areas of the six faces:

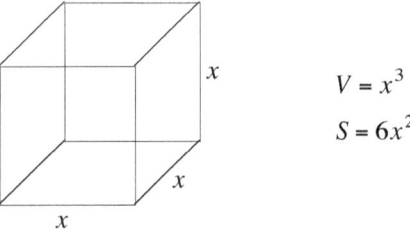

$$V = x^3$$
$$S = 6x^2$$

65. The volume of a cylinder is $V = \pi r^2 h$, and the lateral surface (excluding the top and bottom) is $S = 2\pi rh$, where r is the radius and h is the height:

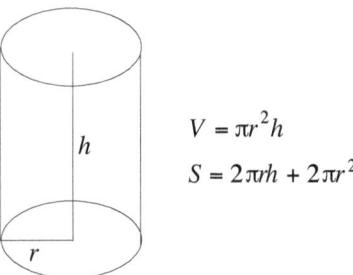

$$V = \pi r^2 h$$
$$S = 2\pi rh + 2\pi r^2$$

66. A line segment form the circle to its center is a *radius*.
    A line segment with both end points on a circle is a *chord*.
    A chord passing though the center of a circle is a *diameter*.
    A diameter can be viewed as two radii, and hence a diameter's length is twice that of a radius.
    A line passing through two points on a circle is a *secant*.
    A piece of the circumference is an *arc*.
    The area bounded by the circumference and an angle with vertex at the center of the circle is a *sector*.

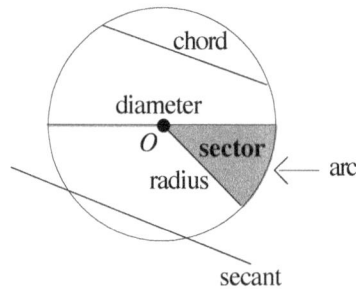

67. A tangent line to a circle intersects the circle at only one point. The radius of the circle is perpendicular to the tangent line at the point of tangency:

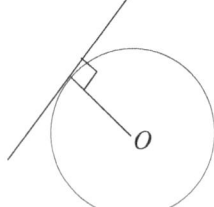

68. Two tangents to a circle from a common exterior point of the circle are congruent:

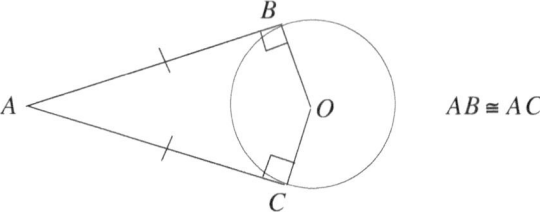

$AB \cong AC$

69. An angle inscribed in a semicircle is a right angle: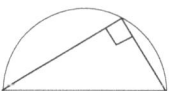

70. A central angle has by definition the same measure as its intercepted arc.

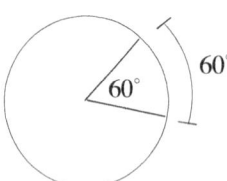

71. An inscribed angle has one-half the measure of its intercepted arc.

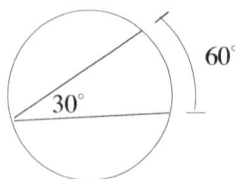

72. The area of a circle is πr^2, and its circumference (perimeter) is $2\pi r$, where r is the radius:

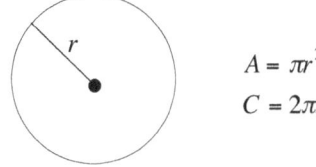

$A = \pi r^2$
$C = 2\pi r$

73. To find the area of the shaded region of a figure, subtract the area of the unshaded region from the area of the entire figure.

74. When drawing geometric figures, don't forget extreme cases.

Miscellaneous

75. To compare two fractions, cross-multiply. The larger product will be on the same side as the larger fraction.

76. Taking the square root of a fraction between 0 and 1 makes it larger.

    Caution: This is not true for fractions greater than 1. For example, $\sqrt{\frac{9}{4}} = \frac{3}{2}$. But $\frac{3}{2} < \frac{9}{4}$.

77. Squaring a fraction between 0 and 1 makes it smaller.

78. $ax^2 \neq (ax)^2$. In fact, $a^2x^2 = (ax)^2$.

79. $\frac{1/a}{b} \neq \frac{1}{a/b}$. In fact, $\frac{1/a}{b} = \frac{1}{ab}$ and $\frac{1}{a/b} = \frac{b}{a}$.

80. $-(a + b) \neq -a + b$. In fact, $-(a + b) = -a - b$.

81. $percentage\ increase = \frac{increase}{original\ amount}$

82. Systems of simultaneous equations can most often be solved by merely adding or subtracting the equations.

83. When counting elements that are in overlapping sets, the total number will equal the number in one group plus the number in the other group minus the number common to both groups.

84. The number of integers between two integers <u>inclusive</u> is one more than their difference.

85. Substitution (Special Cases):
    A. In a problem with two variables, say, x and y, you must check the case in which $x = y$. (This often gives a double case.)
    B. When you are given that $x < 0$, you must plug in negative whole numbers, negative fractions, and -1. (Choose the numbers -1, -2, and $-1/2$, in that order.)
    C. Sometimes you have to plug in the first three numbers (but never more than three) from a class of numbers.

86. Elimination strategies:
    A. On hard problems, if you are asked to find the least (or greatest) number, then eliminate the least (or greatest) answer-choice.
    B. On hard problems, eliminate the answer-choice "not enough information."
    C. On hard problems, eliminate answer-choices that <u>merely</u> repeat numbers from the problem.
    D. On hard problems, eliminate answer-choices that can be derived from elementary operations.
    E. After you have eliminated as many answer-choices as you can, choose from the more complicated or more unusual answer-choices remaining.

87. To solve a fractional equation, multiply both sides by the LCD (lowest common denominator) to clear fractions.

88. You can cancel only over multiplication, not over addition or subtraction. For example, the c's in the expression $\frac{c + x}{c}$ cannot be canceled.

89. Often you can solve a system of two equations in two unknowns by merely adding or subtracting the equations.

90. The average of N numbers is their sum divided by N, that is, $average = \dfrac{sum}{N}$.

91. *Weighted average:* The average between two sets of numbers is closer to the set with more numbers.

92. $Average\ Speed = \dfrac{Total\ Distance}{Total\ Time}$

93. *Distance = Rate × Time*

94. *Work = Rate × Time*, or $W = R \times T$. The amount of work done is usually 1 unit. Hence, the formula becomes $1 = R \times T$. Solving this equation for R gives $R = \dfrac{1}{T}$.

95. *Interest = Amount × Time × Rate*

www.ingramcontent.com/pod-product-compliance
Lightning Source LLC
Chambersburg PA
CBHW080724230426
43665CB00020B/2604